Steve's Adventure with the Peace Corps

Steve Hunsicker

Edited by Maria Dubuc

Copyright © 2012 Steve Hunsicker

All rights reserved.

ISBN-13: 978-1461141891

ISBN-10: 1461141893

DEDICATION

This book is dedicated to all Peace Corps Volunteers, past, present and future!

One hundred percent of the profits from this book will be donated to support the work of current and returned Peace Corps volunteers.

My Stories About Peace Corps and the Kingdom of Tonga

This book is a compilation of stories and journal entries written by Steve Hunsicker from 2006 to 2010, documenting his experiences with Peace Corps from the time he first applied to become a volunteer until his return to the United States. The book was updated in December, 2012.

The views are solely those of the author and do not reflect the position of Peace Corps or the US government.

Table of Contents

Forward	11
Getting Started	14
The Circle Widens	16
A Nicaraguan Video	18
Medical ScreenING Completed	19
The Process Continues	21
A Little Apprehension	22
Happy New Year!	23
The Wait Continues	24
I've got a date—actually several dates!	25
A Fiji in Fiji?	28
It is a bureaucracy!	29
Finally. . . Some News!	32
Jumping Through Hoops	33
Guess where I'm going?	35
Medical Clearance–Finally!	37
Who Knows?	39
The Mediterranean	40
Shrimp and Lobster Allergy Tests	43
Oh Where, Oh Where?	45
I'm going to the South Pacific!	47
I made the Newspaper	49
What a Surprise!	50
News travels Fast	51
More Newspaper Stories	52
What makes a President Cry?	54
The Adventure Begins October 2nd!	58

More about Tonga	60
Three Weeks	63
My bags are packed; I'm ready to go!	64
Heading to LA	67
Malo e Leilei	69
First Impressions of Tonga	72
This is Normal	76
Family, Food and School	79
Vava'u—We made it!	82
How I did something REALLY inappropriate!	85
Here comes the rain (again)!	89
Tongan Prices	91
My New Job	94
Aho Fakatonga (Like a TongaN Day)	98
Secluded Beaches and an Awesome Cave	101
Business in Tonga	103
So Long Vava'u (for Now)	107
Natural Disasters	112
I'm a Volunteer	114
Christmas Eve in Tonga	116
A Tongan Christmas	118
An Island Get-A-Way	121
Tongan Punishment	124
A Serious Problem	125
Oh Happy Day!	126
Case Closed	127
US Immigration and Tonga	128
Privacy Tongan Style	130

Friday Night in Tonga	132
Are you Married?	134
A Record-Breaking Rain	136
Eating the Queen's Food	138
Money Matters	141
An Amazing Weekend in 'Eua	143
A Different (but better) Peace Corps Experience	148
Sailing the South Pacific	151
Weekend Work (And Fun!)	154
Tonga Hygiene	161
Debt Collection	164
Six Months in Tonga	166
A Scary Place	168
Survival of the Weakest	171
The View from beneath the Pacific	173
Getting Robbed in Tonga	175
Business Changes in Tonga	178
An Unexpected Result	181
Memorial Day Tonga Style	183
The Fakaleti of Vava'u	186
The Island of Kenutu, Vava'u	189
Tongan Cooperation	192
Seven Days in Ha'apai, Tonga	195
It was Legendary!	199
The Princess and The Feast	202
Some Great PCVs (Peace Corps Volunteers)	204
Independence Day in Tonga	205
Deep-Sea Fishing in Tonga	206

Poor Customer Service from TCC	207
Vava'u Happenings	209
Preparing for the Coronation of King George Tupou V	211
Na'a' ku Femauakena	212
There goes the Neighborhood	216
And then there were nine!	218
Life in Vava'u	221
The Case for a more Effective Peace Corps	224
Beautiful Brisbane	228
So Long Australia!	232
One Year in Tonga	234
The Outer Island Adventure	236
Vava'u Peace Corps Updates	239
My Return to Television	242
Economics, Earthquakes, Parties and Castration	245
Fishing and Phone Numbers	247
Sailing, Snorkeling and Scary Stuff	250
Election Day in Tonga	251
Watch What We Do in Tonga!	253
Hanging with Group 74	254
Yes, we do work in Peace Corps!	255
Thanksgiving Tonga Style	258
A Tongan Wedding	262
Interesting People and Places	265
The Tongan Paradox	270
Big Fire in Vava'u	276
Breaking a Tongan Taboo	278
A Tale of Two Flights	280

This is Tonga..282
My Peace Corps Experience is half Over................................284
Wardrobe Malfunction..286
Did I Dengue or Did I Not?..289
Swimming with Jellyfish!..291
Changes in Peace Corps Tonga...294
Underwater Recovery...296
Peace Corps Wages and Benefits..300
A Whole New (Underwater) World..302
A Speech Worth Reading...306
A Tongan Funeral (and kissing the dead)..............................307
A Bad Year for Banking in Tonga..310
Peace Corps Surprises..312
Steve and Stan's New Zealand Adventure.............................314
This and That..320
Work slows Down..323
A Day at the Office..324
Biscuits and Gravy...326
Peace Corps Tonga TOP 25...327
Lots of Work to Do!...331
Six Months Remaining in Tonga..333
This All Happened in One Amazing Day!.............................335
The Future of Tonga..339
Looking Forward...342
They Call This Cheating in the USA!....................................343
The Great Vava'u Cleanup...346
A Whale of a Day...349
Spending the Night at the Police Station...............................351

A Very Sad Day in Tonga	355
Grief turns to Anger in Tonga	356
Help on the way for Tonga Ferry Victims	358
The "Facts" about the Tonga Ferry Sinking	359
Food Glorious Food	362
10 Questions (and Answers) about Peace Corps	365
Will You Buy This for Me?	372
A Tongan Tradition I Don't Like	374
Together for the Last Time!	376
Another Australian Adventure	378
The Tsunami in Tonga	382
First Hand Account of the Tongan Tsunami	383
A Scary Welcome to Tonga	385
Swimming with Whales—Absolutely Amazing!	389
A Tongan Drag Show	392
Tonga Development Bank Video	394
My Friends in Tonga	395
Steve's Adventure Ends Today	399
The Adventure Continues	401
About the Author	404
Excerpt from "Other Places: Tonga"	406

FORWARD
December 10, 2012

I'm often asked, "What was Peace Corps like?" and that question is almost always followed by, "Why did you do it?" The "what it was like" is what this book is all about. The "why I did it" question is a bit tougher. Like many of the more than 200,000 people who have served in Peace Corps, the answer is not always simple, and there are often many different factors at play.

That was my situation. I've always had a desire to help others, and some of my more satisfying moments from my 23-year career in TV news were those occasions where I really got to do something that made a difference, either in the life of one individual or an entire community. Early in my career, those moments happened often, but as I advanced in my career, I found myself becoming more removed from the people in the communities that we served. I felt that the only people I was really helping were the owners of the TV station—by putting more money in their pockets. And to be fair, I was also putting more money into my own pockets as my career progressed.

But I also wanted more; I just didn't know initially what I wanted. I thought about starting my own business and even met with Ace Hardware to discuss becoming a franchisee. Nothing seemed to stick, so I kept working in the corporate world until one day I remembered once again my interest in the Peace Corps.

This was not the first time I had thought about the Peace Corps. At different points in my life, I had thought about working overseas and had even thought about the Peace Corps when I was in college. As much as I would like to admit that my motivation was selfless, it wasn't. I had a very selfish desire to see what it was like to live in another country and to look at the USA from outside. I was also incredibly naïve about what it would be like. Before I volunteered with the Peace Corps, the most undeveloped place I had ever visited was Mexico, and all of my travel experiences were either in the USA or Europe.

Even when I began doing my research on Peace Corps, I don't think I fully grasped how different it would be living in a developing country. I thought of it in terms of not having Internet or perhaps being without electricity or running water. I never really grasped the cultural challenges I would face or how I would have to put aside my own beliefs and prejudices in order to adapt.

Those challenges hit me almost immediately after arriving in Tonga. After spending one night in a guesthouse, Peace Corps sent me to live with a host family in the remote village of Fua'amotu, a small community on the southern coast of the main island. My host family welcomed me warmly and told me that later they would be taking us (I was one of two volunteers staying with them) out to dinner.

As night fell in the village, I was in awe of how dark it was there. Even though the homes had electric lights, I could see the stars above with a clarity that I had never experienced before. I ventured out, heading to a small store to buy some water. I didn't know how to ask for water yet in Tongan, but I figured I could point and they would figure it out. As I was walking across the dark gravel road, I heard screams, and suddenly I saw five to seven Tongan kids yelling, waiving machetes, pointing at me and running toward me at full speed. What was happening? Why were these young dark-skinned boys angry, and what were they going to do to me? Should I run or should I stay outside the store? It all happened so fast; my life and my decision to join the Peace Corps suddenly flashed before me. What was I doing here, and what was going to happen to me?

In the USA, if a group of young boys had started running at me wielding machetes and screaming at me in a language I couldn't understand, I would have feared for my life, especially alone on a dark street at night. This was my prejudice, and like all prejudices, it was based on my own upbringing and my own experiences.

Thankfully, I was not in the USA. These young Tongan boys were so excited to see a white person in their village that once they saw me, they had to come over and meet me. They had been husking coconuts with their machetes, and what they were screaming was the word *palangi* which is the Tonga word for "white person." They wanted to touch my skin, to see if I knew any English and to find out what I was doing in their village. I had completely, one hundred percent misread the situation. It was my first reality check. I had to put aside my preconceived notions of what life would be like and get used to a different way of life. As I learned, a Tongan of any age will almost always greet a stranger, will offer them food, and from the moment they meet you, they will never forget you. It would be considered extremely rude in Tonga not to acknowledge someone who is visiting your village.

Unfortunately, I didn't learn my lesson. I had been in the Kingdom of Tonga for less than 48 hours, and even though I wanted to adapt quickly, there were simply too many things to get used to.

At dinner that first night with my homestay sister, I excused myself from the restaurant table to go to the bathroom. About the only Tongan phrase I had learned at this point was *Kofe falemalolo?* which means, "Where is the bathroom?" I found it and entered to find not a urinal and not a stall with doors, but a big trough and a stall with no door. Since I only had to urinate and since I was the only person in the bathroom, I went up to the far end of the stall and started to take a leak. About that time, the door opened and a huge Tongan man came in. My memory says he was 600 lbs., but he was probably only about 350. Now, in American etiquette, if a guy is urinating in the trough, the other guy will either use the stall or he will go to the far end and do his business. That's not what happened. At 6'3", I'm not a particularly small person, but this gigantic guy came and stood right next to me shoulder to shoulder, and again I freaked out. I couldn't go. Why was this guy standing so close to me? What kind of situation had I gotten myself into? Then he spoke. In English (because that is all I knew at this point), he asked me where I was from? I muttered something hoping he would hurry up and leave. He just wanted to keep talking. I finally realized there was no way I was going to be able to urinate, so I just zipped up, rinsed off my hands and walked out. There was no soap, and there were no towels.

I was too embarrassed to tell my homestay sister what had happened in the bathroom, but I soon learned that Tongans don't follow American bathroom etiquette. To them, if you see a stranger, you talk with him or her. To walk to the far side of the trough would be rude. Just like the kids with the machetes, this guy, whom I never saw again, was just being Tongan, and I was just acting like an American.

I was certainly out of my element, but as uncomfortable as both of these incidents were at the time, I was exactly where I wanted to be.

But how I got to Tonga is where I'll begin. Each of the entries on the following pages were written on the date indicated. The conclusions I reached were not always accurate, and anyone who is thinking about Peace Corps service should do their own research and come up with their own conclusions. Also, the application process to Peace Corps changed on August 15, 2012, so many of the frustrations you will hear me writing about on the following pages are no longer the case. However, it is still a long application process, but as you will read, one that I found was well worth the wait.

GETTING STARTED
Wednesday, October 25, 2006

I found out today that I'm going to be nominated to be a Peace Corps volunteer. This is great news and I'm excited. I'm starting this journal to keep a record of the application process and my experiences in the Peace Corps.

I've spent almost 15 years working for the same company and the last 23 years working in television news. I have a good job and a nice life, but I feel it is time to do something different. The Peace Corps seems to fit that bill.

I first remember hearing about the Peace Corps when Jimmy Carter was running for president. I was probably about 15 years old at the time, and his mother, "Miss Lillian," was getting almost as much attention as Mr. Carter. I remember hearing that she had been a Peace Corps volunteer and thinking that Peace Corps would be something I would like to do. (A few years later, I had the chance to interview Miss Lillian, but I didn't ask her about the Peace Corps.)

The next time I became interested in the Peace Corps was during a three-week exchange trip to Germany sponsored by the Radio and Television News Directors Association (RTNDA) and RIAS, an organization that hosts two groups of journalists in Germany each year. It was a great experience and really got me interested in wanting to live in another culture, another place.

Now, fast-forward 10 years later: I'm 46, financially secure and have no debt and really no reason that I can't do this now. It wasn't just one factor that motivated me to make the move at this time, but probably a combination of factors. The industry is changing, like all industries do, but it isn't as much fun as it used to be. As the head of a TV news department, I often feel like I'm more of a personnel manager than a news manager. It has always been the news that I have enjoyed, and I get to do less and less of that each day. My company is also undergoing some transformations. We are now on our fourth CEO since I've been with the company. There are many changes coming, and I'm not sure I really want to shoulder the blame that my staff will give me for some of them.

The process of applying to Peace Corps started online. I came home on September 26th after a stressful day at the TV station, filled out the application and medical history form, hit "send" and was on my way. A little over a week later, I was getting fingerprinted at the police department, retrieving copies of my college transcript and selecting three references who would say good things about me.

That lead to an unusual interview. I met Tricia Siaso, my recruiter, at a Borders bookstore; we walked back into the stacks at the store, found two chairs and chatted for about an hour. I told her that my interest was really in business development and that I would enjoy working with people to either start or develop businesses. I also expressed a desire to work somewhere warm. We briefly discussed the former Soviet states and Eastern Europe, but I think she got the idea that I didn't want to go somewhere cold if I could help it. She told me she thought I was competitive for a position and would be in touch with me that week.

After I got home from the interview, I started what has become an almost nightly task—going online and reading more about the Peace Corps. The night after the interview, I read an article that said almost half of the people who apply to the Peace Corps are turned down. However, I also saw that many of those were people without professional experience. I remained hopeful.

True to her word, Tricia phoned and e-mailed me on Monday to say she had some good news—a business development opportunity in the Pacific. I didn't get the messages until Monday night, so I couldn't call her until Tuesday. I asked more about the position. She didn't have a lot of details except that it was located in the Pacific. She did have one business advising position left in the Caribbean, but she didn't know if it was still open, and she really thought I should be in a higher-level business development program. I said okay, so she forwarded me the medical paperwork and the official nomination.

Until today, only three people know that I have applied for this position, and those are my three references. I am flying up to Virginia this weekend to tell my family about my plans. I believe they will be supportive, and I am going to need their support. My plan is to sell my house before I leave, but I don't want to put it on the market until I receive the official invitation saying I have been cleared. The same goes for my job. I'm not going to say anything until I know for sure that this is happening. Tricia, my recruiter, said that if I get my medical work done quickly, I should hear something by January, though it could take longer. All the Peace Corps will guarantee is that you receive the invitation six weeks before you leave. I'm hoping for a bit more time.

THE CIRCLE WIDENS
Sunday, October 29, 2006

I flew to Virginia this weekend and told my family of my plans to join the Peace Corps. As expected, they were supportive. My oldest sister, Becky, seemed a little apprehensive when I asked my two sisters and my parents to come downstairs because I had something to tell them. Becky's comment was, "You are scaring me." However, once I made the big announcement, she was the first to congratulate me and give me a high five. In fact, later Saturday evening, after everyone had left, Becky and I got on her computer and started looking at the places I could be going.

"Where are you going?" was obviously one of the first questions that my family wanted to know and one which I would like to know myself. However, the Peace Corps doesn't share that information until they give you an official invitation. My recruiter told me she was recommending me for a business development program in the Pacific. The Peace Corps website shows six countries with active programs: Fiji, Kiribati, Micronesia and Palau, Samoa, Tonga and Vanuatu. My best guess is Vanuatu, since it is the only one that specifically lists a business development program. However, my recruiter says that doesn't really mean anything since the programs are constantly changing.

Becky and I, with help from my nephew, Isaac, spent time looking at different websites about Vanuatu, including the State Department site which I had not visited before. Isaac suggested we look at Google Earth, so he could see exactly where Vanuatu and the other islands were located. Becky said she had always wanted to visit Australia and that if she couldn't come to wherever I am stationed, we could always meet there. Isaac promptly announced he wasn't going to get on a plane and go that far away. My niece, Emma wasn't home when I made the announcement, but later told me she thought it was "really cool."

I didn't get to spend as much time Saturday evening talking with Maria, my other sister, and with Mom and Dad, but I'm hopeful they will visit regardless of where I am stationed.

The big hurdle left for me is my medical examination. I am not aware of any medical issues that would prevent me from going anywhere, but you never know what could be discovered. My recruiter had originally requested to be sent to Africa, but was not able to go there after it was discovered that she was allergic to the medicine used to treat malaria. I also have to have a complete dental exam, but that one doesn't worry me. Any dental problems can be fixed.

I've started making a list of the many things that I need to do in preparation for my assignment. I don't want to do anything permanent until I have the official invitation, but certainly I need to do some pre-planning. My parents have agreed to take my dog, Lady, during the time that I am gone, and my sister Maria may also take her pending a discussion with her husband, Andy. Becky and her husband, Bill, an attorney, said they would be happy to serve as my power of attorney to deal with any issues during my time away.

I also have some financial planning to do which I can begin even before I get the invitation. One task is to make sure I receive all of my bills electronically. I'm hopeful that wherever I end up, I will have access to the Internet. Even if I don't have that, having everything paid electronically will allow someone else to check on how things are going and to pay any outstanding bills. Once my house is sold, I should not have any additional bills.

At this point, the circle of people who know of my plans remains limited to my three references and my immediate family. I'm going to keep the circle tight until after I receive my year-end bonus, even if I get the official invitation before then. I probably won't broaden the circle until the invitation arrives, so that word does not leak out to my staff and my company.

A NICARAGUAN VIDEO
Tuesday, October 31, 2006

Several times a week, I look at resume tapes of people who want to become TV reporters. Most are pretty predictable and with rare exception, I seldom watch an entire tape. Today was an exception. In the stack of tapes was a DVD from someone named Ian Wood. It was a documentary he had produced during his time as a Peace Corps volunteer from 2002 to 2005 in Jinotepe, Nicaragua. I didn't have time to watch the entire program at work, so I brought it home and watched it tonight. It was fascinating to see his house, his "outdoor" kitchen and to see the other Peace Corps volunteers who were serving with him. I am making copies of the DVD to send to my parents and my sisters.

I'm not sure if he is qualified to be a reporter with my station, but after watching the tape, I sent him an e-mail telling him I would be happy to meet with him. I'm sure I won't tell him that I've been nominated to serve, but it will be interesting to meet him and talk with him about his experiences.

The Peace Corps also sent me a book today with stories written by RPCVs or Returned Peace Corps Volunteers. I look forward to reading that.

MEDICAL SCREENING COMPLETED
Sunday, November 19, 2006

I've finally completed my medical screening for the Peace Corps. I had read online that this could be a laborious process, and my recruiter had told me the same thing. It was time-consuming, but not for the reasons I expected.

The Peace Corps provides an online site where you can check the status of your application at any time. On November 1st, my site was updated to say that the Peace Corps had shipped my medical forms to me and that I should make my appointments to have the exams completed. I did that almost immediately. I quickly got a medical appointment and went to a walk-in eyeglass exam place. I had to wait awhile for the dental appointment, but I was put on the stand-by list and got in a few days later. As it turned out, I completed all of my appointments before the official forms arrived in the mail. Fortunately, the Peace Corps had a downloadable form online that I was able to take to my appointments.

The eye exam was confusing because they wanted information on fitting me for frames but they only provided pictures of frames, and the optician was not comfortable "guessing" the frame size. The dental exam was a bit time-consuming, but I also had a hygiene appointment at the same time. The medical appointment required some lab work, including an HIV test and a blood type test.

The HIV test turned out to be a bigger deal than I expected. Once I got to the clinic, I had to sign two forms: one consenting to have the test done, and the other, saying the results would be reported to my doctor. It seemed like a bit of overkill to me since it was my doctor who ordered the test in the first place. As far as the blood type test, my doctor told me that it was not a common test, which surprised me. I figured it would be routine. Turns out the test was a good thing. I have never given a lot of thought to my blood type and only vaguely remembered that I had Type O+ blood. Turns out, that is not correct, I'm A+. I'm not sure why I had thought otherwise, but that's what the lab reported.

On Wednesday morning, I was taking my dog out for a walk, and a guy came out of my neighbor's house, pointed at my house and said, "Do you live there?" I said yes and he said, "I'm taking care of the Heller's house, and I just found a bunch of your mail in their mailbox. I put it in your box."

This is my neighbor's second home, and they don't use it a lot. The mail could have been in their box for weeks. I went to my mailbox and sure enough, there were my Peace Corps documents.

Fortunately, the medical and dental forms were identical. However, there were now two additional forms I had to have my doctor complete. One had to do with my physical capabilities, asking if I could sit and stand for long periods of time, lift 50 pounds, etc. The second form contained additional medical questions based on my application. These asked about my allergy to shrimp and lobster and my high cholesterol. They also wanted additional lab reports on my cholesterol.

I got the new forms back to my doctor who filled them out, and I was finally done. I had been concerned that I had not received the paperwork and as it turns out, it was probably a postal error that caused the delay and not a delay with the Peace Corps. Last night, I made copies of everything, then drove to the main post office and dropped my forms in the mail.

Next week is Thanksgiving, so I'm guessing the forms won't even get looked at until after the holiday. My hope is to receive my clearance before the first of February. That is two months away. If I can get my medical clearance and my invitation by then, I should have plenty of time to get my house on the market, resign my job and get my other affairs in order. I'm also hoping to spend some time traveling and visiting family before I depart.

I'm flying to Virginia on Thursday for Thanksgiving Day. Mom and Dad want to spend some time chatting with me about my plans. I'm looking forward to that.

THE PROCESS CONTINUES
Saturday, December 2, 2006

Joining the Peace Corps is definitely a process. I'm sure part of the reason for that is to keep people from making quick decisions and then backing out.

The other reason is probably related to the fact that the Peace Corps is a federal bureaucracy. It has been two weeks since I mailed out all of my medical forms. This morning, I got an e-mail saying that my paperwork was received by the Peace Corps yesterday. That means it either took two weeks for a letter to get from Florida to DC, or it took two weeks for the Peace Corps to open its mail and update my information. Either way, it doesn't really matter to me. I'm happy to know the process is moving forward.

Interestingly, the Peace Corps website shows that my dental review is complete, and I sent that information in the same envelope as the medical paperwork. The site says most applications are reviewed in four to six weeks. That keeps me on my target of wanting to know my status by the first of February. I have already cleared the legal review, the other step in the process. The only step remaining after that is placement.

My hope is that I can resign from work on Friday, March 2, 2007. Assuming a June Peace Corps departure date, that would be three months of paying my own health benefits. Mom and Dad are also planning to visit the first week of March. I'm not sure what else I will do during those months, but I hope to travel and wrap up my personal business affairs before I leave.

I spent Thanksgiving night talking with Mom and Dad about my plans between now and the time I leave, and also about what I want to do when I get back. I am now planning to keep my house. Mom and Dad have said they would come down a couple of times a year to check on the house, and I'm sure my sisters might also be interested in doing that. I am not interested in renting out the house but would very much like to have someone check on the place regularly. There are also home-watch services, and I may decide to employ one of them as well.

Keeping the house is not necessarily the smartest short-term financial decision. I will pay out a good chunk of change on utilities, taxes, insurance, POA and HOA fees, etc. It might make financial sense to sell but then again, perhaps not. Housing prices are in a slump right now. I would have to sell for less than I want, and that amount would probably be more than what I'll pay out over the two years I'm away. And I really do like where I live, and it would be great to have a place to come home to.

The other task I am completing at the moment is moving all of my bills to electronic billing. That way, I can pay bills from anywhere I have an Internet connection, and if I don't have a connection, someone can log in as me and pay them. I'm not doing automatic debit at this point, as that makes me nervous, but I will be able to pay with the click of a button.

A LITTLE APPREHENSION
Thursday, December 7, 2006

The next thing I'm expecting in the mail from the Peace Corps is an invitation to a specific program. I expect that will happen once my medical clearance has been approved. Tonight, I felt a little apprehension when I opened my mailbox and inside was a very small envelope from the Peace Corps.

I immediately remembered my days of applying to college. You knew that if you received a big envelope from a school, it meant you had been accepted, and if you got a small envelope, it meant, "Thanks but no thanks."

I haven't thought a lot about what would happen if I don't get accepted, but it is something I can't help but consider. The Peace Corps turns down something like half of the people who apply, so it would not be unusual.

As I headed inside, I couldn't wait to open the envelope. Was this a rejection I wondered? After setting down my other mail (and giving my dog her nightly treat), I opened the envelope to find a single page letter.

The letter simply told me that I had received my dental clearance. Of course, I already knew that from e-mail and the Peace Corps website.

Because of that letter, I won't worry too much if I receive a small envelope next time.

HAPPY NEW YEAR!
Wednesday, January 3, 2007

It is now officially 2007, and as I write this, I can't help but think about where I may celebrate the beginning of 2008. Hopefully, it will be somewhere in the Peace Corps. I have to admit that I am starting to feel a bit impatient about the process, but everything I have read says to expect a long application period. I had been hoping to hear something mid-January to early February based on what my recruiter told me. However, the Peace Corps says it will only give you six weeks notice before you depart, which means that if I receive an invitation to a program beginning in June, as expected, I might not hear anything until mid-April.

My family continues to support my desire to join the Peace Corps. For Christmas, my parents gave me a nice pair of GORE-TEX boots by Ecco to wear during my service. My sister Maria gave me a watch that doesn't require winding or a battery and is waterproof. My sister Becky gave me several books, including one called, *"So, You Want to Join the Peace Corps . . . What to Know Before You Go"* by Dillon Banerjee.

I read that book cover to cover in one sitting. It had a lot of good information and some useful tips, including suggestions on what to take. For example, the author suggested taking a roll of US stamps with you. That way, you can give letters and small packages to people heading back to the United States that can be dropped in any mailbox. He also suggested external speakers for your music player, so you don't have to wear headphones in your house. Both are very good suggestions. The book also included helpful information about what it was like to be a volunteer and what to expect.

I spent part of my Christmas vacation visiting friends in Orlando. It was somewhat of a reunion, because the six of us had been to Europe together in September 2005. It was the first time we've been together since we left Paris. Naturally, the talk turned to where we should take our next trip. I pushed them to try for a trip in April without explaining why. I must not have been very convincing, since we decided to take a trip in September again.

I felt a bit guilty about not telling my friends what I was planning, but two of them work in television, and it is a very small business. I don't think either would intentionally say anything, but I've kept the number of people who know my plans very small. Once I get the official invitation, I will certainly tell more people.

I'm also sending an e-mail tonight to my recruiter just to make sure everything is okay with my application. Her office was closed today due to President Ford's funeral.

THE WAIT CONTINUES
Thursday, January 25, 2007

Be patient. That's what I keep telling myself as I wait for news of my medical screening and my official invitation. I received this e-mail today from my recruiter, who was responding to my e-mail asking about the status of my application:

> *Hello! I don't think they have started inviting to your program yet. They are focusing on end of Feb/beginning of March at this point. As far as I see, your medical file is still under review. Just hang in there! They have until the end of April to invite to your program, so I'm guessing you'll hear something in March. But it can't hurt to ask. Feel free to check back often with me. As soon as I know anything, I'll let you know!*
>
> *Tricia*

While there is nothing negative in the e-mail, having to wait until March or April to hear certainly would mess up my plans to take several months off before departing. The worst-case scenario would be to not find out until the end of April. While I could leave my job by just giving two weeks' notice, that would mean I would be leaving during the May rating period, which is the most important rating period of the year in television. I'm fairly certain my company would want me to stay on until the end. If I did that, I would have just a week before leaving for the Peace Corps. If I didn't stay for the May book, I would certainly be "burning bridges" by leaving the station then.

If I find out at the beginning of March, I would still have two months to travel and take care of my personal affairs before departing. While the Peace Corps would be a change of pace, there are many things I would like to do with a little time off from working.

I'VE GOT A DATE—ACTUALLY SEVERAL DATES!
Wednesday, February 14, 2007

Today I had a great conversation with my recruiter, Tricia. I've been a bit nervous about my status with the Peace Corps because it has been months since I have had any correspondence from them—actually, more than two months. The Peace Corps website says it usually takes four to six weeks to get medical clearance.

It has been two months since the Peace Corps said it received my medical information and almost three since I sent everything to them. This is much longer than the promised four to six weeks. Of course, I also have to remind myself that I am dealing with a government organization. This is not TV, where we turn everything around in a couple of hours and then go on to our next project.

Tricia told me that NO ONE has been invited yet to participate in the program to which I have been nominated. That means I'm not the only one waiting. She also assured me that it is not unusual that I have not received medical clearance. She says that while it would be great if the applications were handled on a first-in, first-out basis, in reality, the Peace Corps prioritizes the applications based on the departure date of the program. Some people wait until the last minute to apply, and they will get reviewed before others if their program departs sooner. That is apparently what is happening with my application because they are not yet inviting people.

Now to the dates I mentioned. Tricia said I should expect to hear something by February 28th about my medical application. She knows the person reviewing the information and says it is too soon to call. If I have not heard by the 28th, she will call and get an update. She also told me that based on my qualifications, she expects that I would receive an invitation almost immediately after getting my medical clearance. While there is no guarantee, Tricia believes that I am "extremely competitive" and should get one of the first invitations. All invitations for my program will be issued by April 21st. My program will leave six weeks after that, which is around June 3rd. Even though I don't have medical clearance yet or even an invitation, I am very optimistic about my status. It was great to talk with her, and she told me I was welcome to call her every week until I got my invitation.

I did ask Tricia about my shrimp and lobster allergy, which is really the only thing from a medical perspective that could cause me a problem. She said that even though it is a minor allergy, someone might decide that if an area has a diet high in shellfish, they should not send me there. She then added that when she served in Samoa, they almost never had shrimp or lobster, and that is the same region where I have received my nomination. She laughed and said she wished she had gotten lobster in the Peace Corps!

Joining the Peace Corps is a major life change for me. Last week, I went to the Super Bowl, something many people never get a chance to do. I sat in a covered seat and watched as thousands of people who paid thousands of dollars for tickets got rained on. Going was a really fun experience.

Steve Hunsicker at the Super Bowl in Miami

During my career, I've covered hurricanes, space shuttle launches, the World Series, political conventions, presidents, popes, the fall of the Berlin Wall and many other events. I've also met many fascinating people along the way.

Those are events and people I will always remember. That's the fun part of being in the TV business, and I would not trade my experiences for anything. However, it is very obvious to me that it is time to leave TV. I have no ill will toward my present company, where I have worked for the past 15 years, but the job and the TV industry are no longer for me.

Just this week, it was announced that our station manager was being shifted to a new corporate job, and my boss, the woman who hired me, would no longer be the general manager of our TV station. (She had been both GM of my station and president of our broadcast division. Now, she will just be division president.) That means my station will be getting a new boss. I've had several people ask me since the announcement if I will be taking over the station. The question is quite flattering but the answer is NO! A couple of years ago, I would have been beating down the door to get the job; now, I realize it is not for me. And, I also don't think I would get it even if I was interested. I'm sure when it is announced that I am leaving, people will wonder if it is because of the management changes at the station. Regardless of what is said, many will believe that.

However, I am so sure that I want to do something else, that if they offered to double my salary and give me the job, I would still turn it down. After today, I really believe the Peace Corps is going to happen for me. It may happen in two weeks or it could take two months, but when it does, I will be ready.

A FIJI IN FIJI?
Tuesday, February 27, 2007

When I joined my college fraternity, I didn't know very much about Fiji except that it was the nickname for my fraternity, Phi Gamma Delta. And of course, I knew it was an island somewhere in the Pacific. Each year, my fraternity celebrated "Fiji Island," billed as the best party each year on campus at West Virginia University. We built a lagoon, a waterfall, tropical huts and dressed like Fiji Islanders, or at least how we thought a Fijian would dress. Mostly it was about drinking, but it was always a lot of fun.

Now the real Fiji is at the top of my mind again. I've spent a good deal of time looking at different blogs from current and former Peace Corps volunteers since I decided to fill out my application. I have always thought that Vanuatu was where I would be headed as a volunteer. Now, I believe the most likely place could be Fiji. I've looked at the start days for different volunteer groups based on their blog entries. Here is what I have discovered:

> East Timor - July
> Fiji - June
> Kiribati - October
> Malaysia - Unknown
> Micronesia - November
> Palau - October
> Papua New Guinea - January
> Samoa - October
> Tonga - July
> Vanuatu - April

It is also possible that it could be Malaysia. However, I couldn't find much about that area on the Peace Corps website. They link Micronesia and Palau together, which may mean they both depart in October.

Peace Corps service was stopped in Fiji because of political unrest in 1998 but was restored in 2003 once the country settled down. According to one blog, the Fiji dates from last year align almost exactly with the dates I received from my recruiter for this year.

I'm hopeful that I will receive medical clearance this week. I am supposed to call my recruiter on Wednesday if I do not hear by then. I hope that an invitation is issued shortly after that.

If I do end up in Fiji, I would be "a Fiji in Fiji."

IT IS A BUREAUCRACY!
Thursday, March 1, 2007

There is no question that the Peace Corps is a federal government bureaucracy. And yes, I have read all the information about how getting medical clearance is the most frustrating part of the application process. I'm beginning to understand.

Today, I called my recruiter, Tricia, to inquire about my status. She had asked me to call if I had not heard anything about my application by today. She looked in her computer, and it still showed that I'm awaiting medical clearance. Tricia said I should call the medical officer who is in charge of my application, a guy named Dennis in DC.

I immediately called and he answered the phone. Very friendly guy, but the bottom line is that they haven't even looked at my medical application yet. Dennis said they are jammed up, more than normal, and they are having trouble getting caught up. He said once they look at my file, it will happen very fast. They will either call or send me a letter if they need more information, or just approve it. As we were chatting, Dennis mentioned that he and his wife had been in a similar situation with a house and jobs when they decided to volunteer. He told me to be patient and if I haven't heard something in two weeks, to give him a call back.

I'm beginning to think that that may be the standard line—call back in two weeks. Dennis did give me a little nugget of information: He said that while the official rule is that all invitations are given six weeks before departure, it really is more like eight weeks. He said I would probably not be leaving until mid-June, perhaps around the 15th or so for my program. That's about eight weeks from the April 21st deadline that I was given two weeks ago.

That is actually really good news. If I hear around April 21st, I would still have time to give adequate notice at work and have a few weeks to get ready to leave. It would limit my ability to do any substantial trips before I depart, but I can make that work.

While a mid-June departure doesn't line up exactly with last year's Fiji schedule (see previous post), it still seems a good bet. Both East Timor and Tonga have July departures. It looks like East Timor departs early July, according to two blogs, but one lists an April departure. Tonga seems all over the place, but one blog shows arrivals on July 11, 2004. (I also found a blog writer who was given an official reprimand for sharing his opinions online, and he shut his blog down.)

I don't know if my assumptions about the departures being the same every year are correct, but there does seem to be some consistency in the dates.

So what now? I wait two more weeks. And I keep reminding myself that patience is a virtue.

ANOTHER TWO WEEKS
Thursday, March 15, 2007

It has been exactly two weeks since my last conversation with anyone at the Peace Corps. That means it was time today for my bi-weekly round of phone calls. I got voicemail when I called both my recruiter, Tricia, and the medical officer, Dennis. Tricia was the first to call back saying that, no, she didn't have any news but that she really thinks I should hear something soon. She said if I didn't hear back from the medical office, to let her know and she would follow up personally. A while later, Dennis left a voicemail stating again, that my file had not been looked at but should be soon.

This time, neither Tricia nor Dennis said to call back in two weeks, but both told me to stay in contact with them. Tricia said she checks my file every couple of days because there should be some action soon.

Even though I don't know anything yet, I did give my dog, Lady, to Mom and Dad on Monday since they probably will not be back in Florida until after I leave. It's pretty lonely without Lady. And somehow it makes leaving seem a bit more real. I know they will take good care of her while I'm away, and she'll probably get more attention than I could have given her. It's not permanent. If I don't get into the Peace Corps for some reason, Lady will be back here very quickly.

Phil and Shirley Hunsicker at St. George Island, Florida

It was nice to spend time with Mom and Dad. We were at St. George Island in North Florida for the past few days. I also got a chance to see a couple of friends of mine from Tallahassee, who drove down for a visit on Sunday. I told them of my plans to join the Peace Corps. I think my friend Tim didn't believe me at first but was very supportive once he realized I was serious. I suspect I will get that reaction from others as I expand the list of people who know of my plans.

I don't intend to tell anyone else until I know something more concrete; however, it is increasingly difficult to be in the dark about what will happen. Today, I had a conversation with someone at work about something that could happen in November and another about the station's plans for hurricane season. It was tough to have these conversations knowing that if the Peace Corps accepts me, I will be a long way from West Palm Beach this November, and the only hurricanes I'll be worrying about will be in the South Pacific.

FINALLY... SOME NEWS!
Friday, March 16, 2007

I was pleasantly surprised to get a phone call today from my recruiter, Tricia. She said she had called the head person in the medical office and asked him to review my file. He did that and then sent me the following e-mail.

> *Mr. Hunsicker,*
>
> *I have finished a review of your application that you submitted using an outdated form rather than the current form provided with your medical kit. We unfortunately therefore do not have a complete application.*
>
> *Please provide a copy of the results of your hepatitis B surface antigen, hepatitis B core antibody, hepatitis C serology & G6PD titers. These tests are required for all applicants. There are a variety of tests that can be performed for hepatitis B. Insist that these required tests are obtained. There are no substitutes.*
>
> *We require that you provide us with documentation of past or current Td – tetanus/diphtheria (submitted with your application and current), OPV/IPV – Polio polio and MMR – measles, mumps & rubella immunizations. Please obtain copies of this information for your personal safekeeping and review their correctness and completeness before personally faxing copies to 202-692-1561. This invariably prevents unnecessary delays in receiving the required information.*

If this is all that is required, I feel GREAT about my application. I sent him an e-mail tonight telling him that I have made a doctor's appointment for March 26th to have the shots and blood work done. I also asked him to confirm that this was the only outstanding issue with my application.

I may try to see if I can find someone else to give me the shots sooner and order the lab work. I'm assuming that once that is done, I should be good to go. If I can't get this done sooner, then I probably won't be able to send the paperwork in until March 28th and that's two weeks away.

Oh, in case you were wondering about the reference to the outdated form: I had to download the forms from the Internet because it took a month for the paperwork to arrive, and I had already set up all my medical appointments. Tricia told me the delay was because they were changing the form. That sounds like the government!

My other good news: My company paid out the year-end bonuses today. If I had resigned now, I would have lost the bonus, as that is our policy.

JUMPING THROUGH HOOPS
Thursday, March 22, 2007

I thought today I would be finished with my medical application to the Peace Corps. That didn't happen. Last Friday, I had all of my blood work done. I gave the nurse at my doctor's office the e-mail I received from the medical officer detailing the additional tests that needed to be done. My doctor ordered the tests from that e-mail. When I got to the lab, I showed the e-mail to the lab technician, who consulted a reference book and assured me that the tests on the e-mail were being done.

On Tuesday, I went to the public health department and had my MMR (measles, mumps and rubella) shot and a polio shot. The nurse also suggested a hepatitis A shot since I was going to the South Pacific. I agreed. Last night, I e-mailed those records to the Peace Corps. Today, my doctor's office called and said they had the results from Friday. I picked them up and then both faxed and e-mailed the forms to the Peace Corps medical officer. This evening, I got the following e-mail:

Mr. Hunsicker,

Unfortunately, one of the tests performed was not correct.

We asked that you please provide a copy of the results of your hepatitis B surface antigen, hepatitis B core antibody, hepatitis C serology & G6PD titers. These tests are required for all applicants. There are a variety of tests that can be performed for hepatitis B. Insist that these required tests are obtained. There are no substitutes.

The result of a hepatitis B surface antibody test was submitted that was not requested or required; it does not substitute for the result of your hepatitis B core antibody.

Please provide a copy of the result of your hepatitis B core antibody test as required.

This means, I've got to do it all over again . . . at least the lab work. I believe my doctor's office is closed on Thursday, but I'm going to go there in the morning and try and get this done again. If that fails, I'll try to find another doctor to issue the order, and then I'll get the lab work done. It will take a few days once it is done to get the results, which means I probably won't have them until Tuesday or Wednesday of next week.

Unfortunately, the lab orders are written in "code," so it is very tough to see exactly what you are getting. At least now I can say I need the "core" antibody. I have no idea what that means, and I don't really care. My doctor says I don't have hepatitis, not that I had any reason to think I did, and I suspect that won't change with this latest test.

I can't really fault the Peace Corps for this one. Actually, I was pretty impressed that I got the response less than an hour after sending them everything. Of course, I also don't know if this is some obscure test or if both my doctor and the lab just messed up.

If all else fails, I do have a doctor's appointment on Monday, and I'll get the new blood work order done then. I just hate to keep waiting. I have a new boss who is starting in just over two weeks. I would hate to have to resign on her first day on the job. That would fuel lots of speculation that she was the reason I left . . . and I haven't even met her yet.

As we say in TV, "Stay tuned!"

GUESS WHERE I'M GOING?
Friday, March 23, 2007

Tonight, I got home to catch up on my regular blog reading and found several people who are leaving for Fiji on the 23rd of May. I'm guessing that means I won't be going there since I don't leave until June. I'm probably spending way too much time trying to figure out where I will be sent, but I am enjoying it. I'm learning a lot about what it is like to be in the Peace Corps and realize that many others have the same thoughts and concerns that I have.

Here's a quote that I found tonight on Matt's Peace Corps Adventure blog.

> Man, just when you thought it was gonna get easier I totally read over all my paperwork for my invitation to FIJI. . . . The red tape and essays and resumes never end . . . Now I need to file a new updated resume for my in-country officers to check out, and answer a five part essay about what I am planning on getting out of this experience, etc. Guess I had better get used to it . . . It's not that hard, just one more thing on my plate. :) For anyone thinking of getting into the Peace Corps, just know that you will never be done filling out paperwork, filling out forms, getting medically probed and prodded and writing essays or statements!!!!

He seems to have the same feelings I have had recently. The good news is that while my doctor doesn't work on Thursday, the nurse was there and she wrote new orders to have my blood work done. The lab told me the results should be back tomorrow afternoon, so hopefully, I will really be done with my medical application. Of course, I have to get the results from my doctor and not from the lab, so that could delay matters.

There are just six countries in the Pacific Islands with active Peace Corps programs. There is always a chance that my program could be a start-up. Here are actual departure dates I've found on various blogs.

Tonga – October 25, 2006
Samoa – October 14, 2006
Fiji – May 23, 2007
Kiribati – October 2006
Micronesia/Palau – September 6, 2006 (also September 6, 2005)
Vanuatu – June 11, 2003, June 14, 2006 (also September 22, 2006)

So what does this mean? I'm guessing that the larger programs have more than one departure date each year. The June departure for Vanuatu could be my program. If you remember, I originally thought I was going to Vanuatu but then saw the September date. The Vanuatu program is the largest according to the PC website, with 88 current volunteers. If that is the case, it is possible they do two programs a year. And the training for the June group would be done by mid-September, so that could work.

My best guess is now Vanuatu, and they list a business development program. Hopefully, I'll soon know if I'm right.

MEDICAL CLEARANCE–FINALLY!
Thursday, March 29, 2007

Here's how it happened. I was driving to work this morning, sitting at a stoplight and checking e-mails on my Blackberry. There it was . . . an e-mail saying my status had been updated at PeaceCorps.gov. I was still about ten minutes from work, so I immediately logged onto the website on my Blackberry as I was driving. It was slow, but it worked. As I was pulling into my parking space, the status page loaded, and there I learned that my medical screening was complete.

status	◯	Your file is currently under consideration. Please review the information on this page to determine whether Peace Corps is awaiting any information from you.
FORMS required to become an Invitee		
medical kit	✓	Peace Corps mailed you a Medical Kit on November 1, 2006. Be sure to schedule your medical appointments immediately so you can submit your medical forms as soon as possible. TIP: Some medical forms, reimbursement forms, and samples of correctly completed forms are available in the Download Center.
physical exam	✓	Peace Corps received the results of your physical exam on December 1, 2006. In some cases, Peace Corps may request additional medical information. Please respond quickly to these requests.
CLEARANCES required to become an Invitee		
dental	✓	**Complete.** Peace Corps has completed your dental review. There are no dental holds on your account at this time.
legal	✓	There are no legal holds on your account at this time.
medical	✓	**Complete.** Peace Corps has completed your medical review. There are no medical holds on your account at this time.

It was the news I had been waiting to hear since mid-November. Now, just over five months since I received my nomination, I had finally made it through what everyone says is the toughest part. Finally!

I called Mom and Dad and both my sisters to share the news. I immediately looked at the calendar and started planning my next step. If I get the final word this week, then I might be able to resign as soon as Monday. That would allow me to give three weeks' notice and still have two full months before I depart. I wouldn't have to burn any bridges by leaving during the May rating book, which I don't plan to do anyway. I even started writing my letter of resignation in my head.

As I left work today, I came to the SAME stoplight where I had gotten the e-mail this morning. I pulled out my Blackberry and checked my personal mail. This is what I saw:

Dear Stephen,

Greetings from the Placement Office at Peace Corps Headquarters in Washington, DC!

We wanted to get in touch with you to congratulate you on receiving your medical clearance and therefore, for completing a very important part of the application process. Over the next few weeks, we will be conducting a final review of your application materials, and we will be in contact with you in the event that any additional information is needed. Once the application review is complete, we will update you on the next steps of the application process.

We understand that you might be eager to receive more information from Peace Corps at this point, and we greatly appreciate your patience. In the meantime, you can prepare for Peace Corps service and make your application more competitive by: continuing to gain experience through working or volunteering; attending Peace Corps events; talking to Returned Volunteers; and reading books, articles, and other resources about Peace Corps. You can also find resources and learning activities on our website and in My Toolkit.

If you have earned your degree or gained additional certifications since you applied, please fax them to my attention. Also, if you would like to update your volunteer or work experience, your contact information, or your availability date, please let me know.

Thank you for your interest in Peace Corps, and please feel free to e-mail me if you have any questions at this point. Otherwise, we look forward to contacting you in a short few weeks!

Best regards,

Alyssa

It's obviously a form letter targeted to students, but certainly not what I was expecting. I sincerely hope I don't have to wait two to three more weeks to find out. The letter also makes it pretty clear that my invitation is not a "done deal." I still plan to call my recruiter tomorrow to find out what she can tell me. And to complicate matters, tomorrow morning I have my first conversation with my new boss. We have just been chatting on the phone in advance of her arrival, and clearly I can't tell her that I don't plan to be working at the station much longer because there is always the chance that I might be.

WHO KNOWS?
Sunday, April 1, 2007

The list of people who know about my plans continues to grow. I'm still keeping the news from people associated with work, but I'm telling a few more of my friends. This weekend, I met with our long-time family friend Jay McElroy to tell him that I planned to quit my job and that I was "talking" with the Peace Corps.

Jay is 90 years old and lives alone. His family and my family have been friends for more than 75 years. Jay was not at all surprised that I was thinking of quitting my job. He knows it has been very frustrating for me for the past year and was very supportive of me doing that. He did ask me a lot of questions to make sure I had thought my decision through thoroughly and finally said he could tell that I was not making an "impulsive" move. (Jay and I have a running joke that he never does anything impulsive.)

He was not overly familiar with the Peace Corps other than the basics that most people know. He was very happy to hear that I was planning to keep my home, and I told him that while I didn't know exactly what I would do when I got back, I would begin my job search in South Florida. He seemed happy to know that and said he would miss seeing me while I was away. Then he joked that his doctor had told him he would live to be 100, so we would still have time to catch up when I returned. He also asked me if he could tell some mutual friends, Dick and Peggy Pitkin, about my plans, and I told him that would be okay.

I also confided my plans to my friend Bob Pruitt. Bob is an e-mail buddy that I've known for seven or eight years. He and his wife live on St. George Island. In his e-mail back to me he said:

Steve,

Pursue your dream—if it is the Peace Corps, great—if something else, also great! Don't even think about what others may say or think—it's your life—go for it. I am certainly doing that, and I would encourage you to do the same.

That's probably the best encouragement I've gotten yet. It's a pretty strong "Go for it!" I'm hoping to do exactly that!

THE MEDITERRANEAN
Friday, April 6, 2007

I got a call today from the Peace Corps placement officer for the Pacific and Inter-Americas. He covers all of Central and South America, Mexico and the Caribbean along with the South Pacific.

He said the program to which I had been nominated had been "delayed" until October. He also said because of my allergy to shrimp and lobster, he was limited in the number of countries in the South Pacific where he could put me. He then added that there had been one other business development program, but because of the delay in getting my clearance, that program was now filled. This was clearly NOT the news I was expecting to hear. (And by the way, the delay was not really on my end.) I told him that my shrimp and lobster allergy was very mild and that I had had no symptoms in over ten years. I told him I would be glad to take an allergy test if that would help. He said that could possibly get the medical restriction lifted and that I should discuss it with my Peace Corps medical officer.

He said the Peace Corps wanted to make sure they put me in a program where my business skills could be best utilized. He said they don't like to put people like me with a lot of business experience in a program that is very basic. I told him I really was interested in business development.

He then said there was a "high-level" business development program in the Mediterranean working with the Peace Corps and USAID. It was scheduled to leave late June/early July. That was not his area, but if I was interested in looking at that program, he could send my file over there. I asked him a few questions about the program, and he did mention that it had a moderate climate since he had noticed that my file said I didn't want to go anywhere cold. I told him I would be happy to go anywhere in his area, but would like to know more about the Mediterranean program.

I was out of the office at the time I got the phone call. When I got back to work, I called my sister Becky and asked her to call me back when she was near a computer. I have made a point NOT to call up any websites or send any e-mail related to the Peace Corps from my office. She and I spent awhile on the phone and figured the most likely place, based on the location and the program, was Albania. It could also be Morocco or Jordan. However, Albania seemed to be closest to the way the program was described. She called me back a bit later to say there was a USAID program in Albania, which seemed to make it an even better match.

The placement officer said he would call me later today, but I never got the call. When I got home, I had this e-mail:

Subject: Business project in Eastern Europe

Hi Steve,

This email is to let you know that I have sent your skills over to my program managers in the field, for their review. Once I hear back from them on whether they feel the skill fit is right, I will let you know. You would then work with me towards an invitation, or go back to David for other program options.

OK, so that was probably my "call-back" sent via e-mail instead of phone. It was sent at 3:48 p.m. So now I am thinking about a whole different part of the world and an area where I haven't done a whole lot of research: Eastern Europe. I started researching by looking at *The Peace Corps Congressional Budget Justification*, which is a great document to find out about what is going on in each country and region. There are no countries specifically identified as being in the Mediterranean region, but there are just three in the Central and Eastern European region: Moldova, Romania and Ukraine. I don't really consider any of those Mediterranean. Albania is part of the Balkans and North Africa region along with Morocco, Bulgaria and Macedonia.

Unlike the South Pacific, where I would pretty much go to any of the countries, I do have concerns about going to many of these countries. First, having been to Eastern Europe on several occasions, including a visit to the Soviet Union before it fell, I have some idea of what to expect there. I also have some concerns about going to a strong Muslim country. While I would enjoy learning Arabic and more about the Muslim religion, I am not sure how comfortable I would be in a country where some (not all) of the Muslims would be very anti-American. That presents a bit of a problem, as Albania is 70% Muslim and Morocco is 98% Muslim.

I spoke with my dad tonight, and he made a great point: "Don't go just to get away from your current job. Do what is best for you." That was good advice and after doing a bit of reading, I don't think I would be as happy in Eastern Europe as I would be in the Pacific. It would be much easier for me to get home from Eastern Europe than from the South Pacific, but that probably should not be my overriding reason for going someplace. If I have to get home, I'll get home.

I'm going to send an e-mail to the Peace Corps medical officer tonight and ask him about taking an allergy test for shrimp and lobster. Since I've had no symptoms for so many years, it's possible it is not a big deal for me anymore. I used to have pollen allergies as well, but those went away 20 years ago. If I can get the shrimp and lobster allergy removed from my health record, that would free me up to go to any of the South Pacific countries.

I feel pretty certain the Peace Corps invitation is going to happen, and it does appear there is a bit more negotiation possible than I may have thought.

Of course, I also realize I have a bit more experience than the typical applicant.

At this point, I'm resigned to staying at work through May. I've been very careful to make sure that I've done nothing different at work and have made all decisions as if I were staying. Now, I know that was probably a smart thing to do.

SHRIMP AND LOBSTER ALLERGY TESTS
Thursday, April 12, 2007

At the suggestion of the Peace Corps Medical Office, I was tested for shrimp and lobster allergies today. This is a copy of the e-mail I sent to the Peace Corps placement officer this evening after learning the results.

Hi David:

I wanted to update you on a few things since we talked on the phone a week ago. This evening, I sent a letter to the medical officer showing the results of an allergy test I had done today. (I have no issue discussing this medical issue with you or anyone else.) The good news is that all the tests were negative, and I have asked him to please update my file with the new information.

When I spoke with you, I indicated that I needed to make a decision about my current job by last Friday. I have committed to stay in that job until May. If I am offered an invitation, I would not be able to leave the area until after that date.

Once May is behind me, I don't have another critical period at work until the beginning of October. That gives me a tremendous amount of flexibility in departure dates. Ideally, it would be great to receive an invitation soon, even if I have to wait several months before departure.

You mentioned in our phone call that there might be an opportunity in the Mediterranean for business development. I have not heard anything about that, and while I wish to remain flexible, that area would not be one of my first choices. I remain interested primarily in the areas I discussed in my interview, which are the South Pacific, the Caribbean and Central and South America. I would be happy to accept an invitation to any of those areas. (South Pacific would still be my top choice.)

I realize you have a tough job trying to match all the applicants with the various programs available. And while I know you have a copy of my resume, I thought I would close by telling you about something that is not on my resume and which I think would be beneficial in a small-business development program.

About 10 years ago, I was one of the founding members of The Chattanooga Press Club. This was a membership organization where dues were collected. I was elected treasurer of the group. We dealt in small dollar amounts, but I kept very meticulous books, presenting financial statements at every meeting. My years in management paid off on a very small scale because of my ability to think in both micro and macro terms.

During my tenure, one of our members was killed in an accident. We then turned to fund-raising so that we could endow a journalism scholarship in his name. By using smart business practices, we were able to grow the money we received and eventually donate the money to the University of Tennessee at Chattanooga.

It's a small story, but after having read about the work that small-business volunteers are doing in the South Pacific, it seemed like one worth sharing.

I look forward to hearing from you soon.

OH WHERE, OH WHERE?
Friday, April 20, 2007

I spoke with my Peace Corps placement officer on Monday. The program for which I was nominated has officially been cancelled. That means they now need to find someplace else to put me. He said he was having a difficult time finding something for me in my target areas of the South Pacific, Central and South America and the Caribbean. Because I don't speak Spanish, that limits me to certain areas. He said he was sure that we could work something out but wanted to know about other areas where I might be interested in going. I told him I would research the other areas where the Peace Corps operates and send him an e-mail. Below is what I am planning to send him:

Dear David:

Thanks for spending so much time with me on the phone Monday discussing various placement opportunities. As I mentioned, my time frame is much more flexible now. I have spent a good deal of time researching the business development programs by reviewing the "Peace Corps 2008 Congressional Budget Justification." That gave me a good perspective on all the different countries and areas served by the Peace Corps.

I was particularly intrigued by this description for a program in Vanuatu. It sounds EXACTLY like something I would like to do:

One volunteer helped to make coffee a significant income generator for Tanna Island farmers by introducing business management skills into small enterprise farming and developing the country's first rural-based processing factory.

Projects like the brief description of this one are exactly why I would like to receive an invitation to the Peace Corps. During my business career, I have gotten much satisfaction out of finding solutions to problems and implementing strong business skills on different projects. (I even started a separate business for my current company several years ago and kept the books for the first year.)

While I still remain most interested in the South Pacific region, I do realize the need to be flexible. Certainly the business development programs in the non-Spanish speaking countries of the Eastern Caribbean and Jamaica would also be high on my list of choices.

Outside of the areas we have already discussed, I would be interested in the business development program in the Philippines. And while there doesn't appear to be a business development program in China, I would have a lot of interest in going to China. (I realize that is outside of my request to stay in a warm climate.) I was particularly intrigued by the idea of the "English Corner" concept described in the "Volunteer Focus" area, which would certainly put my years of public speaking skills to use. I also like the idea of teaching business skills.

Thailand could also be a possibility for me.

I really appreciate you working with me to find a "good fit."

I look forward to hearing from you again soon.

I'M GOING TO THE SOUTH PACIFIC!
Thursday, May 3, 2007

It has been a GREAT day. I got a call from David, the placement officer for the South Pacific area, telling me he is going to send me an invitation for a business development program in the South Pacific. It was the call I've been waiting months to receive. It is the same program that I was originally nominated for last October that was cancelled. David told me they are combining the twice-a-year programs into a once-a-year departure as it is one of the smaller programs.

I had been expecting a June or July departure based on my last conversation with him. He said instead of trying to rush me into one of those programs, and since I told him I was flexible on my departure date, he was putting me into a program in October. That news was almost as exciting as learning that I was receiving the invitation. That means I have four months between the end of my job and the time I have to leave. It also means I will be around for my parents' 50th wedding anniversary in August. I am totally thrilled.

I knew that David would not be able to tell me where I would be going, but I asked anyway. As expected, he said that information would be contained in the official invitation I would be receiving in the mail by the end of the month. Once I receive it, I have 10 days to accept it, which I'm positive I will do.

I was able to pick up a few clues about where I might be going in our conversation. It's a small program, which means it is not Vanuatu, which I know is the largest in the South Pacific. And it's a business development program. That means it is either Samoa or Tonga. Fiji, Kiribati and Micronesia/Palau don't list business development options. And both Samoa and Tonga are relatively small programs with 46 volunteers in Samoa and 49 in Tonga.

Both Samoa and Tonga have had October departure dates in the past. However, in a previous conversation with my recruiter, who served in Samoa, she said she doubted there would be a June departure for Samoa. That leaves Tonga. I'm totally cool with either one, but tonight, I also received an e-mail from the Peace Corps about Tonga. I'm sure it is a coincidence, as I get one each month, but perhaps that is it.

I also searched the blogs this evening and found departures in past years in June for Tonga but not for Samoa. Here's an interesting little tidbit about Tonga: Tonga lies three degrees east of the International Date Line, which was bent to include Tonga in the same time zone as its neighbors. For this reason, Tonga is the first country in the world to welcome each new day.

While watching the news in my office tonight, one of my employees came in and said she couldn't believe the big smile on my face. I told her I had found out where I was going, and she said she could tell how excited I must be about this. She also said she was "totally shocked" that I was joining the Peace Corps. I've gotten that reaction a lot from people as they learn of my decision, but almost all have said it in a very positive way.

One of my long-time friends called me today because she had heard I was leaving. It turns out her brother was in the Peace Corps in Fiji and did two stints there, even though the Peace Corps usually doesn't allow that. Someone else whom I've known for a number of years told me about his experience in Bolivia in the Peace Corps. It's really refreshing and only inspires me more.

I'm thrilled about the four (almost five) month wait, but I'm ready to get started.

I MADE THE NEWSPAPER
Friday, May 4, 2007

WPEC news director quits job to join Peace Corps

By Melissa E. Holsman
melissa.holsman@scripps.com
May 3, 2007

Steve Hunsicker, executive news director for WPEC and WFLX Fox 29, surprised just about everyone in local TV news by announcing that he's resigning his job to become a Peace Corps volunteer — in the South Pacific. "I'm going to be a business advisor there and I am just thrilled," said Hunsicker, 47, who joined WPEC in 2003, but has been with the station's parent company, Freedom Broadcasting, Inc., since 1992.

His last day at WPEC is May 11. The move, he said, fulfills a lifelong dream he's kept on hold while racking up 23 years as a successful TV news executive.

"I finally just said it's time," said Hunsicker, who began the Peace Corps application process in September. He said he opted not to tell the staff at the CBS affiliate until he knew for sure he'd been accepted. "I didn't even tell my parents for about a month," he noted.

And it'll be another month before he learns which of the six South Pacific countries served by the Peace Corps he'll be assigned to. "I'll be working to help either individuals or perhaps a small business, come up with good business practices and educate them about ways to grow their business," he said.

Initially, he'll undergo three months of in-country training to learn the language and become familiar with the country's customs. "Then you learn where you'll be living," he said.

He endured three months of medical screenings and background checks before learning he'd been accepted as a volunteer. "I had to actually sign a statement that I wasn't applying to work in the CIA, which I thought was kind of bizarre," he recalled.

He said he plans to keep his West Palm Beach home, will pack his dog off to his parents and has enlisted his sister's help to watch over things while he's gone.

"I'm a little nervous," he said. "I'm giving up a career and income to go do this but I feel that I'm not getting any younger and it seemed like the right time to do it and when I got the official word, I was just absolutely thrilled."

Meanwhile, he said WPEC management will launch a search for his replacement.

WHAT A SURPRISE!
Sunday, May 6, 2007

I have been completely blown away by the response I've received to my decision to join the Peace Corps. I knew my family and close friends would be supportive. But I've heard from people I haven't talked with in years. That has been really nice. However, I was totally unprepared for the reaction from perfect strangers.

The *South Florida Sun-Sentinel* in Fort Lauderdale picked up the story of my plans. Right there on its web page were these comments. I'm almost speechless.

> *mary j acker*
> *Oceanside, CA*
>
> Steve, good for you. A humanitarian is certainly an honorable title and this will be one of your best experiences. Good luck and enjoy and please keep us informed.

> *Davie*
> *Pompano Beach, FL*
>
> Best of luck to you on this new endeavor in your life. It is admirable to learn of someone wanting to give back to mankind.

> *vincylucian*
> *Bamako, Mali*
>
> Steve, don't know you or had heard about you before this article, but have to congratulate you on making the bold move. As an "older" volunteer currently serving in Africa, I feel it helpful to share that those first months of training are rough, but once service begins, the rewards are endless and worth all the hardships in the beginning. Best of luck to you!

> *Local*
>
> Kudos to Mr. Hunsicker. He is doing what many have thought of but will never act upon. Good luck and all the best.

The story has also been picked up by *Shop*Talk*, a TV industry newsletter, and other TV blogs.

NEWS TRAVELS FAST
Tuesday, May 8, 2007

My recruiter, Trisha, called me today. She said the Peace Corps public affairs officer had heard about me from someone at CNN. He was thrilled with the publicity that has been generated by my announcement. She then invited me to come to Atlanta on Wednesday to attend a reception with former President Jimmy Carter and the head of the Peace Corps.

> *On May 16th, 2007, the Atlanta Regional Office will host the Lillian Carter Award Ceremony. This award honors a Volunteer who served overseas as a senior (50 years or older) and has demonstrated a commitment to fulfill Peace Corps' third goal in his or her community: helping promote a better understanding of other peoples on the part of Americans.*
>
> *President Jimmy Carter and Peace Corps Director Ron Tschetter will be the featured speakers at the celebration, which will be held at the Carter Presidential Center in Atlanta. President Carter will read from his mother's letters reflecting on her experiences as one of the first seniors to serve as a Peace Corps volunteer in India.*
>
> *Director Tschetter, who served with Miss Lillian in 1966-68, will introduce the Peace Corps' new initiative to match more senior Americans in overseas assignments and celebrate the important contribution they have made since 1961 in promoting world peace and friendship.*
>
> *This year's event will also include the Burundi Drummers and Dancers of Atlanta and the Master of Ceremony will be Jocelyn Dorsey, Director of Editorials and Public Affairs, WSB TV.*

Of course, I'm going to go. My first memory of the Peace Corps was when Jimmy Carter was running for president. I remember hearing of Miss Lillian's Peace Corps service at that time, and I remember that inspired me to want to know more about the program. I also interviewed her at the 1980 Democratic Convention in New York, which I was covering. She was probably the first famous person I ever interviewed. I was in college at the time but was working in radio news.

I also learned a very valuable lesson that day—one I have never forgotten. I asked Miss Lillian if I could interview her. She agreed and we sat down and chatted for about 20 minutes. When I was done, I discovered the batteries in my tape recorder had died, and I had just 10 seconds of usable audio from the entire interview. Lesson learned: Always put in new batteries before you do an interview. It never happened to me again.

MORE NEWSPAPER STORIES
Thursday, May 17, 2007

I don't remember much that happened my first day in television news. That was 23 years ago on July 30th, 1984. I don't think I could have ever imagined that my last day would be as strange as it was. Here is how the day was described in the newspaper:

WPEC Staff Tested for TB

By Melissa Holsman

Former WPEC News 12 executive news director Steve Hunsicker had a rather unexpected, but no doubt eventful, last day on the job Friday, as staff at the CBS affiliate were told they might have been exposed to tuberculosis from an employee who'd contracted the highly infectious disease.

I imagine the staff who were directed to gather at the station Friday morning, were somewhat surprised to see two nurses ready to test them for TB, instead of an occasion to bid farewell to Hunsicker, who left to become a Peace Corps volunteer in the South Pacific.

When I called, Hunsicker declined to discuss details of the TB scare, other than to say he still thought a send-off soiree was in the works. As for the risk of TB exposure at WPEC, health department public information officer Tim O'Connor said it was not an outbreak, and the testing was a required precautionary measure whenever someone tests positive for tuberculosis.

And the very last story I wrote? It was a story about the health department testing the staff for TB. I doubt it will be remembered for its compelling journalism.

I had predicted months ago that some people would jump to conclusions about the reasons for me leaving. That's exactly what happened in the *Palm Beach Post* when the guy who writes the gossip column published the following:

There'd better not be complicated computers at the Peace Corps! Former WPEC-Channel 12 and WFLX-Channel 29 news boss Steve Hunsicker stunned most of his employees when he quit last week for a stint in the Peace Corps. Maybe no one should have been too surprised. I'm told by a source close to WPEC that Hunsicker didn't earn many brownie points from new General Manager Diana Wilkin while overseeing the transition to the new robotic camera system. It allows the station to broadcast news shows with fewer producers — Translation: It saves money! — but on-air glitches have been so numerous that even the unflappable anchor Curt Fonger has had enough . . .

There is no question that the automation process was a mess, and our shows suffered. However, I had absolutely nothing to do with the decision to buy this equipment and strenuously objected to it being implemented on-air before we were ready. (I lost that argument.) What is true is that I knew the equipment was coming when I applied to join the Peace Corps last September. But it had very little to do with my decision to apply. And while I haven't spoken with Curt since the story came out, he had been one of the supporters of the automation.

WHAT MAKES A PRESIDENT CRY?
Thursday, May 17, 2007

"People are more alike than they are different." That was the bit of wisdom delivered by this year's winner of the Lillian Carter Award which honors Peace Corps volunteers who started their service after age 50. Miss Lillian Carter joined the Peace Corps in her sixties and volunteered in India. At today's reception honoring this year's honoree, President Carter reflected on not only the work of his mother, but that of the other returned Peace Corps volunteers in the room.

The former president told the story of how his mom worked for a family in India. The father used to give "Miss" Lillian fresh vegetables. Miss Lillian had no way to pay for the produce, so she taught his daughter English.

President Jimmy Carter speaks at the Carter Center in Atlanta, Georgia

President Carter, who has been active in Habitat for Humanity since leaving the White House, went back to India last year and met that girl. The former president, his emotions showing, explained that the girl was now the president of a university and had earned her PhD. Yes, the Peace Corps does make a difference and his mother made a difference. And even presidents are more like the rest of us than they are different when telling stories about their mothers.

Perhaps the highlight of the ceremony was a performance by an African drum group, the Burundi Drummers and Dancers of Atlanta.

These kids were just terrific, and they got a standing ovation from the crowd of former Peace Corps volunteers and guests.

Today was a great day for me. It was gratifying not only to hear the stories about Miss Lillian, but also to hear those of the current director of the Peace Corps, Ron Tshetter, and the woman honored at today's event, Shirley Maly. I had a chance to talk with several returned Peace Corps volunteers, and I have no doubt that I am about to embark on one of the greatest adventures of my life. I hope I live up to the build-up that I've gotten so far from both the Peace Corps and my friends and family.

Today I had my photo taken at the Carter Center and then was interviewed by a woman from the Peace Corps communication office. She asked me a lot of questions about the application process and what advice I would give other mid-career applicants. (That's PC-speak for people like me who are not at retirement age, but who have been working for a while.) The director of Peace Corps announced a new program today to get more baby boomers to sign up.

President Carter was introduced by his grandson, Jason Carter, who was also a Peace Corps volunteer. He has written a book about his time in Africa. And President Carter's sister has compiled a collection of Miss Lillian's writing. I'm ordering both from Amazon.com when I get home.

The event generated a lot of media attention, with several TV crews there and some print reporters. I made the *Atlanta Journal Constitution* this morning in a preview of the ceremony. Reading the article, which appeared on page one of the local section, I wondered how I was going to be worked into the story. You can read that for yourself.

The Atlanta Journal-Constitution
May 16, 2007

To those 50 and older: Peace Corps wants you

When Lillian Carter approached her children in 1966 about joining the Peace Corps, she expected some resistance. Carter was 68. The Peace Corps was in its infancy, and largely staffed by college-age kids looking to save the world at the time of the Vietnam War. "She was looking for something exciting to do," said Jimmy Carter, then a state senator. "Age was no barrier for her." Lillian Carter spent 21 months in the Peace Corps, working as a nurse in India treating lepers. She returned to America with 10 cents to her name and was so emotionally and physically drained that she had to be wheeled off the plane to Atlanta in a wheelchair. "It opened my eyes to the need in the developing world for better health care, when I was governor, president and now," Jimmy Carter said. "[The Carter Center has] programs in 71 nations. [Her experience] has affected my life profoundly."

This afternoon, the Peace Corps will honor the former president's mother, who died in 1983, by presenting the Lillian Carter Award in a ceremony at the Carter Center in Atlanta. Jimmy Carter and Peace Corps Director Ron Tschetter will present the award to Shirley Maly of Nebraska, who served in Uruguay from 1992 to 1995. Established in

1986, the award is given every two years to a volunteer who was at least age 50 at the time of service. Tschetter said he also will use the ceremony to begin a campaign to recruit more people over 50. Only about 5 percent of the 7,749 Peace Corps volunteers are over 50. The average volunteer is 27 years old.

"We are putting a lot of new emphasis on trying to get the boomers," said Tschetter, 65, who in the 1960s volunteered with his wife, Nancy, in India. Tschetter said he wants 10 percent of volunteers to be older Americans and hopes to recruit up to 500 by next year. Tschetter said recruiting efforts will expand to retirement groups, like the AARP.

"They are the Kennedy people," he said. "They heard about Kennedy's call in the 1960s. But at the time, they thought, 'Wonderful, but I need a job.' Now, they are here, they are healthy, they have resources and they really have a heart to serve." John F. Kennedy, during his 1960 inauguration, laid the groundwork for the Peace Corps with: "And so, my fellow Americans: ask not what your country can do for you —ask what you can do for your country."

Established by a 1961 executive order, the Peace Corps was immediately popular, and by 1966 had 15,556 volunteers in more than 55 countries. "The goals of 1961 are still the goals of today. To take a sustainable skill abroad and bring a better understanding of America," said Tschetter. "It is amazing, when you visit the villages, the work, the connections, the grass roots have not changed a lot." Tschetter said 98 percent of volunteers are college graduates who serve in 73 countries. About 1,800 returned Peace Corps volunteers live in metro Atlanta. "It changes you drastically. You go from being kind of a playful college kid to being a serious person," said Jimmy Carter's grandson, Jason Carter, who volunteered in South Africa in 1998, a year after graduating from Duke University. "The Peace Corps settled me down." A lawyer in Atlanta, Jason Carter will host the event. My great-grandmother turned 70 in the Peace Corps," he said. "Her experience affected our whole family. It is one of the things that drives us."

Tschetter said a bulk of Peace Corps work involves HIV and AIDS. And with an ever-changing global political climate, safety is a top priority. "Sometimes we will leave [a country] for safety and security reasons," said Tschetter, speaking from Botswana.

Julia Campbell, 40, a former journalist, was killed in April in the Philippines. A resident has been charged with her murder. "Safety is our first, second and third priority," said Tschetter. He said despite safety concerns the Peace Corps still has three times more applicants than it can place. "Our volunteerism, application rate and interest have actually gone up since 9/11. We are right around the 30-year high," he said. "The Peace Corps is very vibrant."

Back in 1966, Lillian Carter stressed that she wanted to go "to a country where the people were destitute, darkskinned and needed help." As chronicled in *Away From Home: Letters to My Family* — a book co-written by her daughter, Gloria Carter Spann — Lillian Carter was sent to Vikhroli, a suburb of Mumbai [then known as Bombay]. Carter said his mother, a registered nurse, initially worked in family planning, but soon began helping a doctor at a local clinic. "I was in the state Senate at the time, running for governor. I was able to contact some of the pharmaceutical companies and got free medicine to send over there,"

Carter recalled. "But the doctor was grossly overloaded and would treat between 200 to 300 people a day. She gave away all her money and food. She came back debilitated."

In 1980, Steve Hunsicker, a young radio reporter, interviewed Lillian Carter during the Democratic National Convention. They didn't discuss the Peace Corps, but Hunsicker knew of her work. He went on to enjoy a nice career, rising to news director at a television station in West Palm Beach, Fla. Then he quit. To join the Peace Corps. "I thought maybe this was the time to do this," said Hunsicker, 47, who plans to attend the ceremony. He said he will be assigned to the South Pacific to work in business development. "When I was 28, I knew some things. Clearly, I know a lot of things now," said Hunsicker. "I think I have a life experience and a maturity level that will serve me well."

THE ADVENTURE BEGINS OCTOBER 2ND!
Tuesday, May 29, 2007

Congratulations!! It is with great pleasure that we invite you to begin training in Tonga for Peace Corps service.

That's how the letter began, ending months of speculation and confirming that I will be heading to the South Pacific Kingdom of Tonga in October. Included with the letter, there was lots of information about Tonga and the business development program, plus a few surprises (more on those in a minute).

First, where is Tonga? Tonga is "where time begins." That means it is the first country across the International Date Line, the place where each day begins. The islands are southwest of Hawaii and northeast of New Zealand.

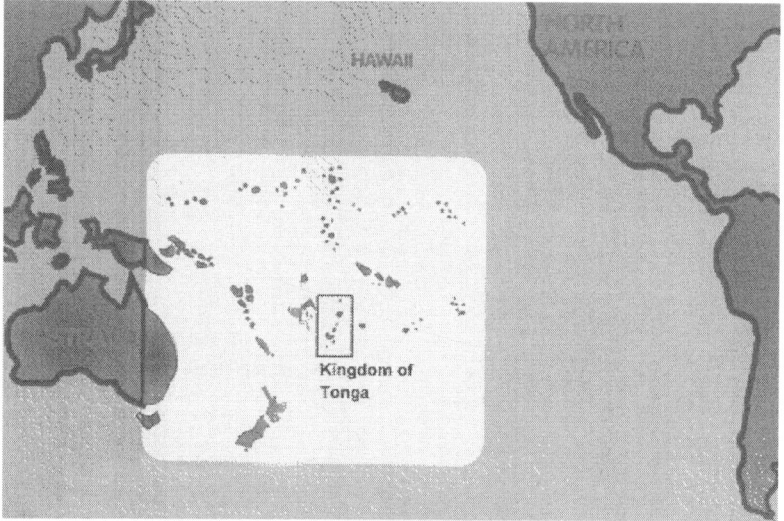

Tonga is a kingdom and is the only Pacific island country never to have been under the rule of a foreign government.

I will be a business educator/advisor in the business education and development program. I won't know until I complete three months of training exactly what I will be doing, but the information from the Peace Corps says it will either be "business education in schools" or "business advising with local governmental and non-governmental institutions." There are opportunities in the "development and sale of handicrafts, agricultural and marine products, and tourism services." Regardless of what I do specifically, I will probably have some business teaching responsibilities in addition to my main work area.

I will gather with the other people in my group, which is called "Peace Corps Tonga Group 73," in the United States on October 2nd and then leave for Tonga on October 4th. My training is scheduled to be completed on January 15, 2008.

I am allowed to have visitors. However, I can't have visitors until at least April 15th of next year.

There are many details about the Kingdom of Tonga and what I can expect in the *Peace Corps Welcome Book* that was sent to me.

I mentioned there were a couple of surprises in the packet.

The first is that I will likely be based on Tongatapu near the capital city of Nuku'alofa or in the city center of an outer island. If I'm on the main island, it is likely that I will have Internet service and even cell phone access. Internet and e-mail are also available in the cities on the outer islands. That would be great if it works out—a pleasant surprise.

The second surprise has to do with the dress code. I am quoting below from the assignment materials I received: "Men wear a cotton button down shirt with a collar (long or short sleeves) and a wrap-around skirt (tupenu) or long pants."

Yes, that did say a SKIRT. It also goes on to say that shorts, my favorite form of dress, are never appropriate in a work setting. This is nothing I can't get used to, but a surprise nonetheless.

I have lots more reading to do and many forms to fill out, including an updated resume, a passport application (can't use my current one) and insurance forms.

In addition to all the Peace Corps paperwork, I'm going to try to make contact with some of the other members of Peace Corps Tonga Group 73.

Steve Hunsicker

MORE ABOUT TONGA
Monday, July 9, 2007

The Peace Corps is celebrating 40 years of service to the Island Kingdom of Tonga. The first group of volunteers arrived in October 1967. Since then, more than a thousand volunteers have worked to help the Tongans. While most of the work has been positive, the Peace Corps in Tonga has not been without its share of controversy. Most recently, there was a shake-up in the senior Peace Corps staff in Tonga and the cancellation of the June business development program. However, the biggest controversy dates back to 1976, when a Peace Corps volunteer was charged with killing another volunteer. But there was a lot more to it than just the murder. Phillip Weiss wrote a book about the incident called *American Taboo*, and CBS News featured the case in 1994 on its show, *48 Hours*.

But that's all recent history and is well documented. Tonga was first discovered by Captain Cook in the 1770's, and it is fairly accepted that it was Captain Cook who first dubbed Tonga "The Friendly Islands"—a nickname still used today. However, there are several versions of how "friendly" the early Tongans really were to Cook and his crews.

Here's what Lonely Planet has to say in its Samoan Island and Tonga guidebook:

> While visiting Lifuke, Cook and his men were treated to lavish feasting and entertainment ... the plan was to gather the Englishmen into a convenient place so they could be quickly killed and their ships looted. There was, however, a dispute (over the time of the attack) ... and the operation was abandoned altogether.

However, the *Moon Travel Handbook* tells it this way in its Tonga Samoa guide:

> When Captain Cook visited Tonga ... he and his men were received with lavish friendliness ... Some say the islanders intended to roast and eat Cook and his men as part of the feast, but Cook's profuse thanks at his reception prompted them to change their minds.

That description may seem a bit outlandish, but early Tonga did have cannibals. However, eating another person was generally seen as a way to take over his or her power and not as a way to satisfy a hungry appetite.

Today, Tonga is considered one of the safest countries in the region, and its people continue to enjoy a friendly reputation. The country is small. There are 176 islands, but the population is about 100,000. Worldwide, there are probably less than 200,000 Tongans, but it's interesting how quickly you can find people who have a connection to this country.

In the past several weeks, I've heard from my first cousin in Texas who says she knows a Methodist minister from Tonga. Another friend, who is a nurse at a hospital in California, had a Tongan patient. I met a woman in Virginia who told me to get ready for some "great rugby" once I get to Tonga. And a friend in Kansas who has visited Tonga several times has adopted a family there, providing them with school supplies.

I also e-mailed a volunteer who is serving in Tonga right now, who tells me that my Peace Corps group will be a combination of both business and education volunteers and that there will be about 30 of us. (I'm guessing they are trying to recover from the June cancellation.) Apparently, we will all be training in the Vava'u Islands, which are warmer than Tongatapu, where the capital city of Nuku'alofa is located.

I've been reading the online editions of two Tongan newspapers recently, and some of the stories are about the same issues that people everywhere face: taxes, low pay, rising prices, crowded roads, private investment and Iraq. That's right, Tonga is part of the Iraq coalition, and President Bush referred to Tonga as his favorite country when it signed up to send a small contingent to join the United States.

Some of the other news is a lot more fun. Rugby is very popular as are the players. And Tonga recently had two beauty pageants. The Miss Heilala Pageant would be considered a typical contest with beautiful women. The second pageant will be a surprise to those not familiar with Tongan culture. The Miss Galaxy Pageant features *fakaleiti* who are young Tongan men who dress up as women. This is apparently an accepted part of Tongan society.

As I've been traveling the past couple of months, I've gotten lots of questions about what life will be like in Tonga. I have some idea, but there is a lot that I don't know. That's part of the excitement of getting to discover new things and of living in a new land. Perhaps the two most frequently asked questions are: "Will you be living in a grass hut?" and "What will you eat?"

The living situation is wide open. I could be living somewhere without electricity on an outer island, but I've read and been told it is more likely that I will be in a city since I'm in business development. That increases the chances that I'll have electricity. One business volunteer right now even has wireless Internet at his house, but that is rare.

When it comes to food, the easy answer is "pork, fish and sweet potatoes." *The Peace Corps Welcome Book* for Tonga says, "Tongan meals consist of staple foods, such as yam, taro, sweet potato, cassava, fish, pork, and canned meats. One of the most common dishes is cooked taro leaves with coconut cream. On Sundays and for special occasions, Tongan families prepare an underground oven called an *umu*."

The government of Tonga is a constitutional monarchy ruled by King George Tupou V since the death of his father on September 11th, 2006. A lavish coronation ceremony is tentatively scheduled for August 2008.

Finally, I'll close with some numbers. The main island, Tongatapu, is 259 square kilometers. That's about 100 square miles. At its longest point, the island is about 20 miles long. The highest point is 82 meters or about 270 feet above sea level. The entire country is about four times the size of Washington, DC. The literacy rate is 99%, and the pa'anga is the national currency, which is worth about 51 cents.

THREE WEEKS
Sunday, September 9, 2007

Three weeks from today, I will officially begin my journey to Tonga to start my Peace Corps training. It has now been a year since I first applied to volunteer. I can't wait to get started. I actually couldn't be happier about the way things have worked out so far with the process.

While the application process was long and frustrating, it has been great to have so much time since receiving my invitation before I depart. I was originally scheduled to leave in early June, but due to a cancellation of the June program to Tonga, I was able to have almost five months to get ready.

It has been four months since I stopped working, and I can honestly say there has not been a single day when I was bored or looked back and wished I was still in television. I've also had a great opportunity to spend time with family and friends and to take some fun trips. I have also had time to get my personal affairs in order.

I will leave West Palm Beach on September 30th for Los Angeles, where I will have a couple of days of training. Then it is on to Tonga. So far, I've had contact with four people from my group and am anxiously looking forward to meeting the others.

According to the latest information I've received from the Peace Corps, "access to email should be available—albeit not necessarily at all times." In addition, it describes phone service as reliable but pricy. However, I may not have phone access during my 10 weeks of in-country training.

It may take four to six weeks for mail to get to me. That means if you were to mail something today, I would already be in Tonga when it arrived. The Peace Corps recommends that mail be sent in envelopes or padded envelopes if possible, as boxes tend to be taxed and opened more frequently.

In just 10 days, I'm going back to Virginia for a few days to say goodbye to my sisters and their families. I'm then coming back to Florida with Mom and Dad, who are going to spend the final six days with me and take me to the airport.

Stay tuned . . . the adventure begins very soon!

'Alu a! (Goodbye!)

MY BAGS ARE PACKED; I'M READY TO GO!
Thursday, September 20, 2007

I will soon be joining 32 other people for the journey to Tonga. The group (33 including me) is larger than I had expected but apparently it includes both education volunteers and business volunteers like me.

Today was final packing day. I'm heading to Virginia to begin a 10-day trek to say goodbye to my family before leaving September 30th for Los Angeles.

I have been out with friends here in Florida every day for the past week to say goodbye. It's exciting for me as the days get closer, but it is also a bit sad knowing that I won't see many of these people for more than two years. A couple of friends have even promised to visit, and I hope they are able to work that out.

Because I've had a bit of time to plan, I have done a lot of thinking about what to take with me and how to comply with the Peace Corps' mandated 80 lb. limit for checked baggage. (No checked bag can exceed 50 lbs. and all bags must be 80 lbs. total.) I'm taking two bags to check and a backpack as a carry-on. Thankfully, there are a number of volunteers who have posted what you need and don't need to bring with you to survive for two years.

The most helpful posting I have found was on "Tak's Peace Corps Tonga." I've made a few changes but am pretty much going with his list. I decided to bring a snorkel and mask but not fins, which are pretty bulky. I figure I can get a cheap pair in Tonga, and those are not as critical as the mask and snorkel. I also took his advice and had my Cingular (now ATT) cell phone unlocked, so I could activate it if I end up in a place with cell service. I already have a Bank of America ATM card, which was a very helpful suggestion. I bought a solar battery charger, so I can charge the batteries for my camera, MP3 player and flashlights without electricity, if necessary. I tried it out here in Florida, and it seemed to work pretty well, but hopefully, I will have a good supply of electricity when I get my final assignment. I am also bringing a bicycle lock, which another person suggested as a handy item to have because you can use it not only to lock a bike but also to secure other items.

The "stuff" that is going to Tonga with Steve Hunsicker
When you look at this photo, it doesn't seem like a lot of stuff for a two-year stint, but I have been able to make it all fit into two bags.

I know I'm over the weight limit, probably by about 10 lbs., perhaps even 15 lbs. Hopefully, I'll be able to sneak through with the extra weight. The airline on which we are flying to Tonga says you can have two bags up to 50 lbs each. If that's the case, then I will be fine. However, I don't know if the Peace Corps has some kind of special deal, or if we will follow the same weight requirements as the airline.

Oh, and I got MORE forms today to fill out for the Peace Corps. These had to do with W-2's and direct deposit. We actually get taxed on the small stipend that they give us as volunteers. It is currently $280 per month or $3,360 per year. We also get a $24-a-month vacation allowance and a one-time move-in payment of $516 to buy basic household items once we get our permanent job assignment. That comes to $4,164 for the first year. It doesn't seem like much but apparently it is more than adequate. You are expected to live at the same economic level as your neighbors and colleagues. One volunteer in Tonga claims to have saved money because she didn't need the whole amount.

HEADING TO LA
Monday, October 1, 2007

After more than a year of paperwork, medical tests and interviews, I'm finally on my way to Los Angeles for staging. Right now, I'm flying somewhere over the Gulf of Mexico, after saying a final goodbye to my parents. Saying goodbye has been a lot harder than I thought it would be—not just to my parents—but to my sisters, other members of my family and my friends. I've certainly been away for long periods of time in the past, but never for two years with little chance of seeing most of the important people in my life during the time away. For the last week, I started saying, "my last trip to Miami," "my last trip to my favorite restaurant," "my last swim in the pool," etc. Of course, it probably isn't really my last ever trip to those places, but it does seem like a long time before I will be back. All the goodbyes have been great, but I've put on a few pounds from all the big going-away meals and drinks.

As I was checking in at the airport counter, they weighed my bags, and I was over a bit more than I thought. After a bit or rearranging, I got my big bag to weigh in at 70 lbs., the maximum Continental allows. I had to pay a $25 surcharge for being over the weight limit. The Peace Corps will not reimburse me for this but I am not sure what else I could have left out at this point. Apparently, I will have to pay $35 for the extra weight on our overseas flight. The good news is I've packed so that I shouldn't have to open the bag until I get to Tonga. Once there, I can store the things I won't need during training.

A couple of days ago, I got an e-mail from the Peace Corps with more details about what I'll be doing for the remainder of this year. I will begin training almost immediately after arriving in Tonga on Thursday (which is Wednesday in the United States). I'll have two homestays during my training. That means I will be living in the home of two Tongan families. The first home-stay will be with another volunteer on the main island of Tonga and will last 18 days. After that, I get to take a 22-hour boat trip to Vava'u, which is north of the main island. I've heard from other volunteers that the 22-hour boat trip is not very pleasant and that we will be on deck for the trip. Once I get there, it looks like the second homestay lasts about six weeks. The Peace Corps e-mail also said I should have access to the Internet and perhaps even to phones during my training. It will be great if I can keep in touch with everyone back home.

My biggest concern about joining the Peace Corps has been learning the language. I've never learned a language, so I don't have a frame of reference on how I will do. I bought the Tongan language CDs and book to start studying, but learning from a CD is difficult, as you don't get any feedback on how you are progressing. I was very happy to read that "instructors teach formal language classes five days a week to small groups of four to five people." I think being in a small group should make it much easier for me to learn.

Assuming that I pass the language test and other training successfully, I will be sworn in as a volunteer on December 13th. Shortly before that time, I should find out my permanent job assignment and where I will be living.

I opted to come to Los Angeles a day early. That way I avoided having to get up at 5 a.m. to get to the airport and get a same-day flight to Los Angeles. I figured I could use one more night of sleep before diving into the Peace Corps' very full training schedule. My uncle, who lives in Palm Desert, is driving to Los Angeles to see me.

MALO E LEILEI
Friday, October 5, 2007

Hello from the Kingdom of Tonga! I'm finally here and have been so impressed with this island kingdom so far. We got in Thursday morning and were greeted at the airport by cheering Peace Corps workers and volunteers. As we cleared customs, we were each presented with a flower lei and given a great welcome.

After flying all night, I thought I would be exhausted, but I found that after a cold shower (that's the only kind here), I was ready to set out and explore some of the island. I didn't get to see much but was amazed at how friendly the people were to us as my roommate and I walked the streets. Almost everyone said hello to us, and school children waved as we walked by. It is fascinating to see a place where culture is still so important. This is most obvious by observing the dress of the native people, which is very much in line with what the Peace Corps had predicted.

This afternoon, we had a welcoming "kava ceremony" from our country director, who is the head person in charge of the Peace Corps in Tonga. Kava is a drink made of the root of the kava plant, ground and mixed with water. Before we had our first taste of Tongan kava, we were treated to the story of how kava came to be such a tradition in the local culture.

I've seen kava described many ways, ranging from "gross" to "tasty." I would have to say that it is about what you would expect a root ground up in water to taste like. I only had a small cup and did not feel any of the effects—a sense of relaxation, according to our training. As a welcome gift, the country director presented us with our own kava cup to use during our tenure here in Tonga.

As the CD (country director) was welcoming us in his opening presentation, I felt a tap on my shoulder. One of the Peace Corps staff asked if I could step away and give an interview to Tongan television. I didn't really want to stand up and walk away, but she said they were getting ready to leave and needed to interview someone. The interview was pretty simple. The reporter, who was also the photographer, asked me to say something about Tonga. I wasn't really sure what to say and was really expecting a question. I started talking, and then he told me he hadn't turned on the camera. I quickly gave an answer about how impressed I was with Tonga so far and how I was really looking forward to seeing more of the island and meeting more of the people. His second and final question was, "Do you have anything else to say?" I responded that I was glad to be a part of the Peace Corps and was looking forward to working in Tonga. That was it. He thanked me, and I went back to the welcome ceremony. He also interviewed a woman from our group. I have no idea if anything I said will actually end up on TV, but one of the current volunteers here told me that I shouldn't be surprised if someone comes up to me and tells me they have seen me on TV.

Several of my fellow trainees got a laugh out of the fact that I was selected to be interviewed since they all know from training that I spent my career in TV news. Of course most of it was on the "other" side of the camera.

Our flight to get here stopped in Samoa, and I wrote the following while we were waiting to get back on the plane to continue our voyage to Tonga.

Wednesday October 2, 2007

It's 5:30 a.m. and our group of Peace Corps volunteers is sitting in a transit area in Apia, Samoa.

It has been an intense couple of days since arriving in Los Angeles for our staging. Our group is pretty diverse. There are 33 of us. In that group are five married couples, 12 single women and 11 single men. There are three volunteers who are older than me. Most are in their twenties and thirties. I was pretty impressed about everything the people in our group have already done. Many have been active in volunteer work and quite a few have lived in another country before. We have two groups of volunteers—one in business and one in education.

I keep thinking about the opening line to *MTV's Real World*: "What happens when you put 33 strangers together?" Actually, quite a bit. Overall, I was pretty impressed with the staging process. There were no surprises, but it gave us a good overview of what we could expect once we arrive in Tonga. The training was more specific to overall Peace Corps practices.

While I've known this group for probably just 48 hours, I know all their names, and I am pretty sure I know where they are from.

Once we finished our staging, we were sent to the airport and then on to Tonga without an escort from the Peace Corps. We appointed four group leaders: one for the hotel, one for the bus, one for the skycaps at the airport and one (me) for the airport and travel. It didn't seem like a big deal to hand out the passports and tickets to everyone at the airport, but we got a bit of hassle at the airline counter. They would not allow us to board the plane since we did not have a return ticket from Tonga. Even after I showed the letter provided by the Peace Corps from the Kingdom of Tonga with our names, they still told us we had to have visas or return tickets before they would check us in. I finally got a supervisor who copied our travel documents and handed them out to all of the other gate agents and told them to check us in. But that wasn't the end of the problems. One of the gate agents didn't get the message and held up two of the people in our group, and I had to come back with the paperwork, so he could make another copy of it, just for him. As it turns out, the paperwork was sitting on the counter in front of him the entire time.

We also had some trouble with the TSA. One of the baggage screening machines at LAX was broken, so the 33 of us with LOTS of luggage had to wait in a line that extended out to the street just to check our bags. (Oh, and I did not have to pay a luggage surcharge even though I was over the limit when I checked in.) It probably took an hour for us to get everyone checked in, if not longer. Those of us at the front of the line spent the time hanging out in front of LAX.

Once we got past the issue with the gate staff, we had a pretty pleasant flight.

FIRST IMPRESSIONS OF TONGA
Wednesday, October 10, 2007

It's hard to believe that I've been here for such a short time. Each day, even every hour, seems to bring a new experience as we continue our introduction to the Tongan culture. So far, the experience has exceeded any expectations I may have had about what to expect. From the beautiful harmony of men singing while sitting around a kava circle, to the friendly hellos you get everywhere you go, Tonga has certainly extended its welcome mat to our group of 33.

During our training, we've heard several times that it is important not to compare what we see in Tonga to our own culture. The idea is that it is important to learn and accept the culture for the way it is without putting our own cultural views on everything. I agree with the philosophy, but for the purposes of my family and friends in the United States, I'm going to break that important rule to help you understand better what I'm experiencing.

We are staying in a small village on the main island of Tongatapu. I'm living with a host family and a fellow Peace Corps trainee. Everywhere we go, we run into other members of our host family or family connections, and "family" has a very broad meaning in Tonga. It goes back generations and includes every aunt, uncle and cousin you can imagine. Adoption also seems to be very common. One of our hosts was adopted into her family of nine children. In some cases, the biological family even becomes part of the family of the adopted son or daughter. I've yet to meet a Tongan who lives alone, and most houses have many generations of family under the same roof or living close by. One Tongan woman, who now lives in the United States, explained to me that reunions are critical in Tonga because if you don't know who you are related to, you might end up dating them. She said two people living in New Zealand might not know they are related if they don't show up for the reunion.

There is a hierarchical rank in every family, but it is very difficult to figure out. A rank can even be passed down from one generation to another. Where you sit during a meal or how decisions are made have a lot to do with the rank within each family. As guests, we have been put at the head of the table and have even been asked to move once we are already seated. This has been explained to us as a sign of respect.

Our host family is truly wonderful. I like them all very much, and they have welcomed us much as you would welcome your own family members. While there are just four family members living in the house, there are often many other relatives and friends here, making it hard to keep track of everyone sometimes.

I had read before arriving about how strongly gender roles are defined in Tonga. And while I have seen quite a bit of that, it would be unfair to think that the typical "a woman's place is in the home" stereotype is always accurate in Tonga. There are women who are the only breadwinners in their families, women who are in high positions in government and those who own their own businesses. My experience has been very limited so far, but it appears that a Tongan woman has more opportunities than what I might have expected.

Having said that, there are places where women are just not welcome. One is kava or a kava circle. This is strictly a man's affair, and the only women allowed are those who serve the kava to the men. Saturday night, our host took us to a kava circle across from our home. There were about 40 or 50 men being served kava by two single women. The women who serve kava are always single, and they are not allowed to drink it, only serve it to the men. In our circle of about 15 men, one was playing the ukulele, another the guitar and two others were singing along with them. Their voices were beautiful, and while I couldn't understand the words, it was great to listen and watch them, as they stopped only to take another cup of kava. Each person who wants more kava passes his cup to the woman serving who pours the kava and hands it back. As *palangi* (foreigners), we were given smaller servings, which I was later told was a sign of respect. In addition to the music, the men sit around and talk, tell jokes and generally enjoy each other's company. This particular kava circle collects five *p'aanga*, which is equal to about US$2.50, from each participant every Saturday night. One of the participants told me they use the money they collect to provide scholarships to the university—a fact that was later confirmed by someone else.

The one place I expected them to collect money but they did not was at church on Sunday. I attended the Free Wesleyan Church, which is the Methodist Church in the United States. I was there with about 20 fellow Peace Corps trainees. The first thing that struck me was the music. Unlike churches in the United States, the Tongans sing with an unbelievable passion. Here's where I'll make a comparison. Think of the finale of a Broadway musical, and you will begin to get an idea of the sound of the congregation. There is no choir at the front of the church, but there is a music director who directs the congregation in each song. There are times it is so loud, you almost want to lower the volume a bit. There were no pianos or organs, just a keyboard player who played softly in the background. In fact, there were many times I thought the congregation was singing a cappella as you could not even hear the keyboard.

Each song was started by the town officer, who was sitting on a pew near the rear of the church. It is not because of his job as town officer that he does this, but it is something he has apparently been doing for years. As is the tradition in the Methodist Church, the first Sunday of the month is Communion. In Tonga, they simply extend the service on the first Sunday instead of cutting something out, as the Methodist Church does in the United

States. The only thing missing on Communion Sunday is the offering, which they do not collect since they are serving Communion. Communion is offered by age, with the oldest people in the church going first and the youngest last. The congregation sings songs from memory the entire time the congregation is taking Communion. And in true Tongan tradition, everyone goes in bare feet to the front of the church. (Everyone wears sandals or flip-flops everywhere, including church, so it's not difficult to take them off to take Communion.)

While I did not understand most of the service, we were greeted in English during the service by three separate people who thanked us for coming to help their country. Another part of the service was the announcements. Instead of just church announcements, the announcements included community news, as the church is the centerpiece of the Tongan community. So, anyone celebrating a birthday this week was called up to the front of the church and the entire congregation sang "Happy Birthday" to him or her.

Food is everywhere and very plentiful. Almost everything is grown in the village where we are staying. There are pigs, chickens and dogs running around everywhere, and there are no fences. (No, they don't eat the dogs, but one of our group did get bitten by a dog. He's okay.) The big meal of the week is the after-church feast on Sunday. We ate outdoors at a table covered in banana leaves, and our food was prepared in an emu or underground oven. Our hosts had two types of *lu*, which is meat, onion and coconut milk wrapped in taro leaves and then wrapped in banana leaves to cook in the oven. We had canned meat in one lu and mutton (lamb) in the other. It was really delicious. It reminded me a lot of the Kailua pig I used to eat in Hawaii. We also ate sweet potatoes, breadfruit and cassava with our fingers. As a drink, we had fresh watermelon mixed with coconut milk, which was really delicious as well. Coconuts are plentiful and used daily in cooking. I've become addicted to the local bananas. They have two types, and both are really sweet and delicious, picked right off the tree in the backyard or served to us at our group events. They make a great snack, and I bet I'm eating five or six a day.

I've been most impressed with the Peace Corps training process so far, and the staff here is terrific. You know they want you to succeed, and they are all working to help us not only learn the language but also better understand the culture and the country. The days are long. We are in class from 8:30 a.m. until 5 p.m. We take a two-hour break for dinner with our host families and then are back again at 7 p.m. However, the instructors keep it moving. The toughest part, at least for me, is trying to retain all the information they provide. I feel like I'm struggling a bit with the language, but every day I learn more, and it is great to be able to come home and understand simple phrases. We are taught in groups of five or six people, so we get a lot of attention. My instructor is great. We'll soon be put in new groups based on our abilities, and I think it will help to have people of similar abilities together.

Steve Hunsicker

THIS IS NORMAL
Tuesday, October 16, 2007

In our village of Fua'amoto, there is an Internet café, except there is no coffee, no drinks and no food at the café. It's actually not a café at all but a house that has Internet service. Inside are about eight computers and space to hook up one laptop. The Internet house, as I've started calling it, is located just behind the building where our classes are conducted each day. The arrival of 33 Peace Corps trainees has done a lot for its business.

But that's not the point of this story. Friday, after class, I stopped by to download my e-mail onto my laptop. I've found it is much more efficient to write offline and then upload and download mail than it is to try to write online, which can be painfully slow. After I was done on Friday, I asked the woman at the door how long they would be open tomorrow. She told me until 12 p.m. Since many Tongan businesses are open only for a part of the day on Saturday and many are not open at all, I figured I would get there early in case they decided to go home early. In Tongan, time is always relative, and you never really know if someone is going to be somewhere at a certain time or if a place will be open. Saturday morning, I finished breakfast with my host family and walked to the Internet house. When I was about two blocks away, a kid yelled at me in English from inside the yard, "Hey Steve, where are you going?" How this kid knew my name, I don't know. Several kids have asked me my name, but I didn't remember him. I told him I was going to the Internet. He said, "It's closed." Now how he knew this, I didn't know either. I thanked him, told him I was going to take a walk and continued on to the Internet House. Guess what? It was closed. There was a man outside who said they would be open later. When I asked what time, he said when he got back from town. I said, "So around noon?" He said, "After lunch." That was his answer. I walked back home a different way, not wanting to offend the kid who gave me the correct information.

Fast forward to about 3 p.m. My host family was preparing to go to the beach for a picnic. I told them I would be right back, that I wanted to go to the Internet. This time, I got all the way there and it was still closed, but I saw a woman across the street. She said they would be open this evening. After a truly memorable trip to the beach, I decided to walk home with a couple of others and walked by the Internet café. It was now open. Of course, it was dark outside and probably close to 8 p.m.

This simple story has several messages. One, why would I walk to this place instead of calling? Because that's the way to do it. I've noticed that when my host family wants something, they don't pick up the phone and call, they go there. Want to talk with someone? Just stop by. Second, the people in this village know a lot about what is going on, from my name to the status of the Internet. We used to talk about the "coconut wireless" when I lived in

Hawaii, but Tonga uses this method of communication to perfection. And finally, don't bank that things will happen on any kind of schedule. It's all normal here, just different to us.

In fact, there are many things that are starting to seem perfectly normal after just a few weeks in Tonga.

- Wearing a skirt or tupenu. All the men wear one to work, school and other more formal occasions like church. I have borrowed a few from my host family, and I now have two of my own. Who would have ever guessed that I would ever go shopping for a skirt for me? While it feels normal to wear one, I haven't quite mastered the art of sitting in one, especially on the floor. The first day I "flashed" several people in my group, making me realize that until I get used to wearing one, it is best to wear shorts underneath instead of just underwear.
- Seeing pigs everywhere—on the road as you walk around the village, driving to town, sitting at the kitchen table and looking out the door or while in class. They are everywhere, and while at first it seems kind of strange, it now seems much more normal.
- Saying hello to every single person you see in the village, and often they want to talk, ask me my name or ask where I am going. Fortunately, I can now answer these questions in broken Tongan instead of English, and even when they ask me in English, I try to remember to respond in Tongan.
- Going to sleep to the sounds of people singing. Whether it is men sitting around a kava circle or a church choir, it is not uncommon to be serenaded as you go to bed and even as you wake up in the morning. The village has lots of noise from roosters to dogs. And of course, there are the people too.
- Drums signal the start of town meetings and other events. You can distinguish them from the constant sound of tapa being tapped by the women of the village. Tapa is the bark of the mulberry tree, which is pounded into a cloth and decorated.
- Church bells ringing all the time to remind people to get ready for church and that church is starting. Most bells ring an hour before the service, and there are services all week long. On Sunday, the first services start at 5 a.m.
- Food is everywhere and served all the time. Most is grown right here in the village, and you only buy what you don't raise or receive from family members.
- Cold showers. They are not as bad as they sound.

Learning about the village, its people and the customs are all very important parts of what we are learning every day.

I will close by saying how impressed I've been with the other people in our group. It is very refreshing to be around so many inspired and intelligent people. It's also great how we continue to support each other as we all adjust to our new surroundings.

FAMILY, FOOD AND SCHOOL
Saturday, October 20, 2007

The concept of family in Tonga takes some explaining. Yes, the families are very large, but the relationship between family members is quite different than what you would find in most American households. There is no such thing as a cousin in Tonga. What we would consider cousins in the United States are called sisters and brothers in Tonga. That means that the children of every aunt and every uncle are your brothers and sisters. Perhaps you have five children in your household, your father's brother has five and your mom's sister has five. That means you have 14 brothers and sisters.

Tongan children also call their parents by their first names and the parents are not always their birth parents. Confused? In the household where I am living, there is a three-year-old who is being raised by our hosts. However, he is the son of our host's brother who lives nearby. Adoption is pretty common here, and it is not always by immediate family.

If you are adopted, you count your biological siblings and your adopted siblings as your brothers and sisters. Now imagine this scenario over multiple generations, and you begin to get the idea of the size of most Tongan families. I've met many of the relatives and the children of my host family, and it is hard to keep everyone straight. Often, a new face shows up in the house, and it's just another relative we get to meet.

If you want to be confused even further, in the Tongan language, brothers call their brothers one word and sisters call their brothers another word. The great part about all this is that you can seemingly go anywhere in Tonga and meet family.

My housemate Justin and I have certainly been warmly welcomed into our family here and are starting to feel at home. Unfortunately, we have to say goodbye on Tuesday, but I am confident we'll remain in contact with our hosts during our service in Tonga, regardless of where we both end up working.

Food is a HUGE part of life in Tonga. Tongans eat all the time, and they eat a lot. I doubt I will ever go hungry here. On Wednesday, Justin and I took a walk down to the beach after dinner. On the way back, we walked by a house where we didn't know anyone. They called out to us, "Come eat!" as they were eating their evening meal. We've heard this is pretty common. If you see someone, even if you don't know him or her, you are invited to come share a meal, and the person will be happy to have you join. We did not join these people, but I have no doubt we would have had a great time.

In the morning, we usually have toast and tea or instant coffee. Occasionally, we will have eggs. The toast is hand-cut from a loaf of bread and piled on a plate. I doubt we could even come close to eating all the toast that is put in front of us. We often have fresh fruit like bananas as well. At school, we have a morning tea, lunch and an afternoon tea.

The lunches are big meals and always include root crops like sweet potatoes, yams and taro. We also get breadfruit almost daily. In addition, we'll have fish, chicken or *lu*, which is taro leaves with canned beef cooked in coconut milk. One of my favorite lunches is curry chicken, which is delicious. We get watermelon with almost every meal and often with our morning and afternoon teas.

When we come home, our hosts make another big meal. My favorite food so far is raw fish marinated in coconut milk with onions and tomatoes. The teriyaki chicken is also delicious. We get root crops with every meal and occasionally rice. I've liked everything so far and can't believe I've eaten as much as I have. I'm learning to limit my portions, so I don't end up gaining lots of weight. Other than walking everywhere, I've had little chance to exercise due to the busy schedule.

School takes up most of our days. We start at 8:30 a.m. with a community meeting which is conducted by several of the trainees, and it can be on any topic. That's followed by class until 5 p.m. We take a two-hour break and go back for one hour at 7 p.m. We have about two hours of language training every day plus the one hour at night.

The language is my favorite part of the day, even though I don't feel I'm progressing as well as I should. Of course, when I remember that we've only been here for two weeks and that I can carry on conversations at about the level of a four-year-old, I guess that is not bad. We are being encouraged to talk in complete sentences now instead of just learning new words and giving single word answers. There are more than 100 pronouns in the Tongan language and remembering all the rules can be difficult. Here are two confusing differences: In Tongan, there are pronouns for single, dual inclusive, dual exclusive and plural. If you are talking about two people, you use one set; if you are one of the two people, you use a different set; and there is a yet another set if you are talking about three or more people. Also, there is one pronoun for he/she/it instead of the three we have in English.

The rest of the school day includes sessions on health, safety, culture and business. Because our group includes both education and business volunteers, we split up for these sessions and go to a different building. The business information is fascinating. It's clear that profit is NOT the motivating factor for many Tongan business owners. On Monday, we are visiting a small business to see how it runs, which should be exciting. The Peace Corps staff is also starting to give us some information about the types of jobs we may be doing. While we haven't gotten anything specific, they are asking us to rank our preferences based on some job descriptions. We are supposed to find out November 13th where we will be assigned. That gives us a month to prepare before we are sworn in as volunteers and start working.

We leave for Vava'u, another island north of here, on Tuesday. We are going by ferry, and it takes 22 hours to get there. Today (Saturday), we all had to jump in the water. We probably were in the water for close to two hours, treading water, towing each other and swimming 100 meters in two minutes. We also learned how to survive in open water as a group. All of this was done without life jackets, but we had guys from the Tongan Navy close by in case any of us got into trouble. I think we were all surprised that it was much more strenuous than we had expected.

Finally, a few miscellaneous things worth noting:

- Many in our group walked in a breast cancer walk this morning through the main city.
- A friend e-mailed and asked me about the mats I was wearing in one of the pictures. The mats are worn over the tupenu (skirts) that we wear every day. Think of the mats like you would a tie. You might wear one to work depending on where you work, and you would always wear one to a formal occasion. I don't own one, but have borrowed a mat from our host family when I have needed it, like to go to church.
- The US ambassador for Fiji and Tonga, who is based in Fiji, met with us Wednesday, as did Deputy Secretary of State Christopher Hill. Both were in Tonga attending the Pacific Forum meetings happening in Nuku'alofa this week. Hill is a returned Peace Corps volunteer.
- Several of the trainees have gotten sick, and a few are dealing with infections from cuts. So far, I've only gotten mosquito bites and haven't had any illnesses or infections. We have a very competent medical officer who is looking out for our needs.
- Friday we had cooking classes. I learned how to make the raw fish mentioned above.

Steve Hunsicker

VAVA'U—WE MADE IT!
Friday, October 26, 2007

The lush green landscape, rolling hills of tropical foliage and pouring rain are all signs that we are no longer on Tongatapu. After a shorter than expected ferry ride, we made it to the northern island group of Vava'u. The ferry ride was an experience to be enjoyed once, but probably not again. As we were waiting to board, I was happy that the Peace Corps required each of us to take a life jacket. The boat looked as if it had seen better days, and once on board, our first impressions were found to be true.

We had secured an inside room for our group of 33, plus three of the Peace Corps staff. However, the room was not nearly big enough for all of us to sit in, much less sleep in. Several people ventured upstairs to the open deck, a decision that some would later regret. I opted to stay inside, and while the occasional ocean spray would come through the open windows, it was a dry trip. I did not take any photos of our cramped quarters, but imagine this: one person with her or his head looking at another person's toes; that person looking at the head of the person next to her or him and so on down the line. There was not enough room to stretch out shoulder to shoulder. Somehow in all of this, I was able to sleep, but not without occasionally kicking or rolling into the people next to me. Of course, I also got bumped plenty of times throughout the night.

We had all been prepped for a 22-hour boat ride. The Peace Corps medical officer (PCMO) issued motion tablets with instructions to take two one hour before we left; two more once we left; another two when we left our first stop; and the final two, four hours after that. The last two were not necessary because we got in about four hours early, and we were all ready to get off the boat, even though it was pouring rain.

We got a great Peace Corps welcome from the current volunteers serving in this region and the Peace Corps staff who had arrived ahead of us. The volunteers had made cookies for us, which I thoroughly enjoyed. Because of the rain, there was a lot of confusion about the luggage. Originally, our bags were to be taken to our villages in open trucks. But that plan was scrapped for those going with me to my village. We all crammed into a bus with all of our bags. We made it fit, but it was a tight squeeze.

We are now in three different groups in three different villages. I'm with 10 other trainees in the village of Ta'anea. (If you have Google Earth, zoom into Ta'anea and find the town hall with a large church next to it. Directly across the street from the town hall is where I am living. Next door to me is another church.)

My new host family consists of a father, mother and 29-year-old daughter. It's a very nice house, and they have been very hospitable. When I first got here, after the initial introductions, my first words were "*kaukau*" which is "bath" or "shower." I was feeling pretty gross after the long boat ride, the sea spray and then the pouring rain. The bathroom and the shower are located in separate rooms that are connected to the main house, but you must go outside to get to them. The shower was awesome. The water did not feel as cold as it did in Fua'amotu, but that could also be because it is quite a bit warmer here. After a delicious lunch featuring two of my favorite foods—fresh pineapple and *'ota 'ika* (raw fish)—I took a very long nap.

After my nap, I visited a bit with my host family and then went for a walk with the daughter, some neighbors and a couple of other trainees. We also stopped and visited another trainee at his house and then visited our language teachers at their house. When I got back, it was time for dinner. Here's where I got a quick education about how Tongans' eagerness to please everyone. I ate alone while the others watched. I've learned this is a sign of respect, and while it takes a little getting used to, that is just the way it is done here. I reached for a slice of bread, and my host mom moved the butter toward me. I asked in English, "Do you have jam?" It was not on the table, and my previous host family always had jam or jelly. She became very flustered, said "*ikai*," which is no, starts yelling for her daughter, grabs some money and sends her daughter to the store to buy me some jam. I tried to stop her saying it was not a big deal, but she kept pushing her daughter out the door. After a few minutes, when the daughter didn't come right back, the mom went to the front door and called for her. By now, I had finished my dinner but not wanting to offend my brand-new host parents, I sat there, with a slice of bread on my plate, patiently waiting for the jam to come. It finally got there, and I enjoyed my bread and jam but learned a valuable lesson about asking for something you don't see on the table.

This village is much smaller and a lot quieter than Fua'amotu, our last village. The quiet is because there are fewer dogs, pigs and chickens. Since arriving in Tonga, I've been sleeping with earplugs to deafen the outside noise. Here, I am able to sleep without using the earplugs. I still awake to the sound of roosters but not as many as before.

My room has a fan, a double bed covered with a lace mosquito net and a table with a chair. It's quite comfy, and I'm looking forward to enjoying it. It would be easy to spend all my time in my room in front of the fan, as it is definitely warmer here, and during the day, there is not a noticeable breeze.

My new language teacher is 71 years old and seems quite patient. I was sad not to keep the teacher I had, but look forward to learning more of the language. Here is a sample of what Tongan looks like. You'll get an "A" if you can translate this!

Ko Steve au. Oku ou ha'u mei Florida pea oku ou saiia 'ota 'ika mo faina. Ko hoku twofefine ko Becky mo Maria. Oku ou ngaue e Peace Corps pea oku ou nofo 'i Ta'anea.

Figure it out? There are a few hints above, but if I did this correctly, it says, "I am Steve. I come from Florida, and I like raw fish and pineapple. My sisters are Becky and Maria. I work for Peace Corps and I stay in Ta'anea."

I was able to write most of that from memory except to check the spelling of a couple of words. However, I've got a LOOOONG way to go. Being able to say it and being able to hear and translate it are two very different things.

I was very sad to leave my previous host family. I got attached to them in a very short time. If I end up working on Tongatapu, I'm sure I will see them regularly. Monday night, our last night at home, we sat around and played cards at the kitchen table. I had brought a deck from home but didn't give it to them until a few nights before we left. We played all kinds of games and sometimes just made up the rules as we went along. They also taught us a Tongan card game called "High Card" and a card trick.

As it started to get late, I began to wonder why we had not eaten. Finally, Sia told us our dinner was coming from town. I told her that we could just get something here, and she said no, this was something special. And special it was. Our family had ordered us two huge lobsters from the International Dateline Hotel complete with French fries and vegetables. There was no way I could have ever eaten one lobster by myself, so we all shared. It was probably only the second time I've ever eaten lobster. (I almost didn't get sent to the South Pacific because I thought I might have had an allergy to shrimp and lobster.) I've avoided both almost my entire life and even after passing an allergy test, I still don't eat much shrimp or lobster. The good news is that it was delicious, and I had no side effects. On Tuesday morning, as we were leaving, the family presented us with flower leis for the trip and gave us each a *ta'avala* (mat worn around the waist for formal occasions).

HOW I DID SOMETHING REALLY INAPPROPRIATE!
Monday, October 29, 2007

During breakfast Saturday, my host sister told me that we were planning to go to another village called Taoa, which she described as far away. We made a very short trip into Neiafu, the main city here in Vava'u, and came home to pick up my host mom for the trip. As we were getting ready to leave, Tiana, my host sister, told me that I needed a tupenu for *lotu*, which is church. I said, "For tomorrow?" She said, "No, for Taoa." That was my first indication that we were going to church. The drive to Taoa was beautiful and was my first chance to see any of the island. During part of the way, I could look out over the Pacific. I was most impressed by how this country has remained unspoiled.

We got to Taoa about 10:30 a.m., and the first question asked was, "Do you want to eat?" This was just two hours after I had eaten a really big breakfast. I declined and then was told I needed to eat. I was led into a town hall next to the church, and there were about eight ministers and other leaders sitting around a table filled with all kinds of food—whole pigs, fish, chicken and sausage. The table was not just covered in food, but food was piled on top of food. My host mom and sister disappeared, and I was put directly across from the minister. After I sat down, the meal began. The minister shared his lobster with me, making it the second time that I have had lobster here. (I now understand why the Peace Corps didn't want to send me to Tonga if I had a lobster allergy.) I tried to eat small portions. We didn't even come close to eating all the food in front of us.

After this meal, the church leaders got into a kava circle, and they invited me to join them. So far, my kava drinking has always been at night. It was only about 11 a.m. Then, I did probably the single most inappropriate thing I have done since my arrival. The minister, in English, asked me how long I was going to be in Tonga. I replied "F—k you." Of course I didn't say that, but I held up two fingers, palm inward to indicate that I would be here for two years. However, this is a very obscene gesture in Tonga and is the same as giving someone the middle finger in the United States. I immediately realized what I had done, jerked down my hand and answered in my best Tonglish (Tonga-English), "Two years." No one sitting at the kava circle gave any indication that they were offended, but needless to say, I felt horrible. Our training has stressed how important it is to be culturally sensitive to our host country residents, and I not only did something really insensitive, but I did it to a minister.

At 11:30, we moved to the church. I was expecting a regular church service, but I soon figured out it was either a wedding or a funeral. It soon became apparent that it was a funeral, as people were crying. An elderly lady was taken to the front of the church, and people started presenting her with gifts. Soon, I felt like I was at a telethon. People started taking money up to a small table, and then they started taking even more money up. The fundraising went on for almost two hours. My host mom took a beautiful mat with tapa to the front of church along with what appeared to be thousands of dollars. She was crying as she did it.

Finally, the leaders took all the gifts and money to the old woman, who said a few words. I assumed she was the widow. I had read that it is customary for people to give gifts when someone dies and that the gifts are eventually distributed back to the family's friends. As soon as the service was over, extremely festive music began playing from the hall where I had eaten earlier. There were women dancing in the streets and people singing. I entered the hall and could not believe the amount of food that had been prepared. There were mats lining the floor overflowing with food and drinks. My host mother motioned for me to sit on the mat. As I was sitting down, one of the church leaders led me up to the head table and motioned for me to sit. Now imagine this: There were probably 150 people sitting on the floor, and I was at the head table with 10 to 12 people. What I had previously thought was a lot of food didn't even compare to the spread before me now. I had a whole pig just for me, not to mention all kinds of other food. People started making speeches, some crying, some joking and then women began dancing to music. The man I was sitting next to did not speak English but was kind enough to speak very slowly, so I could understand what he was saying. Finally, it was over and everyone got up, but there was enough food left to easily feed 300 people.

It was quite a cultural experience, but as I soon learned, things are not always what they seem. Later, I was telling my language teacher about the "funeral," and she told me it wasn't a funeral but the annual church fundraiser. If someone has died in the past year, the families all collect money to give to the church at this time of the year. The people who were carrying up the gifts were all the people who had lost a relative. She told me my host mom's mother had died in the past year, and that is why she was there. When I told her they had put me at the head table, she explained what a very high honor that was. I said that I had understood. However, what I had not understood is that the "appropriate" thing for me to have done was to get up and make a speech and thank everyone for providing the food and allowing me to sit at the head table. That thought never entered my mind. She said it would have been fine for me to have said thank you in English, but I should have publicly thanked everyone for the high honor they had afforded me. So that was my second inappropriate action for the day. However, my teacher assured me that it was fine since I didn't understand the custom.

I'll close this story by adding that when we got home, my family was ready to eat again. I had bread and some rice. There was no way I could have eaten again after all that I had consumed.

Now on to life in Vava'u

Jimmy Buffett sings a song called "Changes in Latitudes, Changes in Attitudes." This title couldn't be more fitting for my current situation. We're living in a new latitude, and there is certainly a new attitude among our group. Gone are the carefree days of living in Fua'amotu where everyone spoke English, had modern plumbing and could access the Internet by walking a short distance. Reality has set in: We know that the next two years are not going to be like that. I'm lucky to be living in a really nice house with running water and terrific host parents. Not everyone is as lucky. One of the married couples only has water a few hours at night when it gets turned on. Another trainee is living in a house with no fan, and it is very hot here. English may be understood but is not widely spoken, and we have all given up the comfort of having another volunteer living with us. If we want to talk, it is pretty much going to be in Tongan. We are also not together. The 33 of us are living in three different villages, so we don't see each other as often either. Not having regular access to the Internet also makes us feel a bit more isolated from our homes and families. The Internet is available in the main town but we have to either hitch a ride or take a bus to get there.

And speaking of buses, on Friday, all 33 of us got together for the first time since arriving in Vava'u. We had school in a neighboring village. At the end of the day, we were on the bus, and less than a mile from the school, the bus had a flat. The driver had no spare and no cell phone, so we all just walked home. It was nice to get the exercise, but of course, it was raining.

Trainees Bria and Enrique walk home after the bus gets a flat

It's easy to see that this is all an important part of our immersion into our new culture. I'm impressed with the way the Peace Corps has eased us into life here. I think if we had come to Vava'u on day one, we would have had a lot of people drop out. So far, all 33 of us are still here, and I'm really hopeful we all will stay together. I do feel like I'm communicating a bit better in Tongan now. Learning the language is pretty much my top priority, and the isolation gives me a lot of opportunity to study and to practice.

HERE COMES THE RAIN (AGAIN)!
Friday, November 2, 2007

Remember the movie *Forrest Gump*? There is a scene where Forrest is in Vietnam and he says, "One day it started raining, and it rained and it kept raining." That pretty much describes the past week in Vava'u. Not only has it rained but it has poured. It's hard to believe this little island in the middle of the Pacific gets so much rain, but that's probably why Tonga has the most fertile soil in the world. Interestingly, I have yet to hear a Tongan complain about the rain. They appreciate the cooling effect. Rain is also the primary source of water for the island.

The water here in Ta'anea is a pretty interesting story. There is a water tank at the top of the hill, and the pumps are controlled by the guy who lives near the tank. When he turns the pump on, everyone has water. If he turns it off, most houses do not have water. (I have water full time thanks to a cistern that supplements the town water.) Everyone in the village pays the same amount for water. If you have 10 people in your house or just three, you pay the same. If there is a leaking faucet or toilet, there is no incentive to fix it because your water bill won't change.

As an assignment, we had to interview people in our village about their opinions on the town's most important needs. While the survey was certainly not scientific, fixing the water was a top priority listed by the older people in the town. However, no one really had a great solution. We might think that installing meters on each home and charging for the water makes sense, but here people wonder who will pay for the meters, and what will happen if someone's bill goes up. For now, the community just deals with it, and it probably isn't a really big problem. I'm learning that when something is broken or doesn't work, Tongans just do without or accept it.

In my house, the kitchen light burned out on Saturday. There was no spare, so we ate by candlelight until Monday when a new bulb was purchased. The light still didn't work, so another light was moved into the kitchen. It's the same with food. If your garden has bananas in it, you eat bananas. If it doesn't, you eat something else. The concept of being able to buy tomatoes, bananas or any other perishable item at any time is foreign to Tongans.

The priorities are also different here. We have one trainee in another village that has full-time Internet access at his house, but doesn't have full-time water. He was able to update me on the World Series, since we hear nothing from home and the rest of us have very limited access to the Internet. (Glad Boston won!)

We've now been here for one month. In many ways, it seems like a lot longer because we have done so much since arriving. Yet it also seems like we have so much more to learn. Many of us were very disappointed to learn that the Peace Corps cut 25 hours of language training out of our schedule. That means we have 25 fewer hours to pass our language test than previous volunteers here in Tonga. Instead, they are giving one extra full week of model school for the education volunteers. The business volunteers will be doing business-related tasks during those two weeks, but we haven't heard the specifics yet. The good news is that each day I start to feel more confident with the language.

I'm really looking forward to next week. We get to spend two full days shadowing a current volunteer. There are only three business volunteers on Vava'u right now, so there will be four volunteers with each one, but hopefully we'll get a lot of insight into what to expect after we become volunteers.

This weekend, we are going to be working on our projects for *Fakatonga* Day (Like a Tongan Day). Each village has to prepare a skit in Tongan and learn a Tongan dance. We also have to individually make one Tongan dish and one Tongan handicraft. I'm going to learn to make ota ika, which is raw fish served in coconut milk. It is by far my favorite Tongan dish. For my handicraft, I'm planning to make a broom with some help from my host father.

TONGAN PRICES
Monday, November 5, 2007

It's not uncommon to discover that residents in many resort destinations get a better price than what the tourists pay. When I lived in Hawaii, *kamaina* prices (local prices) were published just about everywhere. You could stay at a huge resort for a lot less than a tourist, rent a car for less and even fly for less. In Florida, the practice is not as widespread, but you can still get a lower price to the amusement parks and certain other places. In both Hawaii and Florida, the key word is "published prices." The difference here in Vava'u is that the local prices are widely available, but you won't see them posted anywhere.

Friday, I went to an Internet café on the water. This place obviously caters to the "yatchies" who dock their boats just outside in the inlet. There is a sign posted that says Internet access is TOP (Tongan pa'anga) $7 per hour. That's just less than US$4 dollars. I spent an hour online, and when I was finished, I told the woman in Tongan that I was done. After her obvious surprise at hearing me speak in Tongan, she charged me $4 for the hour.

I then joined several of my fellow trainees for dinner at a local restaurant. The owner assured us that she considered us locals, and she would always give us the local prices. What are those prices? You have to ask because they are not posted. Other trainees have found t-shirt shops that offer local prices. It's actually pretty smart business because the locals would never be able to afford to eat or shop in these places, and the concept certainly fits with the Tongan culture of helping out each other. Even for me, the dinner and beer were big splurges.

The Peace Corps expects us to live at the same level as the locals and tapping into our money at home is strongly discouraged. To put it in perspective, as a Peace Corps trainee, I'm given an allowance of TOP$8 a day. One beer cost me $7.50. In other words, I spent almost an entire day's wage just to drink a beer. Of course, if you convert it to US dollars and think what a beer costs in a waterfront restaurant in South Florida, it's a deal. And here's another funny twist to the story: When I walked in, the owner said, "Hi Steve." I've stopped wondering how she or anyone else knows my name. It's very friendly, but also a reminder that you are always being watched, and if you do something inappropriate, it will get talked about.

The culture toward palangi is different here than it was in Fua'amotu, our last village. Fua'amotu never gets tourists unless they get lost. While it is close to the international airport, you wouldn't drive through town, and there are no businesses that cater to tourists. The people here in Vava'u see tourists all the time. Unfortunately, it is not always a positive experience.

Twice, we've had tourists riding all-terrain vehicles through the middle of town at high rates of speed. The ATVs are loud, and the tourists riding them don't seem to care about all the kids and people who are in the street. Vava'u also attracts people with higher incomes. Many are here to either rent yachts or to sail their own yachts. They have lots of money, and I think that many palangi, including those in the Peace Corps, are grouped in with these tourists. It would not be hard for someone to spend more money on a week's vacation than an entire Tongan family would make in a year.

The other side of this is that unlike Fua'amotu, you can escape here and live like an American for a night. A big group got together Friday night to celebrate the birthdays of two of our fellow trainees. Saturday, we quickly learned how fast the coconut wireless can work. And we also learned it's not always accurate.

There was a rumor going around that one of our female trainees had gotten drunk in town. The only problem was that the woman mentioned never went to town and was in the village all night. In the Tongan culture, women are not supposed to get drunk or be seen hanging out with men.

For the most part, women do things together and men do things together. Even married couples go their separate ways in public. At church here in Vava'u, the men and the women do not sit together. Knowing that, you can understand why this woman was upset about her reputation in the village. Our language teacher told her not to worry about it, as there wouldn't be a way to fix it anyway.

I spent most of the past weekend studying for our first language test, which is on October 16th. It will let the Peace Corps know how we are doing and where we need help before we take our final test prior to being sworn in as volunteers. There are three levels—novice, intermediate and advanced. My teacher tells me that she believes I'm past the novice level, but she is not the person who will be giving me the test. To become a volunteer, I need to be at the intermediate level. As far as I can tell, the differences between novice and intermediate have to do with the complexity of the answers. At novice, you can say, "I'm going to town." At intermediate, you can say you are going to town, what you will do there, what time you are going, how you are getting there, who you are going with and when you will be back. I can almost do that, but I do it very slowly. I feel pretty good about sentence structure but still need to learn a lot more nouns and verbs. I have a lot more confidence in my ability to speak Tongan now and believe I will make it to the required level.

I want to show off my host family here in the village of Ta'anea. That's me in the bare feet.

Steve Hunsicker (center) with Siaosi and Tilisa Vaka

I'm living with a retired minister named Siaosi, his wife, Tilisa, and their daughter, Tiana. They have two other children who live in New Zealand and Australia.

MY NEW JOB
Wednesday, November 14, 2007

I will be spending the next two years in Vava'u working with both the Tonga Development Bank and the Vava'u Chamber of Commerce. I am very happy with the assignment but also a bit surprised. We had heard that just one business volunteer would be stationed here, which turned out not to be true. Vava'u is a really neat place and getting to work with small business owners in both organizations should be exciting and challenging. My primary job will be at the bank, which I know a little bit about because we had a presentation on it during our initial training on Tongatapu. They provide development loans to Tongans to either start or grow small businesses.

There is currently a volunteer who is working with the development bank at the main office in Nuku'alofa, and I will actually work there initially for training before moving to Vava'u permanently. (Thankfully, I get to fly; I don't have to take a boat.) The Vava'u Chamber of Commerce is a new organization started earlier this year, and that position is ad hoc at this point. There are about 30 member businesses but no office or full-time staff. I'm going to get to know a lot of business owners in the job, and that will be exciting for me.

My hope was that I would end up in a business advising role, and that is exactly what I got. I really feel like the position is the kind of thing I wanted to do in the Peace Corps. There are several other people from my training group who are also going to be here. Interestingly, James and Stan, who were the first people I met online before we went to staging, will also be here along with Janis, Shannon, Katie and Andrew. Amy will be on an outer island in the Vava'u group.

Janis, Stan, Amy, Shannon, Steve and James will all live in Vava'u

Our program managers put a folder in front of each of us with instructions not to open it until they said it was okay. Once we opened it, we all immediately saw where we were going. As you can imagine, there were a lot of emotions with some people who were clearly ecstatic about their locations and others who were not. While I was happy with my assignment, it was sad to hear that many of my friends from training would be on other islands and that I wouldn't get to hang out with them as much.

Getting a site assignment is really the last "planned" surprise in a long series that begins with your original application to join the Peace Corps. First, you receive a nomination to a program and region, in my case, a business program in the South Pacific. The next surprise is the invitation, which tells you the country and the specifics of your program. Once you arrive in country, you find out where you will be staying during training and who will be your host family. In Tonga, you have two homestays. Finally, you get your site assignment and find out where you will be living. While I would never suggest there will be no surprises for the next two years, this is really the big one and the one for which I have been preparing since filling out the application.

As you might expect, there have been a lot of rumors for the past two weeks about where everyone is going to go. My favorite was that the Peace Corps only had 28 jobs for the 33 of us. The logic was that they had expected five of us to quit by now, but no one had left. Another was that all married couples were going to Tongatapu and that only the most liberal volunteers would be sent to the outer islands. None of these were true. A couple of trainees even had a sheet with every trainee's name on it, trying to guess where each would end up. I don't know yet how accurate they were with their predictions.

Other News

Last week, we got a really nice surprise from the current volunteers in Tonga. They came to our training session to deliver "mail" to us. They said that during training, they had missed getting mail like we do. A volunteer had written each of us a letter, and we each got an envelope of mail containing things like a postcard from a volunteer on an outer island, a page of Sunday comics from the United States, some crossword puzzles to do, a discount on a cup of REAL coffee from a coffee shop and some candy. My favorite item was a bookmark with the following quote: "Some people see the glass half empty, some people see the glass half full, a Peace Corps Volunteer sees the glass and says 'Hey, I could take a bath in that!'" The care package was great and was the first mail I've gotten since being here, even though I know I have some on the way. It was a nice way to show us that our Peace Corps family is not just the people with whom we are training, but also the other volunteers.

The weather has improved tremendously. Saturday, my host mom and sister took me to the ocean for a swim. I got to try out my snorkel and mask for the first time and saw some really beautiful fish, all very colorful. I even saw a bright blue starfish, or at least I think that is what it was. The water here is incredibly clear. Standing chin deep in the water, I could clearly see my toes and everything around them. The snorkeling was really fantastic in such clear conditions. We finished swimming just as the sun was setting, and I got to see my first Tongan sunset before heading home.

We have our first language exam on Friday. I'm hoping to score intermediate low, but will be happy if I make it to novice high. I have to reach intermediate middle before I swear in as a volunteer.

Notes

I spent a good bit of time speculating about where I would be going in the Peace Corps. I found out there were just three countries where the Peace Corps has business programs in the South Pacific: Tonga, Samoa and Vanuatu. Turns out I was wrong. There is a fourth country with a business program: Fiji. If you get a nomination to a business program in the South Pacific, you will end up going to one of those four places.

Of course, programs change regularly, and there is no guaranteeing that there will continue to be just four countries with business programs. The program here in Tonga has changed since I got my invitation. To be relevant, the Peace Corps has to adapt not only to changing business climates, but also to the qualifications of the applicants. The example we were given early in our training was that a country may have a huge need for plumbers and electricians, but very few plumbers and electricians apply to be volunteers. So, it is not practical to have a plumbing program in a country, and the Peace Corps probably couldn't support it with volunteers.

AHO FAKATONGA (LIKE A TONGAN DAY)
Monday, November 19, 2007

While much of our training to become Peace Corps volunteers has focused on the language, a good part of our education has also focused on culture. We are constantly reminded how important it is not only to speak to the people here in their native tongue but also to understand the Tongan culture. For the past few weeks, we have been preparing for what the Peace Corps calls Fakatonga Day or *Aho Fakatonga*. It's a chance for us to thank our host families and villages and also to show off some of what we have learned.

There are three villages with 11 trainees each here in Vava'u. Each village had to do a skit, learn a Tongan dance and prepare handicrafts and food the Tongan way. The handicrafts from our village included mats, brooms, kava cups made from coconuts, baskets, hats, etc. We also had a wide assortment of food. I made ota ika, which is raw fish, but my homestay mother did most of the work. About all I did was stir in the peppers.

Rugby is very big in Tonga. When we first arrived here, there were signs everywhere supporting the Tongan National Rugby team, who had a great season this past year. We decided to do a rugby skit. There is a cheer that the players say before each game, and we customized it to our village.

The men all dressed up in rugby clothes and ran into the room with the women cheering. However, we made a big cultural blunder when we entered the room. On the stage was the principal of a local school and the head of the Peace Corps business program. All of our families were in the rear of the room behind us. We turned to do the cheer to our homestay families and friends, turning our back on the two people on the stage. Our language teacher came running out, made us turn around and perform the cheer with our backs to the audience and facing the two men on the stage. They were the "ranking" people in the room, and it was considered rude to turn our backs to them. The other groups learned from our mistake and played to the men on the stage.

We all knew that this was part of Tongan culture before we entered the room, as we have heard about the importance of rank many times. I'm sure it won't be the last mistake we make either.

For our dance, we did a very special dance that was written for a woman here in Ta'anea when she was a little girl. The woman also happens to be the sister of my homestay father. She spent many hours teaching the women volunteers how to do the dance, and the women of the village went all out preparing the costumes. The song and the dance are really very beautiful.

Our village went for the more traditional dance and skit, but we were certainly upstaged by another village of trainees who dressed up as fakaleiti. A fakaleiti is a man who is raised as a woman and who dresses in women's clothes. It is not uncommon to see fakaleiti working in restaurants or walking around town. Historically, when a family did not have any girls in the family, they selected one of the boys to do a woman's work. The tradition continues today. However, none of the fakaleiti I've seen here in Tonga look anything like the men from our training group who tried to imitate them. They got lots of laughs from the crowd and a lot of good-natured ribbing from the other trainees.

After all the performances, we went to another hall for a traditional Tongan feast. There were hundreds of people there, and I bet less than 25% of the food on the tables was consumed. The tables were so full of food that we had to put our plates in our laps to eat. However, I don't want to give the impression that no food was consumed because massive amounts were eaten. But there were a lot of leftovers as is traditional in Tonga. No one ever goes hungry here.

Other News

Friday, I had a few free minutes and went to the Tonga Development Bank to meet the branch manager, who will be my supervisor for the next two years. We had a nice chat and exchanged phone numbers. I'll be training for about three months in Tongatapu and then will be moving here full-time probably around mid to late March. I do not know where I will be living during my training on Tongatapu.

I had my first language exam on Friday. I scored novice high. I spoke with the woman who gave me the test afterwards, and she told me that I was ALMOST intermediate low, but I didn't use enough conjunctions in my sentences, and I made mistakes when making things negative. I'm still hopeful that I'll make it to intermediate middle before December 12th when we are sworn in as volunteers. It will be a challenge though, as we have only one hour of language training a day for the next two weeks. The education volunteers are in model school, and those of us in business are doing a workshop for business owners here in Vava'u. I'm trying to force myself to use as much Tongan as I can, but I will miss the longer language classes. I did have a great experience Friday. It will sound simple but it was a great accomplishment. I needed a tube of toothpaste and went into a store and saw a tube behind the counter. I was able to tell the woman what I wanted, ask how much it cost and pay her without ever uttering a single word of English, and she never used any English either.

Finally, my host family gave me an awesome surprise Friday night. I came home to find a REAL pizza with lobster and fish on it and REAL cheese. It's the first time I've had pizza since leaving the United States. It was great.

Notes

I finally got mail on Friday. Thanks Mom and Dad for the care package and the awesome chocolate chip cookies. They arrived in great shape. Also, I got two cards, which were much appreciated.

SECLUDED BEACHES AND AN AWESOME CAVE
Monday, November 26, 2007

Even though we have been in Vava'u for more than a month, I have not had a chance to see much of the island except for my village and the main town. Saturday, I found out why Vava'u is the vacation capital of Tonga. Most of the trainees and a couple of the current volunteers all hired a boat for the afternoon. We sailed out on the water and saw many of the islands that make up this beautiful island group.

Our first stop was a secluded beach where we were the only people. It was overcast, so there was not a lot of sunbathing, but there was plenty of time to do some incredible snorkeling. The wide variety and colors of the coral combined with the amazing variety of fish made for a great adventure. I even saw my first colorful bird here in Tonga. Even though you might expect there to be many tropical birds here, there are really very few, or they stay out of sight.

After the beach, we headed to Swallows Cave. This is a huge cave, big enough for small boats to get inside. However, our boat would not fit, so we jumped in the water and swam inside. The swim to get inside the cave was much more of a struggle than I had anticipated, and I found myself winded once I got inside—partly because I was holding my mask and snorkel in one hand instead of wearing them. The swim was worth it. You could lie on your back and look up and see hundreds of swallows flying around. I went to the far side of the cave and climbed up the wall with several of my fellow trainees.

After a short climb up the edge of the cave, you could see into another cave ahead. On the way back down, I went back the way I came, but a couple of others went down on the other side and saw a sea snake in one of the small ponds. We've been told that sea snakes are fearful of humans and that their fangs are so far back in the mouth that they can't actually bite a person. However, the guys took no chances and quickly climbed back to join us.

Before slipping back into the water, I put on my mask and snorkel and was treated to an amazing site as I put my head into the water. The cave was at least 75 to 100 feet deep below me, but the water was so clear you could see the bottom. There was another entrance to the cave, and it helped light the ocean floor. It was truly a spectacular site. I don't own an underwater camera, so I don't have any pictures to share. However, even if I did, I doubt the pictures could do justice to the water. Getting out of the cave and back to the boat was an easy swim, but getting back in the boat was more of a challenge. Since there was no rope ladder, we literally had to be pulled up onto the boat.

We had planned to make another stop at a place called Mariner's Cave, but the weather was not cooperating, and we decided that it was too rough for us to make it. To get into Mariner's Cave, you have to swim underwater and then come up inside the cave. The good news for me is that I'll be in Vava'u and will have other opportunities to come back. For some of the trainees, this may be their last time here since we leave in just over a week to go back to the main island of Tongatapu. That also means we have just over two weeks of training remaining before we officially become Peace Corps volunteers.

Other News

On Wednesday and Thursday, the business trainees did a workshop for several small business owners here in Tonga. It was my first chance to really do what I came here to do—work with businesspeople. I helped out with a session on recordkeeping and then did some private sessions on both recordkeeping and using Excel. Even though we were working on Thanksgiving, it was great to see that we could affect some people, hopefully in a positive way.

We had a great Thanksgiving dinner on Thursday. The current volunteers here on Vava'u made arrangements with the owner of a waterfront restaurant to let us use his facilities. We each chipped in TOP$15, which is about US$7.50, and the Peace Corps country director and assistant country director paid for the turkeys. The volunteers took over the restaurant kitchen, cooking all the food including mashed potatoes, gravy, stuffing and pumpkin pie. Might sound like a typical American Thanksgiving, but you don't find those items here in the South Pacific. We even had cranberry sauce. A local band, which included a Peace Corps employee, donated their time to play for us, and we all chipped in to buy them drinks from the bar. It really was a great evening and a nice break from training. Now here's the twist. After dinner, we took our own plates back to the kitchen and washed our own dishes. It didn't seem strange to do this because the great dinner was well worth doing dishes. (Full disclosure: I didn't actually do my dishes as one of my language teachers took my plate for me.)

BUSINESS IN TONGA
Thursday, November 29, 2007

I've wanted to write about business in Tonga for some time, but it has been hard for me to get a handle on exactly how business is done here. So far, my exposure to businesses has been limited to very small Tongan businesses and those run by foreigners. My exposure has also been somewhat controlled by the Peace Corps because the businesses I have seen are those who have or want to have some kind of relationship with the Peace Corps.

Once I begin my permanent job working with the Tonga Development Bank, and later when I get started with the Vava'u Chamber of Commerce, I'm sure my perceptions will change as will my understanding of how business gets done here.

I won't spend a lot of time talking about the palangi-owned businesses because for the most part, they seem to operate like any business in the United States or elsewhere, except they have to be licensed by the government and be on a list of businesses that can be owned by non-Tongans. I've met the owners of two businesses who are living here on two-year visas, and they have both invested significantly in their businesses. If someone in the government decided not to renew their visas or their business licenses, they would be out of business. It seems to be understood that you don't want to "piss off" the wrong person if you are an outsider, as you may find yourself out of business.

The Tongan-owned businesses are fascinating. For the most part, profit is not a motivating factor. I've spent the past two weeks working with some small businesses and almost none of them were tracking their profit. Some tracked their sales, but none could tell you how much money they were making or even if they were making money. Business is pretty much all cash. If you run a store, you pay for the goods when they are delivered out of your cash on hand. We found one business with about TOP$300 in cash stored in candy jars under the counter because the owner did not have a way to get to the bank to deposit it. If you figure that the employees at this store make just TOP$50 a week (six days), that's a lot of money to have sitting around. (In case you are wondering, TOP$50 is about US$25, which is what employees get for a full week of work.) Tongans don't worry much about theft, and yes, they leave the money inside the store in candy jars when the store is closed.

Even the bank operates on a principle of trust. I have been to the bank twice and withdrawn money without ever showing an ID. All I had to do was give them my name, and they handed me the cash. I finally got an ATM card this week, and when I went into the bank to pick it up, I was given both the card and the PIN without having to show ID. Now, to put it in perspective, businesses do know most of their customers, and I doubt they have many

Americans who come in and want to withdraw money, as most wouldn't even have an account at the bank.

There is little regulation of business here and almost no tax structure. Price fixing is apparently perfectly legal. For example, we learned that there are four bakeries here on Vava'u, and they all sell bread for the same price. Apparently, they are all happy with how much business they are getting, so they agreed to all sell the bread for the same price. The guy who told us this said "In Tonga, it's a free market; you can set your own prices." We found that funny since in the United States we would call it collusion, and it would probably violate anti-trust laws. It would certainly not be considered a free market.

Not only can you fix prices, but on some goods, the amount of profit you can make is fixed by the government. I don't know exactly what goods this rule applies to, but your profit on the regulated goods is limited to no more than a 15% markup. That means if it costs you $1.00, the most you can charge is $1.15.

When it comes to tax loopholes, Tonga has one so big it is amazing that it exists. There is a 15% value added tax (VAT) charged on all goods in Tonga, but you have to sell TOP$100,000 annually for this to apply to you. Want to avoid paying this? Just open a second business. If one business is doing better than the other, just start funneling money from the good business to the bad to keep under the limit. If you are grossing TOP$250,000, just have three businesses and make sure none make more than TOP$100,000 each, and you don't pay the 15% tax. You can even use the same bank account and co-mingle the funds. And get this: You keep the books, and you report how much you earn to the government. Then they tell you how much tax to pay. As one business owner told me, "You just have to know how to keep the books."

In addition to the business tax, there is an income tax here, but it only applies to people who make more than TOP$617 per month, which excludes many people. The bottom line is that many businesses and residents pay no taxes and from what I've seen, there is no real structure to enforce the laws that do exist.

So you might ask, if this is the case, why don't a lot of businesses locate here? Mainly because foreigners can't own land, they can only lease it. That's one of the primary reasons I believe there are no international companies located in Tonga. And as mentioned above, only certain businesses are allowed to be owned by non-Tongans. This policy meant that for many years Tongan-owned companies could pretty much do as these pleased. Stores often kept irregular hours and if something was out of stock, Tongans just did without it. Customer service as we know it in America didn't really exist.

Now here is where it gets really interesting. A few years ago, the former king sold passports to some Chinese citizens. Once they paid for the passports, they were Tongan residents and were allowed to own any kind of business. While the passport selling quickly stopped after a huge international outcry, the Chinese who bought the passports are still here, and they operate thriving businesses. They keep regular hours; they buy their goods in bulk and have cheaper prices. In just about any town in the kingdom, the best-stocked store is likely to be owned by Chinese. This has caused many Tongan-owned businesses to suffer, and now those that survive often find they are buying their goods from the Chinese just so they can stay in business and compete. As you might imagine, this has led to some resentment towards the Chinese.

Here's where the Peace Corps comes in. I see the role of the business volunteers as helping Tongan businesses compete and grow, not just against the Chinese, but everywhere. In one store we visited, we showed the managers of the store how to keep better books. The next day, we went back, and they had redone their records for the past day, not only doing it the way we had suggested, but actually taking our suggestion and making it better. Just one store and just one day, but if they keep it up, I believe it will help them better manage their business in the future. I doubt everyone will be as receptive, but the women at this store were very smart and seemed to immediately grasp the importance of better recordkeeping.

Other News

This is my last post from Vava'u, at least for a while. On Tuesday, I will be saying goodbye to my wonderful host family, as we are returning to the main island of Tongatapu to complete our training. We'll be staying at a guesthouse in Nuku'alofa until we are sworn in as volunteers on December 12th. After that, we all will go to our assigned posts, except for me. I will be staying on the main island for approximately three months before coming to my permanent job here in Vava'u. Right now, I don't have a place to live. I might be staying with another volunteer during my three months, or I may get my own place. It is not finalized yet. (My housing here in Vava'u is not finalized either.)

I did get more information about what I will be doing during my first three months. The Tonga Development Bank is looking for assistance on launching a new website, and they also want some help with developing radio and TV advertisements. Both sound pretty interesting to me. I'll also be learning skills to bring back to the Vava'u branch.

It has now been two months since I left my Florida home, and in some ways, it seems like such a long time ago. However, I think that is because we have had so much information thrown at us in those two months. I couldn't even begin to count the number of new people I've met, I've learned the basics of a new language and I've had a lot of fun along the way too. The time in training has gone by quickly (except for two really bad sessions), and the

Peace Corps staff here is truly amazing. I really feel like all the staff really works hard to make sure that each of us will be successful volunteers. There is a very supportive atmosphere here, and I think it will really pay off for all of us. After spending almost a year going through the very long and tedious Peace Corps application process, it was refreshing to come here and find so many committed people. Having said that, I'm tired of training and ready to begin my work as a volunteer.

SO LONG VAVA'U (FOR NOW)
Sunday, December 2, 2007

Tongans are known for giving speeches at just about every event. It's very common for people to stand up and say what is on their mind at many different kinds of functions. Friday was fellow trainee Janis's birthday. Her host parents invited the 11 of us who are living in Ta'anea to dinner. As we were eating, her host parents gave several very emotional speeches about how much they are going to miss all of us. Our language teacher also got up. This started the long process of saying goodbye to the people with whom we have lived for the past six weeks. Janis, Shannon (another Ta'anea trainee) and I will be back and will certainly see our families again. But the others may not be back, as they will be living on other islands for the remainder of their Peace Corps service.

On Saturday, the minister of the Wesleyan Methodist Church asked several of us to participate in our final church service on Sunday. I was asked to lead the congregation in a Tongan hymn. Now for those of you who don't know me, singing is not exactly one of my strengths. And speaking Tongan, especially poetic Tongan, is not a strength either. However, unlike in the United States, when you lead a hymn here, you simply read the verse and the congregation sings it back to you. We sang three of the four verses of the song, and it had some pretty big words. The sentence that I had the most difficult time with was: "*Kau 'ofa ki he me'a kotoa Tukuingata ke 'aonga neongo pe ho hai.*" In Tongan, *ng* is considered one letter, and I always seem to struggle with the pronunciation of words with *ng*. The above sentence has three words that use *ng*, so it was pretty tough. I know I butchered it when I read it aloud, but I just kept going. As far as I know, I didn't say anything inappropriate. The sentence means something like "try to be helpful in everything you do," but that is not an exact translation.

Steve Hunsicker in his "Sunday Best."

I put on a tie for the first time in Tonga. The last time I wore one was just after leaving my job, when I attended a Peace Corps ceremony hosted by former President Jimmy Carter. Of course, I didn't wear a skirt and go barefoot then, like I did on Sunday.

Sunday night, the goodbyes continued, with the village throwing us a two-hour going away ceremony at a local church. The youth did a number of dances for us. The men from the kava circle sang, and at the end, everyone sang (in English) "We Wish You a Merry Christmas." It was a very nice send-off, and I don't think any of us were really expecting it. We didn't even find out about it until Sunday morning when they told us to be at the church at 7 p.m. We all arrived and discovered that each of us was expected to give a speech. I really wanted to thank everyone, but I had trouble remembering all the words I wanted to say in Tongan, so I quickly said hello in Tongan, switched to English and then wrapped up at the end in Tongan. I probably only spoke for about a minute, but it seemed much longer trying to remember all the Tongan words. A couple of the trainees had found out that they were going to have to give a speech and had written it out in advance. I didn't know, so I just winged it.

Monday, my host family prepared an awesome goodbye dinner with some of my favorites, especially the fish curry and the chicken curry. They topped it off with cookies-and-cream ice cream. It was a nice evening, and it also gave me a chance to thank them one last time for all they have done for me. This time, I wrote it down in Tongan so I could get it right, and they seemed to understand me. I look forward to seeing them again when I return to Vava'u in a few months.

Tuesday morning, we left early and my host mom and sister wanted to drive me to the airport to personally see me off. They waited with us until the plane finally arrived. They both cried as I was leaving, and I gave them both really long hugs. That's not exactly culturally appropriate here, but I wanted to do it and it seemed to be fine.

The plane that flies between Vava'u and Tongatapu

The flight was on a very small plane. To get on the plane, we each had to stand on a scale with our carry-on bags to make sure that together we would not be over the plane's maximum weight allowance. We were then assigned seats based on weight, so the plane would be balanced. We were each allowed a maximum of 22 pounds of carry-on and checked luggage.

The rest of the bags were put on a boat and will arrive in a few days. When it came time to board, we walked directly to the plane. There was no security check-point, no airline official who announced the flight and no rules about walking onto the runway. We got on board and there were no flight attendants. During the entire flight, we flew with the cabin door open, and because I was in the second row, I could clearly see the gauges in the cockpit.

The flight was actually pretty amazing. We got to see Vava'u for the first time and flew over our home village of Ta'anea. It was incredible to see all of the islands in the chain and to have a bird's-eye view of the island that has been our home for the past six weeks. It was a beautiful day, and we flew at a fairly low altitude so it was pretty easy to see. After about 30 minutes, we flew over the Ha'apia Islands and got to see one of the active volcanoes on the west side of the plane. I tried to take a picture, but there were clouds in front of it and it didn't turn out. We finally landed in Tongatapu, right on schedule at 9 a.m. We will complete our training here and will become official Peace Corps volunteers on December 12th.

Vava'u from the air

Wednesday morning, seven of the guys played in a basketball tournament, losing one game and winning one game. I surprised myself, scoring the very first time I touched the ball. Unfortunately, it was the only score I made after that. We lost 10-8 to a group of Tongans. (Baskets count as one point and what we would consider a three pointer is a two pointer here.) Our fellow trainees did a great job cheering us on. The second game we won against a Chinese team, but they were really tough to keep up with and moved a lot faster than the Tongans.

After the game (and a shower), I got to go to the main office of the Tonga Development Bank, where I'll be working for the next two months. I met with some of the bank executives and the Peace Corps volunteer who currently works at the main branch. They put together a great overview of the bank for me and gave me a tour. As I was watching the PowerPoint presentation they did for me, I realized that I would soon be stepping back into the corporate world that I left May 11th. It's going to be a completely different experience of course, but it brought back memories. It was great fun to sit in there and learn about their business strategy, financial condition, market share, etc. My first day will be December 17th, and I'll have three weekdays off at Christmas and three weekdays off at New Year's.

Other News

In Tongan, there are many words that have the same meaning, and you just have to figure out the context. When we introduce ourselves, we are encouraged to give some of our background. I generally say in Tongan that I managed a TV news department. The word for manage is *fakalele*. However, the same word also means diarrhea. That means I say, "I managed a TV news department," or "I diarrhea a TV news department." I can already hear my former co-workers laughing and saying that managing and diarrhea have a lot in common.

NATURAL DISASTERS
Monday, December 10, 2007

In the past 24 hours, we have been threatened with a cyclone, and we had an earthquake—the first quake I've ever felt. I was lying in bed at a guesthouse when I felt a vibration. It kept going, and I asked my roommate Justin, "Do you feel that?" He said yes and I said, "Is this an earthquake?" Turns out that even though he is from the West Coast (Oregon), he had never felt one either. I asked, "Should we just stay here?" which we did. When it was over, we went outside and asked the owners if it had really been an earthquake, and of course it had been. Interestingly, several of our group were walking back from town at the time, and they didn't even feel it. According to the weather service, "A magnitude 7.6 to 7.9 earthquake deep in the seabed north of the Kermadec Islands was felt in Nuku'alofa at around 8:30 p.m. Tonga time, Dec. 9, 2007." And the cyclone never happened. "A Tropical Cyclone Alert has been cancelled for central and southern Tonga as Tropical Cyclone Daman has weakened overnight and is expected to curve southwest away from Tonga today, Dec. 9, 2007."

Other News

We swear in as volunteers on Wednesday. We had our last class today (Monday), but I have FIVE final interviews to complete with the Peace Corps staff later this afternoon. After that, I'm done until we have our ceremony. I spoke to my first homestay family this weekend, and they are planning to come to the ceremony

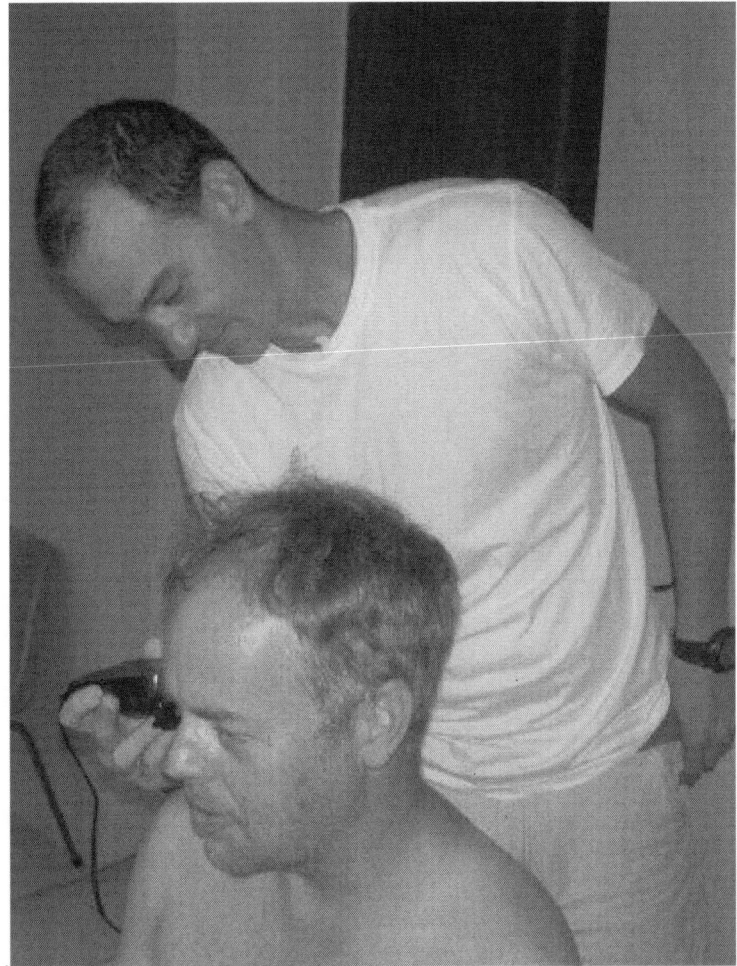

Scot Fitzgerald gives Steve Hunsicker a haircut

I got my second hair cut here in Tonga. The first time, my homestay dad trimmed it for me. This time, I had my friend Scot shave my head. It is the shortest I think I have EVER had my hair, or at least the shortest I can ever remember. You can't see it in the photo, but there was an audience watching as my hair went away. I'm still getting used to having no hair, but I've had several positive comments about my new look from my fellow trainees.

I don't have a place to live yet either here or once I get to Vava'u. We are supposed to move out of the guesthouse where we are staying on Thursday. I hope to gain more information about what is going to happen during one of my interviews today.

I'M A VOLUNTEER
Friday, December 14, 2007

It's official. I'm now a PCV or Peace Corps volunteer. My entire group of 33 trainees made it to the swearing in ceremony on Wednesday night. The highlight of the night for me was that my host family from Fua'amotu showed up for the ceremony and presented flower leis to both Justin, my roommate, and me. We also got to have dinner with them. It was great to see them again, and they told us that we aren't going to get an invitation to come visit them because their home is our home, and you don't need an invitation to visit your own home. What a nice gesture! We will both be taking them up on it soon.

Sia Tupou, Volunteer Justin Doneth, Tau Tupou, Steve Hunsicker

You might notice that Justin and I look a little different in this photo. While the swearing in ceremony is a pretty formal affair, some of my fellow trainees decided to have some fun. For the past several months, many of the male trainees have been growing facial hair. We saw a photo of a volunteer group from the late 1970s posted in the Peace Corps office. We decided we wanted to look just like them with their mustaches. We all wanted to show up for our official photograph looking like we walked out of the 1970s. A bunch of the guys really got into it. I started to participate and grew hair for about a week before I got tired of it and shaved it. (It was also pretty hot.) Then this past weekend, I decided not to shave and with the help of an eyebrow pencil, showed up with a mustache. (It came off Thursday morning.)

The women also got into the act, feathering their hair and dressing like women did in the 70s. It was pretty funny for me because many of them were dressed like women from my college days.

After swearing in, we all went out for one last night together. We won't see each other again until April. Thursday, we started saying goodbye as people started leaving for their new homes. It was pretty hard because we have all seen each other almost every day for the past 10 weeks, and many friendships (and a few romances) have formed. I'm staying here in Nuku'alofa for a few months and said goodbye to my fellow Vava'u volunteers. They flew to Vava'u Thursday morning, and I moved into a house where I will be staying during my time here.

I'm living in a small house on a college campus in the main city of Nuku'alofa. However, it's a very small campus, about the size of a small elementary school in the United States and classes are out until mid-February. I have a small house with indoor plumbing and amazingly(!), Internet access. I'm pretty happy with my situation. It is a short walk to the Tonga Development Bank where I will be working for the next two months, and the bank provided me with both a refrigerator and a stove. I'm scheduled to move to Vava'u at the end of February, which is where I will live for 18 months. I don't know if you can see the house on Google Earth, but if you want to check out the neighborhood the coordinates are: W175 11.809 S21 08.244

Steve Hunsicker in front of his Tongan fale' (house)

I woke up in my own house Friday morning and had REAL Tongan coffee from my French Press, which had been in storage, and ate bananas from the tree in my yard. It was a great way to start the day.

CHRISTMAS EVE IN TONGA
Sunday, December 23, 2007

Living in Tonga, it is hard to believe that it is almost Christmas. It has little to do with the warm—make that hot—tropical weather, but more to do with the complete lack of Christmas commercialization here. There are no advertisements promoting last-minute Christmas sales and no obvious indication in the shops that Christmas is just about here. But make no mistake, this is a very Christian country, and Christmas will be celebrated in a big way. We've heard it has been impossible to get a seat on an airplane to Tonga because so many of the Tongans that live overseas are coming home for the holidays. There are Christmas trees (all artificial), and some homes have outside Christmas lights. For most Tongans, Christmas will be a day to spend at home with family and friends.

Friday night was the Christmas party for the bank where I work. I went with Craig, a Peace Corps volunteer who has been working at the bank for more than a year. We were told it was a dress-up occasion, so Craig and I both wore long pants, a dress shirt and a tie. Craig also wore a jacket. (I didn't bring one with me.) We walked in and saw people in t-shirts, jeans and very casual attire. We were the most over-dressed people there. But it didn't really matter, and we had a great time. The bank managers even introduced me so that everyone would know me. Of course, since I was one of just two guys in the place with a tie, I wasn't hard to spot.

On Saturday, Craig played Santa at a fair in Nuku'alofa. The organizers said they wanted him to do it because Santa is "white." I thought that was kind of interesting because who says Santa couldn't be Tongan?

"Santa" Craig Harner with Tongan kids

The Christmas holiday is officially a two-day event in Tonga, with Christmas on the 25th and Boxing Day on the 26th. However, for schools, many government agencies and businesses, the celebration of Christmas can begin more than a week before the holiday and stretch into the New Year. Tonga is the first place in the world to welcome every day since we sit just west of the International Dateline. That means we are the first to celebrate Christmas and will be the first place to welcome 2008 on New Year's Eve.

Other News

As you might expect, things were pretty slow for me my first week at work. While the bank was open, many of the bank employees were not there last week. Current volunteer Craig Harner has designed a lot of the programs the bank uses to advise small businesses here in Tonga. Since it is a development bank, the bank's role is not just to provide the loans but to make sure the businesses are successful. A lot of this is done in workshops conducted for anyone who wants to attend and in one-on-one consultation with the business owners.

Interestingly, once a business becomes successful, it will often leave the development bank and move to one of the three commercial banks since they offer a full range of banking services not offered by the development bank. I'm looking forward to getting out and working with the businesses and prospective businesses once the holidays are over.

A TONGAN CHRISTMAS
Tuesday, December 25, 2007

Imagine sitting on a beautiful beach in the South Pacific, palm trees waving freely in the wind, freshly caught fish simmering over an open fire, waves gently caressing the white sand beaches and a glass of wine in your hand as the sun sets over the sparkling blue water. That pretty much summarizes how I spent most of my Christmas Day in Tonga. I wasn't sure exactly what to expect for my first Christmas here in the kingdom but knew it would be different than any Christmas I've celebrated in the past.

My first clue that we were in for something different happened as Justin and I were riding to the village of Fua'amoto with our homestay family. As we entered the village, Tau did not take the turn to the house and instead took the road to the beach. At no point had he mentioned that we were going to the beach. As we started the drive down to the shore, he told us they had camped at the beach last night (Christmas Eve) and that everyone was already there. We drove to the grave of his father, which is next to the ocean, and found a home away from home—two tents, a grill, a gas stove and most of the extended family. The kids were in the water swimming, and everyone else was just kind of hanging out.

There didn't seem to be anything unusual to me about camping next to the grave of Tau's father, and his mother was there with us. Justin and I took a nice walk through the tropical blue ocean out to the reef—something you can only do at low tide. We drank juice made from freshly picked pineapple and coconut milk and eagerly watched as Tau's brother turned a spit holding a freshly killed pig over an open fire. Dinner time came and we "pigged" out. I had not eaten much—an orange for breakfast and a couple of bananas for lunch—so I was very hungry. In addition to the freshly roasted pig, we had BBQ chicken, snapper that Tau had caught earlier in the day, crab and raw fish. Quite a feast! And what a beautiful place to relax on Christmas.

After dinner, we watched the sunset and started drinking wine. I was actually surprised by the presence of the wine. It was the first time I had seen any of the people there take a drink. It was also time to turn on the generator. Yes, an electric generator. They had decorated the grave of their father in Christmas lights and brought a generator to power the lights.

The grave of Tau Tupou's father decorated for Christmas

As the sky grew darker, out came the fireworks. The kids were running around, holding Roman candles and bottle rockets in their hands, setting off firecrackers and generally having a great time. Now imagine this: The oldest kid was 11; everyone else was younger, and at first I couldn't believe that they were allowed to handle the fireworks with no adult supervision. However, they didn't do anything stupid and no one got hurt.

After a couple hours of fireworks, it was time for Santa Claus. Santa (Sia) gathered all the kids on a mat on the ground and handed each a gift—nothing fancy or elaborate, but everyone got something. Tevita, the three-year-old, got a bag of Cheetos, which he quickly devoured.

Sia Tupou hands out Christmas gifts on the beach

There were a few more fireworks, and then Sia asked us if we were ready to go back to the house. Justin and I said we would be happy to stay with the family and camp at the beach instead of going back to the empty house. There was a gentle ocean breeze keeping everything cool, and we were really enjoying ourselves. However, we didn't really rough it. Sia made up our "rooms" in the tent with a mattress covered in a sheet, a pillow and a top sheet. I don't know what time we went to bed, but we got up very early the next morning with Sia calling our names before 7 a.m.

It was really a very memorable Christmas, and as I was riding back to my house, it occurred to me how completely comfortable I had felt. The Tupou family has really made us feel like part of their family. I know enough Tongan to be able to pick up on what is being said, and they also know English pretty well. I knew the names of all the kids, just like I might at my own family gathering, and it was great fun to play with them and to see the joy in their eyes as they received their Christmas gifts. Christmas in Tonga is a day to spend with family and friends, and that's exactly what we did.

AN ISLAND GET-A-WAY
Wednesday, January 2, 2008

The Kingdom of Tonga is not really an "island" nation, but a nation of islands. There are four main island groups: Tongatapu (which includes 'Eua), Vava'u, Ha'apai and Niua. Within each of these island groups are many small, mostly uninhabited islands. As you stand on the shore of the major islands, you can often see the small islands that dot the ocean landscape. In Tonga, you really can have an island all to yourself, at least for a day. All you need is a boat to get there.

And if you live on an island, where do you go to get away? Why a smaller island of course. Friday, I made my first trip to a smaller island to celebrate my birthday. I went to the island resort of Pangaimotu. Don't get confused by the term resort. It is not what most Americans would classify as a resort. There are beach *fales* (huts) where you can spend the night, but they have no electricity, and the water comes from a cistern. The only electricity here is from a generator the resort uses to keep the freezer and fridge running in the restaurant. Most people come for the day, as it is the closest beach to Nuku'alofa. (While the capital city of Nuku'alofa is on the water, it is a port and not a beach.)

To get to the island, you get on a small boat. However, there wasn't room for the boat to dock, so we walked across another boat to get into the launch to the island. As Peace Corps volunteers, we are required to carry our own life jackets anytime we get on a boat. We followed the rules and certainly stood out, as we were the only people with life jackets on the boat.

After the short one-mile ride to the island, we pulled up at a dock that looked as if it had seen better days. It was high tide, and the dock slanted toward the water. One slip and you would get wet. We walked the remainder of the way to shore, paying TOP$15 to get off the dock. That's the fee for using the island for the day. Our first stop was the bar, where two glasses of red wine from a box cost us TOP$17. The wine was not cheap, but you are not allowed to bring your own food and drink to the island. Lunch was more affordable but featured basic bar food like hamburgers and fish and chips.

The Bar at Pangaimotu

The bar is in a place called Big Mama's Yacht Club. It's very quaint and looks like something you would expect to find in the South Pacific. Off the deck in the water is a shipwreck. Kids take turns climbing up and diving from the top of the vessel. There are rope swings and plenty of beautiful sand beaches.

My friend Craig, who has been to Pangaimotu many times before, and I decided to explore the island, finally stopping at an isolated stretch of beach where we could safely break out a contraband bottle of wine that we had smuggled onto the island. We didn't get caught.

Swimming in the ocean was pretty amazing. The beaches are littered with seashells, and the ocean floor has a lot of life. I picked up starfish and numerous shells with the creatures still alive inside. I even found a perfect sand dollar, still alive. We tossed it all back of course, but each sweep of the hand brought a new treasure.

We headed back and then treated ourselves to pizza at one of the few pizza places in Tonga. The pizza was surprisingly good, and while we certainly overspent our Peace Corps budget for the day, it was a great way to spend my birthday.

The next night, I got a nice surprise from some of my fellow volunteers. One of the current volunteer's birthday is on the 30th. They surprised the two of us by baking brownies, putting candles on them and singing "Happy Birthday" to us. The brownies were great. The mix had been shipped to Tonga in a care package from the States.

Other News

I may have a place to live on Vava'u once I move there at the end of February. My friend James sent me a link to some pictures he took of the house where I might live. It's not official yet, but the bank manager and the Peace Corps staff have been talking about it with the landlord. The house next door is James'.

Steve Hunsicker's new house in Vava'u

Our group of 33 is still intact as we now celebrate three full months in Tonga. However, two people are actually out of the country for medical reasons. One was sent to the United States and the other to Australia. Medical care is downright scary in Tonga, and if you need anything, even a simple MRI, you are going to be sent elsewhere to have it done.

TONGAN PUNISHMENT
Saturday, January 5, 2008

In many ways, it is sometimes easy to forget that I live in a developing country. Sometimes, it doesn't feel that different. However, there are times when it really hits you in the face that things are different here. During my interview for the Peace Corps, I remember my recruiter, Tricia, asking me how I would handle myself if I saw something that I thought was inappropriate but was culturally acceptable. I hadn't thought much about it until my last week on Vava'u when the issue smacked me right in the face.

We were sitting in language class on Saturday morning on the porch of our trainer's house. All of a sudden, we heard children shrieking at the top of their lungs. We looked over into the next yard and watched a woman beat her daughter, who was perhaps two years old, with a switch. She kept hitting her and hitting her. Then she picked up a large stick and went after her son, who was probably four years old, and hit him repeatedly. The children were in tears, and we all just sat there and watched. My emotions quickly ran from astonishment to anger to helplessness. In Tonga, it's perfectly acceptable for a parent to hit his or her children. I had previously seen some children who had had their ears flicked or who had gotten a light spanking, but nothing like this. And clearly, in my opinion, kids that age could not have done anything that warranted the beating they received.

One of my classmates remarked that children who misbehave in school also get hit and that one teacher she had visited kept a stick in the room to keep order.

After the beating was over, we all just sat there for a minute in stunned silence. Finally, our teacher, a 71-year-old Tongan woman, said, "Some parents are not very educated." Her remark made me feel a bit better that what we had witnessed might not be the norm, but I've had a hard time getting the sight of those two little children being beaten out of my mind.

In the United States, we would have called 9-1-1 on that woman, and her children probably would have been taken away. Now, I know why Tricia asked me that question.

Other News

I now have a place to live on Vava'u. The bank told me this week that they have rented the house for me that I mentioned previously. In Tonga, housing is provided by the host organization, so the bank will pay my rent for the house while I'm working there. I am flying to Vava'u on February 29th and will start working at the Vava'u branch of the Tonga Development Bank on Monday, March 3rd. I'll continue to work out of the main branch here in Nuku'alofa until then.

A SERIOUS PROBLEM
Tuesday, January 15, 2008

I woke up early Saturday morning, reached for my water bottle and discovered I did not have the strength to pick it up. This was my first indication that something had happened to my left arm. On Monday, a doctor diagnosed that I had just one-fifth of my normal strength in my arm. Peace Corps is now sending me to Brisbane, Australia for a complete exam. If the problem does not improve or can't be quickly corrected, this will be the end of my Peace Corps service.

The good news is that my arm is much improved today (Tuesday), and I'm a lot more optimistic that whatever happened is going to be correctable. I was able to lift my arm over my head this morning, and while it is a struggle, I am able to use my fingers to type these few words.

I do not want to leave, but getting the use of my arm back is clearly a lot more important in the grand scheme of things. I am hoping that it will continue to improve each day, and I'll be back in Tonga soon.

Jason, a member of my training group, was just medically separated this weekend. He is the first from our group of 33 to leave, and we are all going to miss him.

OH HAPPY DAY!
Tuesday, January 15, 2008

It's Wednesday morning, and I am so thankful, relieved and happy today. I woke up this morning and the full range of motion in my left arm has returned, and while my strength is not 100%, it is close. After visiting with the Peace Corps medical officer this morning, she cleared me to return to work on Friday with no restrictions. I still have to go to Brisbane and have tests done, but that will probably not happen until February now. She says because we don't know what caused my arm to weaken, it's important to have it examined in case it should ever happen again.

When I wrote about my arm yesterday, it was still difficult for me to type, so I didn't explain what happened to me at the doctor's office on Monday morning. The doctor was an Australian doctor, probably in her late 50s. After examining me, she suggested acupuncture to see if that would help my arm. I agreed to give it a try. I figured it certainly wouldn't do any harm.

At the clinic, there is only one exam room, so she moved me into the clinic pharmacy, which opens onto the waiting room and has a big open window between the rooms. She stuck six needles in me, one in my head, the rest in my hand, arm and shoulder. I asked for a glass of water and was left alone in the pharmacy. After about five minutes, I started to feel faint. I screamed for help and a stampede of people came rushing in, including other patients who were waiting to see the doctor. They grabbed me before I fell and put me on the floor. I spent the next 20 minutes lying on the floor of the pharmacy with needles sticking out of me. I can only imagine what would have happened if I had fallen on top of one and jammed it into my body. Afterwards, the doctor told me that about one out of every 50 people becomes faint when they get acupuncture. It's hard for me to imagine that those little needles could cause that feeling. Of course, I also don't know if it was the acupuncture that made me get better or if I would have improved anyway. Doesn't matter. I'm just happy to be almost back to normal and thrilled that I'm not going to have to end my Peace Corps service.

CASE CLOSED
Wednesday, January 16, 2008

"I was poisoned." That's the official verdict from the Peace Corps medical office in Washington, DC about the problems I've had with my arm over the past week. This means I no longer have to take a trip to Brisbane, Australia, and I have no need for any further medical attention. After reviewing the symptoms, I believe this is probably a proper diagnosis. I was probably suffering from ciguatera fish poisoning, paralytic shellfish poisoning or scombroid fish poisoning.

A week ago today, I had lunch at the Catholic Basilica and ate fried tuna. Within two hours I started to feel bad. I left work early and did not work on Friday. I did not eat again until Saturday morning, which is when I woke up unable to use my arm. I had numbness in the fingers on both hands and also had numbness on my tongue. What's strange about the illness is that I never threw up, which is the first thing I always associate with food poisoning.

It's scary to think how much poison I must have ingested for it to still be affecting me a week later. Last week was not the first time I had eaten at the restaurant at the Catholic Basilica. And it probably was not anyone's fault that I got sick there. All three of the poisons mentioned above are impossible to detect, and the fish comes out of the water contaminated.

US IMMIGRATION AND TONGA
Sunday, January 20, 2008

Even though I'm a long way away from the United States, I'm very aware that immigration is a hot issue right now. I'm not writing this to weigh in on what should be done or even to offer any personal opinions on immigration, but instead to provide a Tongan perspective on USA policies.

If a Tongan wants to visit the United States, he or she needs a visa. Pretty obvious, right? Actually, it is a lot more complicated than it might appear. Because there is no embassy in Tonga, anyone who wants to visit the United States has to fly to Fiji, which is the closest embassy, and apply in person. That's an expensive trip for most people, but it is the only way they can legally visit friends and family in the United States or just vacation there. Prior to September 11th, the embassy used to make occasional visits to Tonga to process visa requests. However, the process now involves being fingerprinted, and the machine they use for fingerprinting cannot leave the embassy in Fiji for security reasons. (At least that is how the US ambassador to Fiji explained it to us during our training.)

Once a Tongan gets to Fiji, she or he may get a visa or not. Many visas are issued for a year, but you can get a two-year visa and occasionally a ten-year visa. The reason many people get turned down is because the United States believes they might stay in the country. But if you have a good job, a house and a family in Tonga, you will probably get a visa. But if you are a young person, just out of school with no strong ties, you'll probably get turned down. Contrast this with New Zealand, which has an open visa policy for Tongans, and it is easy to see why someone might opt to visit there instead of the United States. Of course, it is also a lot closer. Getting a visa to visit the USA is difficult, but it's even harder if someone wants to immigrate to the States. That involves entering a lottery conducted by the State Department.

But this is only one side of the issue of immigration in Tonga. If a Tongan is arrested in the United States, they are deported back to Tonga. It might be after serving a jail sentence or as a way to avoid jail. From the USA perspective, this probably makes a lot of sense. From the Tongan perspective, these deportees are often the proverbial "fish out of water."

Many of the Tongan deportees have grown up in the United States; some only speak English and coming back to Tonga is a very tough adjustment. During our training, we met a deportee on Vava'u who runs an organization called the Ironman Ministries. That group tries to help deportees adjust to life in Tonga, which is very different from life in the United States. I've met deportees here who are actively involved in their communities and have completely turned around their lives. Others have jobs while some resort back to their previous lives of crimes.

I recently heard a story about a deportee who was spending his first Christmas outside of jail in 20 years. The week of the holidays, he got arrested by the police here.

I was introduced to a Tongan not knowing he was a deportee. I greeted him in Tongan, and he had no idea what I was saying—not because my Tongan was so bad, but because he was just back from the United States and didn't know how to speak the local language.

It is no wonder that many of the deportees find themselves comfortable around Peace Corps volunteers. We all speak English, and many of them consider themselves more American than Tongan.

PRIVACY TONGAN STYLE
Friday, January 25, 2008

I remember at a very young age learning that there are just some things you don't discuss in the USA—like age, income and religion. If you are an American who avoids those topics, then you will be in for a big surprise in Tonga. There really is no such thing as privacy here. Tongans will talk about almost anything, and most of what they do is readily visible to everyone else. Here are some examples that may surprise you.

• Each year, the churches in Tonga have a fundraiser. This is the primary way that the church supports itself. During the fundraiser, the church announces to the entire congregation how much money each family has donated down to the penny. A family will often hit up relatives overseas to help them come up with big donations, so they are not embarrassed at the church fundraiser.

• Each year, Tonga National Radio broadcasts the exam results of seniors who pass their final test. If you fail the test, your name is not read. Thus, everyone in the country knows how well you did in school.

• Age is not considered private. Tongans will ask your age and marital status all the time. In fact, during our training, we were taught that we should introduce ourselves by telling everyone how old we are and whether or not we are married. This is especially true when addressing a group. It is not rude to ask people how old they are.

• At the bank where I work, I sit at the desk of someone who is on leave. Posted on the wall for anyone to see are the amounts that each of the bank directors and managers receive for utilities, housing and entertainment.

• Each day the bank sends a mass e-mail to all workers that says who is sick, who is on vacation, who is attending workshops, who was late to work that day and whether or not each person called in to say she or he would be late. It also lists the names of people who are returning to duty after being sick, and in some cases, what sickness they had.

Medical information is freely discussed. If you are "puke" or sick, expect to explain in detail exactly what is wrong, and if you are well, be prepared to hear details about anyone who is sick no matter what the issue may be.

• A co-worker at the bank interviewed this week for another job. Everyone from the head of the department to his immediate supervisor knew about the interview, including how much money he would make if he got the new job.

• And finally, this one might fall into the "too much information" category, but in many bars and restaurants, they do not have urinals in the men's room. It is usually just a trough. If you are using the bathroom, Tongans will walk right up, stand directly next to you and start carrying on a conversation—often looking right at you as they talk.

Other News

We said our goodbyes to Jason Schneider this week, who was medically separated because of an injury to his shoulder. He is the first person from my training group to leave. Jason is probably freezing back in Michigan by now. We went out last week to a local ice cream shop and ordered the special, which is one scoop of every flavor they offer. His fellow volunteers from 'Eua took the boat to Tongatapu and joined us in eating every bite.

Then, on Jason's last night, almost all of the Tongatapu volunteers showed up for a farewell dinner to see him off.

FRIDAY NIGHT IN TONGA
Saturday, February 2, 2008

On the first Friday of every month, the Australian High Commission in Nuku'alofa hosts a reception called "Sundowners" for the volunteers who serve in Tonga. This includes the US Peace Corps volunteers, the Japanese volunteers and, of course, the Australian volunteers along with some Australian and New Zealand residents who work here in Tonga or who may be here on a visit. It's a great chance for us all to get to know each other and for those of us who are in the Peace Corps, to see each other. We had a good crowd this Friday, and the Aussies even extended the reception an extra hour because everyone was having such a great time. They had a cash bar with beer and wine selling for TOP$3.00 and liquor for TOP$5.00. That's about US$1.50 and US$2.50, so it's a great deal since most of the volunteers have tight budgets. They also have a BBQ.

It is interesting to talk with the volunteers from the different countries and to hear about their training and how their organizations are structured. Without a doubt, Peace Corps provides the most training in culture and language and has the longest training schedule. The Japanese get language training, but they attend intensive daylong classes for a much shorter period of time. The Aussies actually get paid a salary, and they rent their own homes, whereas the Peace Corps volunteers here are provided housing by the organization for which they work. Both Japan and Australia provide grant money for projects in addition to the volunteer labor. New Zealand provides just grant money, but that money can be used to hire people as needed depending on the project. The United States doesn't hand out grant money here but instead makes its focus more grassroots through Peace Corps. Our mission is to help the Tongans develop skills on their own.

However, here is where it gets interesting. As a United States Peace Corps volunteer, I can apply, or help an organization apply, for grants from Australia or New Zealand. And those grants often get approved. It helps to remember that the top sources of income in Tonga are grants and remittances from overseas. These come not just from countries and aid organizations, but from Tongans who live abroad and send money back to help their families.

I don't know the history of the Sundowners reception, but it's a great idea, and this is the second one I have attended. However, it will also probably be my last. I am moving to Vava'u at the end of the month to start my permanent job there. I'm actually excited about the move and am eager to get settled in my new home. It will also be great to see my fellow Vava'u volunteers again.

Other News

Friday was the second anniversary of the death of Tessa Horan, a Peace Corps volunteer in Tonga who was killed in a shark attack in Vava'u. Here in Tongatapu, we all observed a moment of silence for her. Most of the volunteers who trained and served with Tessa have concluded their service now, but a tribute to her is prominently posted in the Peace Corps office.

One of the married couples from my training group is now on medical leave, and both are out of the country. We hope they will be back. We are now down to 29 members of our original training group of 33.

ARE YOU MARRIED?
Thursday, February 7, 2008

One of the Peace Corps volunteers serving here in Tonga lives near a vegetable stand. He often stops there to pick up a pile of tomatoes or a stack of cucumbers. As would be expected, he has gotten to know the people who work at this stand and considers them friends. Occasionally, he'll stop by just to chat or even have a drink with them.

That was the case Monday night—a friendly visit, some Tongans and an American, just hanging out. Or at least, that is how it seemed. As the volunteer was talking to his Tongan friends, he saw a big flatbed truck pull up, and in the back, there was a young woman dressed "to the nines." He had seen her before, but never spoken with her. The truck pulled up in front of the vegetable stand. The young woman, who was probably somewhere between 18 and 20, got out and came over.

The following conversation took place in Tongan, but went something like this:

"Are you married?"

"Not yet."

"Will you marry me?"

Yes, you read that right: "Will you marry me?" The woman asked the volunteer to get married. And yes, she was serious. We were warned during our training about this, but it's the first time I've actually heard about it happening. I've often been asked if I am going to marry a Tongan woman as have most of the guys in our group. In fact, asking someone if they are married is a pretty common question. My language teacher told me that when I am introducing myself at a meeting or workshop, I should tell a little joke, and she suggested that when I say, "I am not married," that I add, "but perhaps I'll marry a Tongan."

There are many reasons that a young woman may want to marry an American. Even though we live on next to nothing and live at the level of most Tongan people, it is hard to overcome the reputation of being a "rich American." For many, America is still the land of opportunity, and getting married to an American is a quick way to get to the USA and have a better life. And sometimes, it is just that the person is more attracted to Americans than Tongans.

In this case, we'll probably never know the motivation. Because in case you were wondering, they won't be getting married.

Other News

On Thursday, I got to visit three of the bank's clients at their businesses. All three were having problems with recordkeeping, and we went to show them how they could improve this skill. None of the three were actually tracking their profit, only how much money they had at the end of the day. The businesses were very diverse: a liquor store, an electrician and a tyre (that is the correct spelling here) shop.

I really enjoyed getting out and meeting with these Tongan business owners. Getting to help these folks is one of the reasons I joined Peace Corps. Hopefully, I will get to do a lot more of this when I get to my permanent job in Vava'u. (I move three weeks from today.)

A RECORD-BREAKING RAIN
Saturday, February 9, 2008

"The greatest rainfall ever recorded." That is how Friday's rainstorm in Tonga is being described by government officials. And it was quite the storm. It started Friday about 2 p.m. and lasted until 7 p.m. Imagine the intensity of a typical Florida summer storm, except lasting for five straight hours.

At one point, I started to get worried that the water was going to flood my home. Another inch or so, and it would have been in my house. Luckily that didn't happen. However, one of our volunteers, Patrick, wasn't as lucky. He got flooded but says all is okay now. He is the only Peace Corps member I know that had a flooding problem, but I haven't heard from everyone.

Here is how Matangi Online described the rain:

> The Tonga Defence Force's quick reaction team responded last night to several calls for help as low-lying areas around Nuku'alofa were submerged during the greatest rainfall ever recorded in the kingdom.
> At 10 am today (Saturday), the Fua'amotu weather station measured a total of 289.2mm (11.3 inches) of rain in the 24 hrs. from 10 am on Friday, February 8, to 10 am on February 9. The Nuku'alofa weather station recorded 250.5mm in the same period. "This is the greatest rainfall we have ever had in the kingdom," said the duty forecaster, 'Ofa Taumoepeau, this morning. It is more than the very heavy rainfall experienced in Tonga in 2006. Another climatologist working for the Tonga Meteorological Office said it was without doubt "an extreme event." This daily fall compares to mean rainfall for the whole month of February of 221mm for Fua'amotu and 210mm for Nuku'alofa.

By Saturday, a lot of the water had subsided, but there is still a lot of water everywhere. John, another volunteer here, told me he actually saw fish swimming on the road near his house.

Other News

Saturday, I met up with a bunch of my fellow volunteers at a local restaurant. As we were eating, the US ambassador for Fiji, Larry Dinger, came walking in with a few other folks. His embassy is also responsible for Tonga, Kiribati, Nauru and Tuvalu. He came over and chatted with us for a while before going back to his table. His visit coincides with the visit of the U.S. Navy ship *Reuben James*. The ship is here on a goodwill mission, and the sailors aboard are doing everything from picking up litter to playing rugby with Tongan youths. Some of the projects were suggested by Peace Corps volunteers.

The naval ship was not the only boat in Nuku'alofa on Friday. The 1,800 passenger cruise ship *Aurora* was docked here. This is the third cruise ship to arrive so far this year. Before the rain started on Friday, there were tourists and sailors everywhere.

By the way, the next cruise ship scheduled to arrive is the *QE2* (*Queen Elizabeth II*) on February 18th.

Steve Hunsicker

EATING THE QUEEN'S FOOD
Sunday, February 17, 2008

In Tonga, all land is owned by the king and is either controlled by the royal family or a noble. In exchange for being allowed free use of the land, the Tongans agree to provide some of the crops they grow to the people who control the land. In Fua'amotu, where I stayed when I first arrived in Tonga, the land is controlled by the royal family. There is also a palace in Fua'amotu, just above the beach. And while the current king apparently doesn't visit this palace, it is still often used by his mother, the queen.

When the queen is in residence, the people of Fua'amotu provide her with food, and several of the women will spend the night at the palace in case she needs anything during her visit. I spent this weekend in Fua'amotu as did the 82-year-old queen. She stayed at the palace, and I stayed with my homestay family. We never met, but that didn't stop me from eating her food.

My homestay father, Tau, is the spokesman for the king in Fua'amotu. This is also called being a "talking chief" in Tongan society. When there is an issue involving the royal family, Tau is the guy who communicates the wishes of the family to the people of the village. His wife, Sia, helps out by cooking and occasionally sleeping at the palace when the queen is there. That was the case this weekend. Tau and his brother caught a lot of fish, and one of the biggest and best was cooked for the queen—along with some pig and other Tongan food. Like every meal in Tonga, there was more food than anyone could eat. So after the queen had her meal, the fish came home with Sia and Tau. It happened to get there about the same time that Justin, my roommate during my homestay, and I arrived in Fua'amoto. The fish was certainly "fit for a queen" and delicious.

Never did I think I would eat "royal leftovers" in Tonga, but that's exactly what I did. Actually, we had a lot more than just leftovers. I think all we did the whole weekend was eat. We did get to the beach, and Tau, Justin and I spent some time lying on a mat outside the house just talking. (We were outside under a tree because it was a lot cooler than being inside.) It was quite a nice way to spend the weekend, and I will certainly miss my Fua'amotu family once I move to Vava'u at the end of next week.

Other News

I got my third haircut in Tonga, but this time, I went to a barber. My first haircut was done by my Vava'u homestay father, the second, by my friend and fellow volunteer Scot. This time, I stopped during lunch at a small shack that houses a barber. He never asked me how I wanted it cut, and after I sat down, he just went to work. He cleaned the shears with a toilet brush before he started. Of course, I was just hoping that the brush had never seen the inside of a toilet bowl. Then he trimmed me up with scissors and finally got out a knife and used it to shave any loose hairs. The blade looked like something you would see in a slasher movie, but fortunately, he never drew blood. When I was done, I asked him in Tongan how much it cost and he replied, "Five dollars." I looked at my money and found I had four ones and a twenty, so I handed him the twenty. He couldn't make change, so he took the four dollars. When I got back to work, I borrowed another dollar and took it back to him. I'm sure he had no doubt that I would actually return and pay him the rest of the money. As I've mentioned many times before, Tongans are very honest, and credit is freely extended if someone doesn't have enough money.

But as you can see in this photo, that wasn't the end of my hairstyling. This weekend in Fua'amotu, Tevita (that's David in Tongan) decided I needed some additional help.

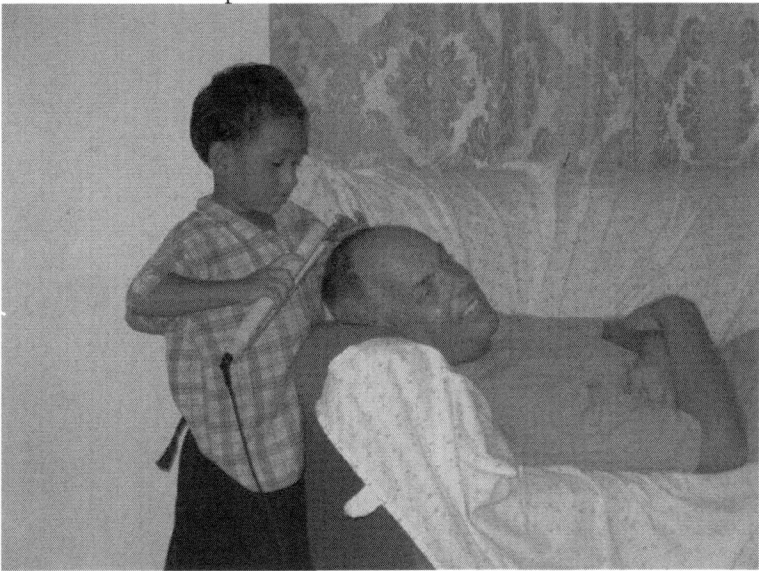

Tevita Tupou "styles" Steve Hunsicker's hair

The other news this week is that there has been a major increase in the cost of electricity in Tonga, and Vava'u, where I will be living, is the most expensive place for power in the country. Rates there increased 20.7%. Tongatapu has a lower rate, but increased more, with bills on the main island going up 21.4% per kilowatt-hour. Many of the volunteers have to pay for their own power, so this is a big hit. We live on less than ten US dollars a day. We've heard rumors that we might get an adjustment because of the higher bills, but nothing official yet.

Tina and her one day old baby

Tina, a woman who lives next door to my homestay family, gave birth to a baby boy on Saturday. She was home from the hospital on Sunday proudly showing off her one-day-old baby to all the neighbors and family. We got to know her during our stay in Fua'amotu.

MONEY MATTERS
Thursday, February 21, 2008

There are many things in Tonga that make no sense. That's a topic for another day. But there are also many things that make perfect sense, some so much so that you wonder why we don't do the same in the United States. And believe it or not, many of the things that make sense have to do with money.

Tongan currency is pretty much issued in the same denominations as US currency: There are $1, $2, $5, $10, $20, $50 and $100 notes. However, the big difference here is the use of the $2 bill. I probably use the $2 bill more than any other denomination, and it makes great sense. If you buy something that costs $6, you can give the clerk three $2 bills or $10 and get back two $2 bills. I don't understand why the $2 bill has not caught on in the United States. When we see a US $2 bill, we tend to save it because it is special. In Tonga, it's an important part of their currency.

Another thing about currency that makes sense is that each bill is color-coded. The ones are green, the twos, pink, etc. It makes it very easy to tell what kind of bill you are using without having to look for the number on it.

Coins are also designed logically. The bigger the coin, the more it is worth. Coins are issued in 1¢, 5¢, 10¢, 20¢ and 50¢ amounts. The 50¢ piece is the largest and like the $2 bill, widely used. By contrast, you almost never see a 1¢ coin. At stores, the amount is always rounded to the nearest 5¢. If your bill is $22.02, you will pay $22.00. At $22.03, your total becomes $22.05. The one exception is if you pay with an ATM card, which is usually only accepted at the larger stores. In that case, you pay the actual amount. (Almost no one accepts credit cards.)

Another money matter that makes a lot of sense to me is the way items are priced. The total price includes the sales (consumption) tax. If an item costs $2.10 in a store or at a restaurant, you will pay exactly $2.10 for it. No additional tax is added at the end. At the larger stores, the receipt shows how much tax was actually paid, but the amount out of your pocket is the amount posted.

Finally, at least from a consumer perspective, the way that Tongans pay for cell phones is very practical. You buy a phone, any kind you want, as long as it has a SIM card. Next, you go to one of the two phone providers and buy a SIM Card, which costs about $5. That gives you your phone number. Then you purchase calling cards in values ranging from $5 to $20 to put credit on your phone. If you make $5 worth of calls one month and $40 the next, you simply pay for what you use. You have a year to use the balance on your phone, and each time you recharge it, it extends your credit for another year. There is no fee for having a phone. You just pay for the minutes.

Of course, there are only voice and text messages here, nothing fancy like the Internet or e-mail, but a system where you pay for what you use seems to be a lot fairer than signing a contract, paying for minutes you don't use and getting a phone for "free" but then having to pay for it in higher per-minute charges.

Next week is a big week for me as I will say goodbye to many of my friends here in Tongatapu. (I'm scheduled to come back in late April for an in-service training session.) My stuff gets shipped to Vava'u on Monday, and we have the workshop on Wednesday. Next Friday, I fly to Vava'u and will get there just in time for a Vava'u volunteer meeting. That means I'll get to see almost everyone shortly after I arrive. Can't wait!

AN AMAZING WEEKEND IN 'EUA
Monday, February 25, 2008

The island of 'Eua is about a two-and-a-half-hour boat ride south of the main Tongan island of Tongatapu. While Tongatapu is flat, 'Eua is a South Pacific paradise with tall majestic mountain ranges, sharp cliffs and lush tropical rain forests. 'Eua boasts the most varieties of plants in all of Tonga. It also has the only river in Tonga and one of two bridges in the entire kingdom. What makes 'Eua so attractive though is its almost total lack of tourists. Most tourists to Tonga either come to the main island or to the kingdom's top tourism destination: Vava'u. Very few venture to 'Eua. My friend Craig and I spent the weekend on 'Eua, and our tour guide for the weekend was Taha, the 'Eua branch manager of the Tonga Development Bank where we both work. We left Nuku'alofa on Friday afternoon, arriving before the 'Eua branch closed for the day. We were able to meet many of the staff who work there before venturing out to the island's one resort called The Hideaway.

The Hideaway would not fit most people's description of a resort, but they do serve food and have six rooms and two small fales right on the water. It's very rustic but the owner, Taki, is personable and speaks great English. We dined on fresh fish. A funny thing happened to us when we first got to The Hideaway. A Tongan man approached us and said, "Are you the two palangi from the bank?" Clearly the coconut wireless was in full operation, as we had never seen this guy before.

Saturday, it was sightseeing time, and Taha picked us up, taking us first to a small waterfall. From there, he put his truck into four-wheel drive, and we headed into areas that looked like no one had been there in years. After winding through more roads and mud than I could have imagined, we got out and hiked down to one of the most beautiful waterfalls I've ever seen. (And remember, I used to live in Hawaii!)

Smoker's Cave waterfall on 'Eua

What made the waterfall so attractive was that it was completely unspoiled. Except for a rope that you could hold on to to keep from falling into the pit that dropped hundreds of feet below, there was no sign that man had ever been there before. This waterfall was far away from civilization, and there were no signs indicating that it was there.

We drove back on more winding roads and took another hike, this time up to a lookout where we could see the cliffs on the southeast side of the island. It was truly a spectacular site. We were so high up that we could look down and see birds flying below us. The forest below was green and lush and the sounds of the waves crashing into the white sand beaches traveled upwards to where we watched. The ocean was as blue as any I've seen.

Next stop was the state park at the tip of the island. From there, you could look across the Pacific Ocean and see Fua'amotu, where I had my first homestay in Peace Corps. It's on another island, but it doesn't look that far away.

In the state park, we headed up another trail. Taha didn't tell us where we were going and we hiked behind him. There were no signs. We finally ended up at another overlook, but this time we were looking at a natural land bridge with a view through it to the ocean blue. Another spectacular site.

From there we went back down into a natural rock garden in the park, and we stood along more cliffs. They were not as high as the ones we saw previously, but we were a lot closer to the water, and it was a bit scary to think about what would happen if you slipped.

Our final stop with Taha was at a beach. We went down a road that was only accessible by four-wheel drive and spent time just relaxing and wading in the water out to the reef.

There are four Peace Corps volunteers permanently assigned to 'Eua, and we had dinner Saturday night with three of them. (The fourth was on Tongatapu because she had contracted dengue fever.) Both Bria and Krystal

Craig, Bria, Steve and Krystal have dinner in 'Eua

were in my training group, and I don't get a chance to see them very often. We ate outside Bria's house and got a chance to catch up.

On Sunday, we ate a couple of sandwiches at The Hideaway and then met back up with Taha. He took us to a drop-off point where we could climb the mountain to see the largest banyan tree in Tonga and also visit Rat's Cave.

The first stop was the banyan tree, which actually has a cave at the bottom. Craig climbed the tree while I explored the cave. It was pretty amazing to see something that size.

From there we began the long hike up the mountain to Rat's Cave. We both had seen a picture of the cave in a Lonely Planet guidebook. It was a good climb, and while we did take the wrong road once, we finally made it to the cave. When we first arrived, we were disappointed. It was a narrow cave with a hole at the end that looked out to a fabulous view. We actually thought we were in the wrong place at first. Then we realized you have to drop yourself through the hole into the cave below. And remember, we were on the edge of a cliff, so one false move and it was over. Getting into the cave was a challenge for me. I was just a bit too tall, but finally made it. It was well worth the trouble.

Steve Hunsicker inside Rat's Cave

We spent a good amount of time enjoying the cave and the breathtaking views. Finally, we realized it was starting to get dark, and we had better head back. We arrived at the main road just as it got completely dark. From the main road, we walked all the way back to town. Along the way, two young Tongans approached us, and we chatted with them for part of the walk. They were very curious as to what we were doing and where we were going.

The only bad part of the trip was Monday morning. In order to get back to work, we woke up at 3:45 a.m. to catch the 5 a.m. ferry back to Tongatapu. When we arrived at the boat around 4:30 a.m., we got the last two seats. The ferry was a little late leaving, and it was a pretty rough ride, but we made it.

And get this, during our Sunday hike, we were gone for seven hours. During that time, we did not see another person. It was really "getting away" and was another amazing weekend in Tonga.

A Tongan molakau

Tonga has very few hazards. There are no snakes, except the sea snake, and its fangs are so far down its throat that it is almost impossible for one to bite a human. There are no alligators or other dangerous animals in the forest. In fact, the worst hazard is probably a large centipede called a molakau. Until last week, I had only seen very small ones. Thursday night, a large one made it into my home.

The molakau are tough to kill, so in addition to spraying it with insect spray, I got a knife and chopped it into pieces. I've heard that bug spray will not kill them sometimes, so I didn't take any chances. Even after cutting it up, it kept moving, so it got another dose of spray, which seemed to finally do it in.

Notes

I move to Vava'u on Friday. My stuff was picked up today, but the boat that was supposed to transport it is not sailing this week, so now it will not arrive in Vava'u until next Wednesday.

A DIFFERENT (BUT BETTER) PEACE CORPS EXPERIENCE
Tuesday, March 4, 2008

While I have been in Vava'u for a short time, arriving only last Friday, I can already tell that my Peace Corps experience here is going to be much different that the two and a half months I spent on the main island of Tongatapu. Not only are there fewer volunteers, but there is a strong sense of teamwork and commitment from those who are serving here. My first official function as a volunteer was a meeting of all the volunteers on the island, and all but one were there. It's a diverse group of people with a couple of volunteers who are older than me and many who are still in their twenties. There are 14 of us, and I'm one of just four male volunteers. It struck me as we were talking how much everyone is involved in their communities. Several people talked about new projects they were starting and asked for help to make something happen. It really inspired me to want to get started with my own projects and perhaps work on some of the projects that are already underway. As we went around the room, people talked not only about what they were doing but also HOW they were doing. It was pretty easy to see that it is a very supportive environment.

I couldn't have asked for a better welcome on Friday. In addition to being my first day in Vava'u, it was also the birthday of Justin, one of the volunteers who happens to be a leap-year baby. Friday was just the sixth time he has celebrated his birthday. (This is not the same Justin I lived with during my homestay.) My friend Shannon, who was in my training group, baked a cake for both Justin and me, which was a great treat.

Things are off to a good start at work as well, and I'm actually busy. On my first day, I quickly learned how much Tongan vocabulary I have forgotten. Unlike the head office where I have been working, the people here do most of their talking in Tongan. The people I'll be working with greeted me warmly, and they seemed happy to have me with them. It has been a long time (more than 10 years I think) since there was a volunteer working at the Vava'u branch. Tuesday, I met with the managers of the three commercial banks here in Vava'u and offered my services to them as well. I also paid a visit to the only TV station in Vava'u, which just signed on the air in December. I will be going there again later tonight to teach them non-linear editing. Right now, they air everything the way it is shot by the camera. And I even have my first business project. I'm going to be teaching the bartenders at a local bar how to use a cash register. While that might sound simple, they have only tracked sales on paper and are nervous about making the change (pun intended).

I'm pretty happy with my office at the bank. I have a beautiful view of the harbor with the mountains in the background.

And thankfully, there is air conditioning and a ceiling fan—something I was not expecting. The branch manager told me that most of the year they just open the windows—except for when it is really hot, like it is right now. In fact, it is miserably hot. However, the days should start to get cooler soon as the summer season winds down.

My new house is pretty awesome. The other volunteers tell me it is probably the second nicest house for a Peace Corps volunteer in Vava'u. Stan just got a new house and while I haven't seen it, it sounds pretty nice. Some of the things that excite me about my new house are going to seem pretty basic to most people, but I'm thrilled to have a sofa (actually I have two) and an armchair. In the place where I was staying in Nuku'alofa, I had neither, so anytime I wanted to read or sit, I either had to sit on my bed, which was actually a mattress on the floor, or sit at the kitchen table. If I watched a movie, I usually lay on the floor.

I also now have two bedrooms, each with double beds. The best new addition is a washing machine. The washing machine is not like the kind you would find in the United States, but it is wonderful to have it. I spent a good part of Saturday with James—the volunteer who lives next door to me—doing laundry. The machine is stored in the house, but you take it outside to use it. You use a hose to fill the tub, add soap and clothes, plug it in and it agitates for 15 minutes. Next, you drain the tub into the grass, fill it back up with a hose and agitate again to rinse the soap out of your clothes. Then you drain it, take two or three items at a time and put them in the spinner, which is separate from the washer. Finally, you hang the clothes on the line to dry. It takes a lot longer to do your clothes than washing by hand, but they come out much cleaner. In fact, I was amazed at how dirty the water got just from each load of clothes. James doesn't have a washer, so after I did my laundry, he did his.

I haven't really moved in yet, as my stuff doesn't arrive until tomorrow. I have just enough clothes and toiletries to last me until the boat arrives. I picked up a few things in town on Saturday and immediately noticed not only the higher prices on everything I bought compared to Tongatapu but also the lack of selection. At the market, there were no tomatoes, cucumbers or avocados—all things that I was able to purchase last week in Nuku'alofa. In fact, the only item I bought at the market was bananas. That was a first for me, as I had a banana tree at my last house. Things like milk, pasta and canned goods are all more expensive here.

On Sunday, my landlord, who lives right by me, surprised me with a big plate of Tongan food. It was enough for both lunch and dinner on Sunday and lunch on Monday. I split the remaining root crops with two other volunteers for dinner on Monday night. Portions here are always huge, and I've learned to not even try to eat it all. And if you are eating with Tongans and clean your plate, you'll just be expected to eat more.

Other News

I had a nice final week in Tongatapu and got a chance to say goodbye to many of my friends there. At the bank, my supervisor bought pizza for our department on Tuesday. On Thursday, there was a going-away tea for my counterpart at the bank, who is leaving after 17 years to take another job. While the tea was mainly for him, they also wished me well in Vava'u, and I made a short speech (in English) thanking everyone. Giving speeches is a part of Tongan culture, and if you are the honored guest, it is pretty much expected that you will say something.

Last Wednesday, the bank sponsored a business development workshop in the village of Kolovai. These workshops are a big part of what I will be doing in Vava'u, and this was my first chance to attend one.

There was no English spoken, but fortunately all I had to do was introduce myself, which I did in Tongan. I even got a round of applause afterwards, so hopefully they understood what I said.

Tonga Development Bank workshop

I plan to start language lessons again soon so that I will be able to do more next time.

SAILING THE SOUTH PACIFIC
Sunday, March 9, 2008

I get it! If I didn't "get" it before, I now completely "get" why sailing enthusiasts from all over the world come to the Vava'u Islands here in the Kingdom of Tonga. I spent my Saturday sailing aboard a huge catamaran and got a chance to see more of the magnificent beauty of these islands. I don't even have the appropriate adjectives to describe everything we saw. If you can imagine what a perfect South Pacific island might look like on a perfect day, then you will begin to understand.

We sailed about 25 miles away from the main city of Neiafu and anchored near a small resort called The Blue Lagoon. This island gets its electricity from four windmills we could see in the distance. There is a beautiful reef just off the shore with steep underwater cliffs of coral and many species of multicolored fish. The snorkeling was a lot of fun, and I couldn't help but notice the constant temperature changes in the water. One minute you were in very warm South Pacific water and the next you felt a much cooler river rushing by you. The coral here is largely untouched and unbroken, making for some magnificent formations.

We spent a good part of the day anchored off shore. Finally, the boat captain told us it was time to leave, so we all climbed back on board and started sailing again.

The South Pacific in Vava'u

Our next stop was a place called Mariner's Cave. Mariner's Cave has been at the top of the list of things I have wanted to do since arriving in Tonga more than five months ago. I had previously visited Swallows Cave during our Peace Corps training and was really excited that I was now getting to go to the most famous of caves in the Vava'u area. The only way to get into Mariner's Cave is to swim down and enter an underwater passage, swimming hard before coming up inside the cave. As excited as I was about getting there, I started to get a little intimidated as I swam up to the point where you have to dive down. Once you commit, there is really no going back, and obviously, you can't come up for air until you actually get in the cave since you are swimming through a submerged passageway. The first time I began to dive down, I started swimming just as a wave started pushing me back. I didn't want to swim against the current and quickly aborted before starting the dive down. You only dive down about six or eight feet to swim through the tunnel, but since I wanted all the advantages I could get, I waited and started timing the waves so that I could get a little extra push to get through the passageway. The second time, I went for it. As you swim into the cave, it's pretty dark, and you can't really tell when it is time to come up. I slowly started swimming up, not wanting to bang my head on the ceiling of the passageway. Once I came up, I realized I had swum a lot further into the cave than I needed. But there really is no way to tell. Better to be safe than sorry.

Inside the cave was amazing. The most unexpected aspect was the change in pressure. As the waves came in, my ears popped from the pressure changes, and the cave filled with mist. I swam over to a ledge and just sat there for a few minutes taking it all in. I was very glad I had come, and I would certainly recommend it. I was wearing a mask, but no flippers.

Getting out was a lot easier. You could see the bright blue water illuminated by the sun as you swam out, and it was easy to tell where to surface. I didn't have an underwater camera, so I don't have any photos to share from inside the cave, and from the outside, you couldn't even tell the cave was there.

Saturday's sailing trip and the swim into Mariner's Cave are certainly highlights of my Peace Corps experience so far. My weekend in 'Eua would be another. I think one of the great things about Peace Corps is not just the work we do or the people we get to meet, but the chance to explore new places in a foreign land. I think it is pretty unlikely I would have ever visited Tonga if I had not volunteered for Peace Corps service.

Other News

I've wrapped up my first week at the Vava'u branch of the Tonga Development Bank. It was a really great week, and it is amazing to me how many people I've met and what I've been able to do in such a short time. My biggest project this week was programming a cash register for a local bar. Since I've never done this before, I spent a good deal of time reading the manual and then asking the owner about her business. I learned a lot about retail from that. Next week, I'll be going back and teaching the staff how to use it. I've tried to keep the feature set to a minimum and have turned off a lot of features that I don't think they will need. This includes things like passwords, age verification and even receipt printing. It is now set up to do inventory management and of course, record sales. Hopefully, it will be an improvement over the paper system they are currently using.

Next week, I'll be conducting my first staff training—on understanding cash flow reports—for the bank's employees. I spent part of the week putting together the PowerPoint presentation that I'll be using. I can't claim full credit for all the content—some of it came from a presentation I found sitting on the hard drive of a computer at the main bank office in Nuku'alofa. It was probably put together by a previous volunteer.

I have an amazing view from my office at the bank. Without question, it's the best view I've ever had in any office in my life. Here's a photo that gives you the view from my desk.

The Port of Refuge in Neiafu, Vava'u

My stuff arrived on the boat on Wednesday. I saw the boat pulling in from my office and knew it was time to head to the wharf to pick it up. Everything made it in good shape except for a jar of mustard.

WEEKEND WORK (AND FUN!)
Monday, March 17, 2008

Garbage and litter are big issues in Vava'u. There is no garbage collection. Most people burn their personal garbage and commercial businesses take their garbage to a landfill. It sounds fairly simple, but it gets complicated because there are no public trash cans anywhere on the island, and most Tongans just throw their litter on the ground or out the car window. Apparently, there was an attempt to put some garbage cans in public areas a while back, but the plan failed, not because the cans didn't get used, but because Tongans started bringing their personal garbage and dumping it into the public cans. This overwhelmed the cans, and they were eventually removed. There is recycling of aluminum in Vava'u, but there are not that many recycling bins and they don't get used a lot. The bottom line is that there is a lot of litter here and no easy solution on how to deal with it. Early Saturday morning, I joined nine of my fellow volunteers and a Tongan women's group to pick up litter in downtown Neiafu.

Vava'u volunteers help clean up Neiafu

I filled an entire bag with aluminum cans in less than an hour and that was just in a three-block area. The truck in the photo above was quickly filled with all kinds of rubbish. As I was collecting litter, several of the women called me by name. I couldn't figure out how they all knew my name even though by now I should be used to that. As it turns out, the women had all attended a presentation on personal budgeting that the bank manager and I had given on Friday night.

After our early morning litter collection, the Peace Corps "boys" and the Peace Corps "girls" all went their separate ways. The women were cooking a women's-only dinner at the house of one of the volunteers, and the guys went to the eastern tip of Vava'u to hang out and see the cliffs.

Lava pools in Vava'u

We caught a ride as far as we could and then hiked through the woods to get to the top of the cliffs where there is a nice meadow with a great view out to the ocean below. As we stood on the top, we pointed about 45 degrees to our left and said, "America is that way." We then headed down to the water. The climb is not as treacherous as it might look from the photo, but you certainly would not want to slip. At the bottom there are small pools where you can immerse yourself in the cool waters of the Pacific. You can only do this at low tide, and as the tide started to come back in, we quickly realized we needed to get out of there and start climbing back.

A little work and a little fun. Not a bad way to spend a Saturday in Tonga.

Other News

When President John F. Kennedy created the Peace Corps, it was designed with three goals—goals that the agency still lives by today. People are most familiar with the first goal, which is to provide help where requested. The second goal is to teach people of other cultures about Americans, and the final goal is to provide Americans with information about other cultures. Basically, this last goal says to bring the world home to Americans. By writing about my experiences, I hope that I'm helping to fulfill the third goal, not just for US citizens, but for people everywhere who happen to stumble across these pages.

One person who has become a regular reader is a Canadian by the name of Larry MacDonald. Larry is actually a friend of a friend even though we've never met. Larry and I both share an interest in Tonga, and we've exchanged e-mails. We also share an interest in writing about Tonga. While I write about what it is like to serve in the Peace Corps in Tonga, Larry has written about what it is like to come here as a tourist. Larry gave me permission to share a story he wrote that I hope provides you with a different perspective on Tonga. Sharing his story seems like a great way to further the third goal of Peace Corps.

Timeless Tonga
Charter Sailing in a Polynesian Paradise

By Larry MacDonald

When one thinks of Tonga in the South Pacific, the mind conjures up images of a Polynesian paradise—lush tropical islands with white sand beaches sprinkled like emeralds on a turquoise sea. Supplement that image with quiet anchorages, warm breezes and crystal-clear waters, and it's understandable why Tonga is considered one of the world's premiere sailing destinations.

Tonga's remoteness, about 1,300 nautical miles northeast of New Zealand, may be partly responsible for the islands retaining their unspoiled beauty and timeless character. However, for Canadian charter sailors, it's a long way off; 17 hours flying time from Vancouver on three different airlines . . . we know, we've been there; and would return in a heartbeat. It's amazing how quickly travel fatigue is dissipated by the excitement and anticipation of visiting a new culture.

Sandy and I, with our friends Barry and Joan, scheduled a bareboat sailing charter with The Moorings for two weeks in March. We booked our flights from Vancouver, via Los Angeles, to the main island of Tongatapu. However, we wisely decided to use Pacific Travel Marketing (a Tongan travel agency) to book our inter-island flight to Vava'u, the primary sailing area. When our flight from LA was delayed, our agent Ruby rescheduled the inter-island flight, booked us into a comfortable B&B on Tongatapu, met us at the airport and toured us around the island. This fortuitous adventure gave us an opportunity to experience the bustling capital city of Nuku'alofa, a world away from life back home. Our one-hour flight on Airlines Tonga to the Vava'u island group would take us even further back in time.

After a restful night's sleep at the Paradise International Hotel and their sumptuous breakfast, we proceed to The Moorings base. Sirocco, our 41' Beneteau gleaming in the sunshine, is awaiting our arrival. We stow our gear and receive a thorough boat and chart orientation; then take a short cab ride into downtown Neiafu to purchase provisions. The experience is enlightening, and most likely amusing to the locals. Following a visit to the ATM, we fill the trunk with items from several small grocery stores, a bakery, meat supplier, wine store and an outdoor market. The sun is hot; the pace slow; considerably slower than our frenetic efforts to finish the shopping so we can go sailing. We enjoy practicing the language and learning the currency, which initially involves holding out a handful of cash and allowing vendors to pick the correct amount!

Vava'u is a cluster of 50 islands scattered across 15 miles of ocean, protected from swells by outlying reefs. The Moorings' navigational chart of this area identifies 42 designated anchorages, half of which are approved for overnight in prevailing southeast winds. The area is small enough that one can sail from one end to the other in just a few hours. Yet, in two weeks it is impossible to see it all. However, we do manage to visit a few villages and more than a few deserted islands for beachcombing, snorkeling and replenishing our souls.

The Friendly Islands

Waves lap softly against our hull; a rooster crows; church bells ring. I peek through one eye at my watch. It's 0500. What? Who goes to church at five o'clock on a Sunday morning? In the village of Matamaka, everyone does—all 350 islanders, young and old, attend church at 5 a.m.; again at 10 a.m.; and then again at 4 p.m. Religion, we're about to discover, is a very important part of Tongan culture.

Late yesterday, we anchored just off a crescent beach bordering the village. This morning, after tying our dinghy to a coconut tree, we amble ashore to explore. Almost immediately, we receive a warm welcome from Fa'aki and her husband Ben, who live in a small house with their five young children. All are dressed in their Sunday's finest, clean and colorful. We ask if we can visit their village. In very good English, they graciously offer to show us around. Six churches, a school, playground, Kava House and an array of small houses line the dirt path that meanders through the village. Only the churches and the Kava House have electricity; which means there are no refrigerators, stoves, washers or any other electrical conveniences that we Canadians take for granted. Domestic pigs, dogs and chickens wander about. Columns of smoke rise from outdoor cooking pits. Everyone we meet smiles shyly and says hello ("Malo e lelei"). Captain Cook, in 1777 called Tonga "The Friendly Isles," and we can certainly see why. We feel like we have been transported back a couple of centuries, when people lived off the land and sea, bonding together to ensure survival.

Since it is nearly 10 o'clock, Fa'aki invites us to join her family at their church service. We accompany them up a hillside to a small building made of coconut tree 2x4's with open doors and windows. While we sit on woven floor mats with a dozen faithful villagers, the young minister plays guitar and everyone sings along. Their voices are incredibly clear and inspirational. After a passionate sermon in Tongan by the minister's wife, punctuated by "Hallelujahs," the minister thanks us for joining them and wishes us a safe journey. The young girls pick wild flowers and present them to Joan and Sandy. A young boy offers his hand to help Sandy down a slippery bank, a spontaneous gesture so characteristic of Tongan kindness.

As we pass the Kava House, Barry asks: "What goes on in there?" Ben invites us into the small building occupied by a half-dozen men sitting in a circle on the matted floor. Kava is a brown, watery drink made from the dried roots of a pepper plant. It is widely used as a ceremonial drink throughout most of Polynesia. The Kava House serves as a meeting place, mostly for men it seems. After introductions, we are offered half coconut shells as cups and invited to try it. We describe our first taste as bitter with a slight tingling of the lips and tongue. The men smile approvingly with stifled laughter. Apparently, after a few drinks, the effect is a feeling of calmness, which to Tongans represents renewal. After our drink, some conversation, laughter and an awareness of the importance of this tradition in the daily lives of Tongans, we bid farewell and continue back to the boat.

On the way, Ben and Fa'aki invite us for lunch and we agree, but only if they join us on board. They arrive in their small fishing boat with fresh mussels cooked in coconut milk, boiled tapioca root and a mango-coconut cordial. We are extremely honoured by their generosity, sharing their meager food supplies with relative strangers. In return, we offer them a roll of aluminum foil, dry pasta, canned goods, a Canuk's hat and some lollipops and gifts for their children. After they leave, Joan and Sandy conspire to "adopt" this lovely family and immediately start planning a care package to be sent to them at Christmas.

On the most western island of Hunga in front of Ika Lahi Lodge, we tie to a mooring buoy for $10 Tongan, about $6 Canadian (a small price to pay for sound sleep!). In anticipation of a visit to the village school the next morning, we gather together some school supplies and various children's toys. Our visit is delightful. David, the principal, holds an impromptu recess and invites us inside. Although the children are initially reserved, Sandy and Joan soon have them gathered around, intent to learn some Canadian English, eh? And to sing along, "If you're happy and you know it, clap your hands. . . ." Later, in the village, we meet an elderly woman who proudly shows us her beautiful flowers and then offers us a few mangos. She reluctantly accepts our handful of change.

Simply Breathtaking

The Moorings arrange a Tongan feast on a centrally located beach for their charterers, a score of sailors from various countries. Guitars and drums accompany graceful young dancers, followed by an authentic meal of local foods. Conversation mostly involves things to see and do in the islands. Everyone has his or her favourite snorkeling reef or secluded sandy beach.

One of our favourites is Maninita, a small island furthest south, designated as a bird sanctuary. Under sunny skies and brisk easterlies, we beam reach for a couple of hours with two other charter boats. Along the way, a school of spinner dolphins play in our bow wave. A serpentine turquoise path through a matrix of coral leads to a sheltered lagoon. Boobies, petrels, terns and various other sea birds circle the forest canopy as we respectfully explore this special place blessed by Nature. The shallow reefs are teaming with colourful fish; the beaches look and feel like granular sugar. Designated as a "day anchorage," we reluctantly weigh anchor and retrace our route to yet another picturesque island.

Another breathtaking experience, literally, is Mariner's Cave. The entrance to this submerged cave is three metres down (at high tide) and four metres horizontally beneath an overhanging rock. The assent is another three meters before surfacing inside a cavernous limestone grotto. Some local knowledge and commitment are required for this dive. Jim and Simon, fellow charterers who had dove it last year, supply the local knowledge. Since there are no signs indicating the entrance, they dive first and don't return, which means either that I am in the right spot or they're never coming back! I take a deep breath and commit . . . popping up inside like a walrus gasping for air! Standing on a ledge, our ears plug each time the misty air is compressed by the incoming one-metre swell. Going out is less intimidating as we can see sunshine through the opening. Incidentally, one can practice for this feat by diving underneath the boat keel from one side to the other, or better yet bow to stern. Nearby Swallows Cave is another popular natural feature. This large cavern at the waterline can be entered and explored by dinghy, which suits my non-committal crew just fine!

Each morning on VHF Ch 06, sailors are provided with tide and weather information, including a forecast. Most days we get a mixture of sun and cloud with 10 to 20-knot breezes providing comfortable sailing. On our last day 30-knot "breezes" prompt a reefed jib and main sail. Charging back to The Moorings base, we're totally pumped and at the same time saddened by our adventures coming to an end. After lifting off the runway and gaining altitude, we peer out the window at our now familiar playground with the hope that this pristine paradise will always remain timeless and welcoming to future sailors.

Sidebar: Trouble In Paradise?

The Tongan government is one of the few absolute monarchies in the world. For the past 40 years, a beloved and benevolent king ruled the island country. His death in 2006 and the succession of his son to the throne set off previously unheard of civil disobedience in the capital city of Nuku'alofa. Angry rioters, expressing dissatisfaction with the lack of democratic reforms, damaged a significant number of buildings. During our visit four months later, the town was rebuilding and islanders were more inclined to "give the new king a chance."

On Taunga Island in the Vava'u group, a groundbreaking ceremony took place just prior to our visit. A group of foreign investors are building a large five-star hotel on the same island that is also home to a tidy little village; the same village in which Joel proudly showed us around, in which Alice gave us a bag of mangos and in which Betty sold us her handmade woven baskets and bracelets from a panga (small boat).

One can only hope that future directions will not compromise traditions or values of these beautiful people.

Update

During Larry's visit a year ago, he met Sarah Kate, one of the Peace Corps volunteers with whom I now serve. Sarah Kate remembers meeting Larry and especially meeting his wife. She says Sandy was a great teacher and taught the kids to point out where Canada was located on a world map. She says it's amazing that now, a year later, those kids still remember where Canada is located, but they can't find their own country of Tonga on the same map.

Larry also mentions the groundbreaking for a new five-star resort. As of early March, that project was on hold due to disputes over land rights with some of the people on Taunga. Warwick Hotels, which has resorts and hotels around the world, is the company who wants to open what would become the first real resort in Tonga if the disputes can be settled.

TONGA HYGIENE
Saturday, March 22, 2008

Food plays a big part in Tongan culture. Almost every event—from church to meetings to schools—either involves or revolves around food. The food is always plentiful, and no one will ever go hungry here. However, there is another side to all this food that may make you cringe. It's the way the food is prepared. There is no hot water here, so everything is prepared and cleaned in cold water. You will often find a bathroom with either no running water or running water and no soap. Yes, you go to the bathroom, you can't wash your hands and then you sit down and eat with your hands. For most Americans, that would be completely unacceptable, and it is why you'll see many of the Peace Corps folks with bottles of hand sanitizer or something like the "Wash and Dries" my mom stuck into my suitcase before I left the United States.

However, that's just the beginning. Not every house has a refrigerator and even those that do, don't use them like we would in the USA. Here are a couple of examples: I previously told the story of how my host mother during training sent her daughter out to get me jam when I first got here. Here's Part II of that story: The jam sat on the counter for my entire homestay, and yes, I still ate it. If you don't eat something for lunch, especially on Sunday, expect to find it still sitting on the table for dinner. If someone leaves food on her or his plate, it could find its way back to the serving dish for the next meal. Eggs are left on the counter until cooked, and food waste is thrown into the yard for the dogs, pigs and chickens to eat. One of the volunteers who has been here for a while helped clean out pig intestines for a funeral feast. When everyone was done, they all sat down and ate. There was no hand washing!

During my stay at the head office of the bank where I work, they provided bottled water for everyone to drink. However, there was just one communal cup on top of the water bottle. Everyone drank from the same cup.

As you can imagine, this lack of hygiene has been a topic of discussion. Based on everything we have learned in the United States, the Tongans should be suffering from food poisoning all the time or getting diseases from fecal matter. While that probably happens occasionally, it's not prevalent. And there is really no way to know for sure because they don't keep statistics on those types of things, and Tongans don't go to doctors or hospitals the way we do in America. Perhaps the Tongans have built up immunity to many of the germs, and/or Americans have lost their immunity from using soap and anti-bacterial products. A more likely theory is that we are simply trying to put Western standards to a country that isn't "Westernized."

Most Tongan homes are open but also very clean. I have never smelled a Tongan with body odor, and many Tongans shower multiple times a day. Clothes are washed often and ironed before being worn. Tongans generally look nice when in public and especially so in more formal settings like school, business and church.

Because the houses are open, there are bugs and ants inside, but families go to great lengths to make sure the bugs stay away from the food, and any food left on the table is always covered. Dogs, chickens and pigs are never allowed inside a home, and when they try, they are immediately shooed away. Even flies are shooed away during meals. (However, when roaches and lizards are in other parts of the house, they are pretty much ignored.) Even here at my house in Vava'u, it is a struggle to control the ants. I cleaned out used tin cans, filled them with water and put the legs of my kitchen table into them. It's not the best-looking solution in the world, but it keeps the ants from crawling up the legs of table.

I don't think all Tongans understand that some food will spoil if left out. One day during training, I picked up a plate of chicken with something on it wrapped in tin foil. The chicken was nice and hot, but when I opened the foil, I found very warm raw fish inside. Needless to say, I didn't eat it. The idea that you should keep something like raw fish cold didn't seem to matter to the people who prepared the lunch. I told the story to the head of our training program and suggested that we have buffet-style lunches instead of pre-prepared plates. The next day, the staff brought us a nice buffet, and we all served ourselves family style. It was great. However, that was the only day we got the buffet, for the rest of training, we were back to the plates already prepared.

Other News

Vava'u ran out of gas and diesel fuel this week. That's right, no fuel except for what was already in people's cars. The gas was the first to run out and then the diesel. At the bank, we have one diesel car and one gas car. We used the diesel car once the gas was gone. The fuel all comes in on a boat, and right now there is only one boat that comes once a week. The second boat apparently lost its license and won't be back in service until next month. Tongans took it in stride. Like everything else here, if you don't have something, you just do without.

We got a new Peace Corps office in Vava'u this week. We previously had shared an office with the Vava'u Youth Congress, but we now have our own building, which is closer to town. My friend Justin and I spent Thursday afternoon setting up the computers in the new office and moving in. The big moment was the hanging of the sign outside our new building.

Steve Hunsicker puts on a sign on the Peace Corps Vava'u office

I joked that I was going to write that my friend Justin and I were selected from all the volunteers for the great honor of hanging the sign, but the truth is, we were the only two volunteers there and we did it on our own.

Notes

I hosted a Saturday Easter brunch at my house. We opted to have it on Saturday instead of Sunday since we thought Tongans might think it was a party. We have a four-day weekend for Easter, so I don't go back to work until Tuesday.

DEBT COLLECTION
Friday, March 28, 2008

I think I would hate being a debt collector in the USA—knocking on doors, trying to get deadbeats to pay you the money they had borrowed. I'm sure you would get doors slammed in your face, in addition to being physically threatened and probably cursed a lot. It would get even worse if you were threatening to foreclose on people's homes, forcing them out into the streets. Imagine my apprehension when the manager of the bank asked me to accompany him to visit ARD clients. ARD stands for Asset Recovery Division, and if your loan is in ARD, it means the bank is going after the assets you put up to borrow money. This is the final step and usually only happens after months and sometimes a year of nonpayment.

We headed out in the morning, and our first stop turned out to be a person who lives just a block away from me. I was thinking that this was not a good thing. I don't want someone who lives that close to me being pissed off. I stayed in the car and it turned out there was no one home.

We made a couple of other stops and the same thing: no one at home. It was around 10 a.m., which is actually late in the day for Tongans, who often wake up at 4:30 or 5:00 a.m. We then headed to the very edge of Vava'u. It's as far from the main city of Neiafu as you can get in a car. This time, there was someone home. It turned out to be the son of the people who owed money. He volunteered that his parents were now living in another village, and he told us the name of the village. He was polite but was not the guy who owed the money. I wondered if he really told us the truth.

We made another stop, in another village. The neighbor told us the man we were seeking was doing some work across the street from the church. We turned around and went to the church. There he was. He came over to the car, greeted us like old friends and carried on a conversation with the branch manager in Tongan. The manager handed him a letter to sign, which was from the bank's attorney saying his assets were about to be seized. He signed it without reading it, and as we were leaving said, "*Malo*," which means "thank you." No confrontation, no shouting and no threats. Of course he knew he owed the money, but then again so do people who are behind on their bills in the USA. I wondered if this really is one of the "Friendly Islands," even when the bill collectors are after you.

We made a couple of other stops, not finding anyone home. Finally, we headed to the village where the son from earlier had told us his parents were now living. We pulled up to a random house where we saw people standing outside and asked if they knew the couple. Of course they did. They gave us directions to the couple's house. We got there, and it appeared that someone was home, as all the doors and windows were wide open. We called out their names because in Tonga, you don't knock, you just stand outside and call out a name. No answer. I thought, yes, here was someone who was clearly avoiding us. A neighbor came out of her house and said the man was not home but the woman was down the street. Neighbors always know everything. She offered to go get the woman for us. Much to my surprise, a few minutes later the woman came walking up to the car. She was very pleasant and again signed the letter without reading it. She said her husband would be back that evening and that they would call the bank's lawyer the next day. As we were leaving, she said, "Malo."

This same scenario was repeated several more times as we found a few more clients. None were irate and all were pleasant. Perhaps being a debt collector, at least in Tonga, isn't that bad after all.

Other News

If you have Google Earth or some other similar program, you can check out my house and the neighborhood where I live. Here are the coordinates: west 173 degrees, 59.193 minutes; south 18 degrees, 39.007 minutes.

I have not actually done this myself (due to a very slow Internet connection), and my home is only about two years old, so it is possible it is not there yet. The building and big field across from my house are the soldiers' barracks.

Steve Hunsicker

SIX MONTHS IN TONGA
Thursday, April 3, 2008

Today, April 4th, marks six months since we first arrived in Tonga. In many ways, it seems like such a long time ago, but then I also am amazed that the time has gone by so quickly. A little later this month, I will have completed one quarter of my twenty-six-and-a-half month commitment to the Peace Corps. The 33 members of my group, Group 73, arrived in Los Angeles complete strangers. Now, we know each other better than many of us could have ever predicted. There are 29 of us left as we hit the six-month mark. At the end of this month, we will all get together for the first time since we completed our training and were sworn in as Peace Corps volunteers last December. It will be great to see everyone, and we'll certainly miss the four who are no longer here. (Three of the four were medically separated, and the fourth was married to someone who was medically separated.)

After six months, you certainly start to accept some things that may have been difficult to accept when you first arrived. This weekend, a big storm hit Vava'u beginning on Friday, and it rained really hard all day Saturday and into the night. We were without power for about 18 hours before it was restored on Sunday. On Saturday, Sunday and Monday mornings, I woke up to no water. That meant a trip outside to the *sima vai*, which literally translates to "cement water." It's the tank where the rainwater accumulates, and it is what we drink. For the days with no water, it was also what I used to flush the toilet, clean dishes and take sponge baths.

I was actually surprised that the power was restored on a Sunday. Everything here closes on Sunday, and I assumed that no one would work to correct the problem until Monday. However, crews were out on Sunday and we got our power back. I live about two blocks from the only hospital in Vava'u, and I wondered if that might be the reason I got power back on Sunday.

After six months, my diet has changed considerably. When I lived with my host families during training, I almost always had traditional Tongan food. Since becoming a volunteer, I can better control my diet, but I'm still at the mercy of what is available. I haven't seen tomatoes in weeks, and lettuce is very rare, but you can still get it at the market occasionally. I've been buying green peppers, avocadoes and of course, bananas, which are always plentiful. When I eat meat, it is almost always chicken that is imported from New Zealand. And it is always the dark meat—I haven't eaten or seen a chicken breast since I arrived.

On Sundays, my landlord brings me a plate of Tongan food that he has cooked in his outdoor oven, called an umu. It usually consists of lu pulu, which is very fatty canned beef, soaked in coconut milk and wrapped in pele leaves. Pele is a lot like spinach. Also on the plate are some sort of root crops, usually ufi, which is like a potato, but much drier. Occasionally, he brings kumala, which is my favorite Tongan root crop. Kumala is a green sweet potato and is really good.

I still struggle with the Tongan language, but there are times when I start to feel like I am getting it. Last Friday night, my friend and next-door neighbor James and I were walking through town and a Tongan started walking with us. He told us he was going to drink kava, but had stopped by the store to get some food so he wouldn't get sick. We told him we were going to Mermaids, a local restaurant and bar. He commented on how nice the weather was, because it was breezy, and I replied that it was better than the very hot weather last week. The conversation was nothing special, but it was entirely in Tongan—no English spoken and I understood all of it, and he seemed to as well. We also used phrases that James and I both knew, like "Where are you going?" and "The breeze is nice."

At work, the Tongan is more of a challenge because it involves complex thoughts and sentences. I'm taking language classes three days a week, but I doubt I will ever get to the point where I can fluently carry on a conversation.

Being a volunteer is certainly not all work, and I've had some great times during my first six months. The weekend I spent in 'Eua, the sailing trip and dive into Mariner's Cave and celebrating Christmas with my first homestay family are certainly highlights. However, I think the best thing about my first six months has been getting to know the other volunteers, both those who are in my group and those who were in the earlier group. There are some really dedicated and amazing people here. I'm proud to be associated with them.

Other News

I will be doing my first workshop here in Vava'u next Wednesday. I've spent most of the past week getting ready for it. We are inviting 30 people to attend and will be teaching business concepts.

A SCARY PLACE
Wednesday, April 9, 2008

My friend Justin and I went to the hospital on Friday. No, we weren't sick; we went to get our teeth cleaned. In Tonga, the dental office is at the hospital as is the morgue.

It was my first trip to a Tongan hospital and one I won't soon forget. The Price Ngu hospital is just a couple of blocks from my house, but stepping inside it was like stepping back in time. The two-toned walls greeted us as we entered the open-air lobby. The walls were emerald green at the bottom and what once was white above. Behind the peeling green paint, you could see the blue that was probably the color the last time the halls were painted. And bigger cracks in the wall showed that before it was blue, this hospital had mauve-colored walls.

As we walked down the turquoise floor, we could look back and see our footprints, along with the footprints of those who had been there before us, in the dust that covered the floor. Against the wall sat dirty, white, plastic lawn chairs, more gray than white with specs of missing plastic.

A nurse wearing a long pink dress with a white nurse's hat on her head pointed us down the hall toward the dental room. We passed empty exam rooms that looked more like something from the movie *One Flew over the Cuckoo's Nest* than what you would expect in a modern hospital. We walked past a rusty table with wheels that I assumed was used as a stretcher but should probably have been in a medical museum instead. There was a giant water hose reel hanging on the wall next to the electrical box—the cover slightly ajar. That had to have been a safety hazard.

But perhaps not. Looking above, there were wires hanging where there once were lights. Finally, we entered the dental room where a ceiling fan circled overhead, keeping a slight breeze in the room and drawing in a bit of air from the open windows. The dental equipment was modern, as in 1980s modern. The rolling tables were covered with clean linen—probably not just for sanitary reasons, but also to disguise the rust that showed on the steel.

We both knew the dentist we were going to see. She is a volunteer with Japan's version of the Peace Corps. We were very happy to have a Japanese dentist to clean our teeth. There was a sterilizer in the room for the dental tools, and the dentist wore a mask and gloves as she cleaned. As she leaned me back in the chair, she told me that the suction wasn't working so I would have to sit up and spit when needed. I lay back and looked at the ceiling. There were black specs on it. I wondered if it was mold or just some dark spots.

The cleaning was a bit different than in the USA. She had me rinse with a stain that showed the plaque and tartar in my month. I remember doing this many years ago when I was very young, but not since. She proclaimed that I had a clean month even though it had been six months since my last cleaning. Out came the polishers and before long I was on my way, back down the scary hall to the safety of the outdoors.

Other News

Saturday, I joined five other people on a camping trip on the northern side of Vava'u. We went to a place called Utula'aina Point, which is near the village of Holonga. Holonga is one of the three villages that hosted my group during our training last year. It was only the second time I had been to the village and the first time I had been out to the point. We didn't decide to go until late in the afternoon and got there just as it was starting to get dark.

Amazingly, our taxi was able to drive us right to the spot where we camped. Because of the easy access, I assumed we would see lots of signs that people had been there before, but we did not. We decided to make our fire up on the point and to camp just below. There is not enough room for one tent, much less three tents, up on the point, and it would be a scary place to camp because it is a cliff straight down to the water.

We started gathering wood as darkness began to set in and then put up the tents. There was no moon and the stars were amazing. We cooked dinner and then carefully made our way down to the tents to call it a night. The next morning, we were all up at sunrise.

Sunrise at Utula'aina Point

While we had seen a little of the view at night, it was spectacular to watch the sun come up and illuminate the cliffs and the beach below. After a breakfast of oatmeal and marshmallows, we broke camp making sure to leave no traces, other than the ashes from our fire, of our visit. We then hiked down to the beach for a morning swim before heading back to our homes.

SURVIVAL OF THE WEAKEST
Thursday, April 17, 2008

Living on an island is different. Being surrounded by water with no way to get things except for the once-weekly boats causes all kinds of social and economic issues. But this is not a story about island fever or even the more obvious advantages or disadvantages of living on an island. It's actually about livestock. What? That's right, livestock. I recently had the chance to chat with the man who heads up the local office of the Tonga Ministry of Agriculture, Food and Fisheries or MAFF for short. We got into a fascinating discussion about pigs and chickens.

In a nutshell, almost all livestock here in Vava'u and throughout Tonga are the results of inbreeding and something I'm calling "survival of the weakest." Because we are on an island, there are not a lot of choices for livestock breeding. A pig has baby pigs and as those pigs get older, they breed with their brother and sister pigs or their cousin pigs. The bottom line is that most pigs here are from the same gene pool and as we know, all that inbreeding makes for weaker offspring.

But that is just half of the story. As the man from MAFF pointed out, when a chicken or pig actually outperforms its own gene pool, it gets slaughtered. Tongans will take the biggest piglet or the fattest chicken and butcher it to eat, leaving the weaker and smaller animals to breed the next generation. Multiply this by generations and generations of animals, and you will start to understand why Tongan chickens and pigs are often a lot smaller than their species in other places.

It's both an education problem and a breeding problem. MAFF is trying, for the most part unsuccessfully, to convince Tongans to let the big healthy animals live so they can breed, and to slaughter the smaller weak animals. However, MAFF is also trying to introduce some new animals to the gene pool. Right now, they have just imported 20 sheep from New Zealand. Ten are here in Vava'u and 10 are on Tongatapu. Once the females are pregnant, MAFF is going to swap the males from each island. That way, they end up with sheep pregnant from different fathers. If successful, they will keep bringing in new sheep to further expand the gene pool.

Right now, there are not a lot of sheep raised here. The hope is that if these sheep can grow and develop, sheep production will increase. And there is certainly a market for it. The single biggest Tongan delicacy is something called *sipi*. Sipi is nothing more than mutton chops from sheep. It's very fatty and very bony and terrible for you, but each Sunday, you'll find the majority of Tongans eating it. The sipi they eat is all imported, primarily from New Zealand. If the sheep project is successful, Tongans might one day be able to make their own sipi.

And even though there are chickens seemingly everywhere here, almost all of the chicken that is eaten is brought in from New Zealand. The Tongan chicken is very small and the meat is tough to eat. (And I'm sure the New Zealand chicken is probably pumped up with all kinds of hormones as well.) Most of the chickens here either are used for eggs or simply to eat garbage. At a recent workshop sponsored by the bank where I work, a group of women showed up who wanted to start a chicken farm here. They came looking for information on what they needed to start a business and to get financing.

After the workshop, we provided lunch to all of the 27 participants who attended. No sipi on the menu, but we served a huge plate of fresh local fish and chicken imported from New Zealand. Who knows, if the women are successful in future years, it might be locally grown Tongan chicken on the menu instead.

Puppies

The house where I live is on a piece of land with two other houses. One house is occupied by James, a fellow Peace Corps volunteer. The other house is our landlord's, Kepu. Kepu is a former rugby star who rents out both houses. He is also raising his grandson, Peta, or Peter in English. Peter is in second grade and goes to the Vava'u Side School where James is a teacher. At that school, all lessons are conducted in English. Kepu's dog, Ripple, just had four puppies, three of which survived. They were born under my house. James and I each plan to take one of the puppies as soon as they are old enough, and we'll leave the one female for Kepu. I've already picked out the runt, and I am probably going to call him *Matataha*, which actually means "one eye" in Tongan. He has two eyes, but has a spot over one of his eyes making him look like a one-eyed pirate.

Taxes

As a Peace Corps volunteer serving overseas, I have until June 15th to pay my taxes. I thought that was great until just a few days ago, when I found out that even though I don't have to file until June 15th, the IRS assesses interest on any amount I owe beginning April 15th. Not such a great deal after all. I quickly filed my taxes online and got them in on time. I had hoped that this year I would be able to avoid the dreaded Alternative Minimum Tax or AMT. No such luck. Even in Tonga there is no escaping it. By the way, my total Peace Corps income for the three months I was here in 2007 was US$450. That's right; I lived for three months on $450.

THE VIEW FROM BENEATH THE PACIFIC
Tuesday, April 22, 2008

One of my favorite movies as a kid was *20,000 Leagues Under the Sea*. As an adult, *The Abyss*, especially the director's cut, became one of my favorites. Both are about living underwater. While I'm not sure I would ever want to live underwater, I thoroughly enjoy snorkeling and have for many years. One of my other passions is photography. Until now, I haven't been able to combine the two. But after our last sailing trip, I decided to buy an underwater housing for my camera. (Stan has one for his camera, and I enjoyed playing with it last time.) Getting the underwater housing for my camera to Vava'u was not easy or quick. I ordered it online and had it shipped to my parents. They reshipped it to me, and last week, it arrived. That seemed as good a reason as any to go sailing this past weekend.

I joined nine of my fellow volunteers onboard the Orion, a catamaran. We sailed off into the Pacific, past islands in a section of the Vava'u Island Group where I had not been before. Once we anchored, I spent a good amount of time just playing with the camera. Most of the first pictures I took were overexposed. I also had to deal with some condensation build-up inside the housing. I didn't get any pictures that I really liked at the first stop.

From there, we sailed another 45 minutes or so to an area with lots of coral and fish. It was a much better place to snorkel than our first stop. The fish here were really spectacular.

It is really different taking photos underwater. It is much more difficult to compose the shots and for the video, it's hard to hold the camera steady in the ocean currents. I'm sure I will improve with time. Unfortunately, it may be tougher for us to go sailing for the next several months. During the off-season, we can negotiate really good deals because the boats are sitting there not being used. But as more tourists start arriving, the boats are more in demand and the prices increase beyond what we can afford as Peace Corps volunteers. Already, you can tell there are a lot more people here when you walk through town, and most of the businesses that have been closed during the off-season are either open now, or will be open by the end of the month.

Vava'u Runs Out of Milk

Saturday, Vava'u ran out of milk. The only milk that is ever sold here is the boxed kind that can be stored without refrigeration. Occasionally, I've been able to buy boxed skim milk, but this is the first time that there has been no milk of any kind anywhere since I've been here. I went to four stores Saturday in search of milk and all were sold out. Because there are no boats until next Wednesday, that means no milk for five days. It's part of living on a remote island. A few weeks ago, the island ran out of gas for several days.

While I'm very happy living in Vava'u, I do miss the selection and the prices we had when I lived in Nuku'alofa. Every single item I buy here, except for fresh eggs, is more expensive than the same items in Nuku'alofa. And we do not have anywhere near the selection in the stores or the market that you can get in the capital city. I'm going back to Nuku'alofa for a Peace Corps meeting at the end of the month, and I'm looking forward to stocking up on the stuff we can't get here and saving money on the other stuff. It's funny how your perspective changes. When I was in Nuku'alofa, I missed the selection we had in the United States.

Scott Is Getting Married

We said goodbye to Scott this week. Scott is a former Peace Corps volunteer who completed his two years of service earlier this year. He was the last of his group to leave because he's engaged to a Tongan woman. He had to fight through the bureaucracy to get her a visa, so they could return to the United States and get married. Scott and his fiancé spent $1000 to fly round-trip to Fiji, so they could apply for a visa. It was granted. They came home and left Vava'u on Saturday.

Volunteers gather at Steve Hunsicker's house

This is a group picture from inside my house on Thursday night. Scott is the guy sitting behind my right shoulder. This was the second tour of duty in the Peace Corps that Scott has completed. He previously served as a volunteer in Mongolia.

GETTING ROBBED IN TONGA
Tuesday, May 6, 2008

I had my laptop, camera, passport and other valuables stolen on Thursday while staying at the Friendly Islander Hotel in Nuku'alofa. I didn't know it at the time I checked in, but I quickly learned that this is not a safe place to stay. In fact, Peace Corps removed all 29 of us from the hotel because of safety concerns and moved us to another hotel. Unfortunately for me, I was one of the victims.

We checked into the Friendly Islander Hotel on Thursday for what Peace Corps calls HILT or High Intensive Language Training. The hotel is located in an industrial area across the road from the ocean. It's a collection of small fales and at first appearance looks like a neat place. However, it's a bit far from town, which is why Peace Corps chose that location, so we could concentrate on our language and not get distracted.

I checked into the hotel early and dropped my backpack in the room. I came back later with the rest of the volunteers in my group and noticed that all of our luggage was sitting on the curb, not inside the lobby. I grabbed my bag and went back to the fale where I would be staying. Because they all looked alike, I wasn't sure which one was mine, so I went to what I thought was my fale, inserted the key and the door opened. It was NOT my fale. It belonged to a group of single women volunteers. I then made my way back out, found my fale, inserted the key and the door opened. On the bed, where I had left it, was my backpack containing my laptop, camera and lots of other things. I plugged my cell phone in and hung out for a while with the three other guys with whom I was staying: James, Stan and Bobby.

We decided to go to dinner, so we all showered and changed, leaving our belongings locked in the room. I double-checked the door personally to make sure it was locked. After dinner, Stan and I decided to pick up a couple of beers while James went back to the hotel. When we got back, I found James coming towards us saying, "I think we have been robbed. I need you to come check your stuff." At first, I thought he was joking, but clearly he was not. I walked in and my clothes were everywhere. Both my backpack and James' backpack were gone, along with my cell phone. We left the room, and I went to talk to the manager while another volunteer called Peace Corps security.

My conversation with the owner/manager went something like this.

Me: "Hi, someone broke into our room and stole our stuff."
Manager: "Was your door locked?"
Me: "Yes, I personally locked it before I went to dinner. I think someone used a key to get in."
Manager: "None of my employees did this."

Of course, as soon as she said none of her employees did this, it immediately made me suspicious. She then told me, "We've never had a problem with Peace Corps before." I went outside and waited for Peace Corps security.

As soon as the security agent arrived, he called the police. When the police arrived, the officer told me he had been to the same fale where I was staying three other times for break-ins. Perhaps none happened when Peace Corps was staying there, but clearly they have had problems. Later, when I told the owner what the cop said, she said, "Oh that was a long time ago."

Most of the volunteers were awake and hanging around. We started talking about the keys, and we soon discovered that one key would open almost every fale at the hotel. This freaked out a few of the female volunteers who feared for their safety.

At the suggestion of Peace Corps, James, Stan, Bobby and I were moved to another fale identical to the one where we were robbed except it was closer to the main building.

After we had moved and the police had left, Stan and I opened our beers and the four of us sat down in the room to decompress. The door to our fale was open and to our surprise, in came the owner. She didn't say anything, didn't knock, just came in and walked into the bedroom where James and I were staying. We couldn't see what she was doing, but then she walked out with a handful of clean towels, stopping to collect the clean towels from Bobby and Stan. I asked her why she was taking the towels, and she said we could use the old ones from the other fale. She then left.

I hadn't gotten upset about anything that had happened yet. But this really pissed me off. I mean, we just had all of our stuff stolen, and she was worried about clean towels.

We drank our beers and went to bed. The next morning, James and I got up and headed to breakfast. As we walked in, one of the other volunteers told me that he was robbed at knifepoint last night while he was sleeping in his bed. The thief took his bag along with some clothes from a couple of other volunteers. He said he didn't wake us because he figured there was nothing we could do. The Peace Corps staff, including our acting country director (the country director was out of town), were there, and they told us they had made arrangements to get us out of the place. They also said that barring some major security updates, they wouldn't be putting volunteers at the Friendly Islander Hotel in the future.

The Peace Corps took James and me away to start dealing with the logistics of the incident, and they cancelled classes that morning for everyone. While getting all of my stuff stolen sucks, the amount of support I got from my fellow volunteers and from the Peace Corps staff was amazing.

By Monday, I had filed the police reports, filed an insurance claim and had ordered most of the replacement items. It had been stressful, but I reminded myself that it was only stuff. Everything could be replaced.

And by the way, the owner of the Friendly Islander Hotel is NOT typical of most Tongans. At work and at the guesthouse where we ended up staying, the Tongans were very sorry about what happened and offered to do whatever they could to help.

Steve Hunsicker

BUSINESS CHANGES IN TONGA
Thursday, May 15, 2008

Foreign Competition and Great Marketing

There is very little foreign investment in Tonga, and almost all businesses are small and locally owned. That changed in a big way last Thursday when cell phone giant Digicel entered the local market. From a business perspective, the way they did it was masterful.

There have been two cell phone companies in Tonga. The largest, called UCall is owned by TCC, the Tongan Telephone Company. TCC is probably the largest business in the kingdom. The other company, called Tonfon, was owned by the king and other investors. Last year, Tonfon sold out to Digicel. Since taking over, they have been quietly adding cell towers and improving their infrastructure. This process has taken months and until last week, they operated Tonfon as it had always been run. I don't know the exact market share for each company, but I would have to guess that until last week, TCC controlled the market and Tonfon was a distant second.

Early last week, while I was staying in Nuku'alofa, Digicel started promoting a free concert with reggae star Shaggy. At times, there were four commercials an hour on the radio for the concert with just a mention that it was being brought to you by Digicel. There was no explanation as to who Digicel was or why they were having the concert, only that it was free and everyone was invited. That started the buzz. Concerts are VERY rare in Tonga especially from performers who are known outside of Tonga. One person told me it had been several years since the last concert was held here.

There were no signs all week indicating that Digicel was about to launch in a very big way. I went to bed Wednesday night without seeing a single Digicel sign or advertisement. When I got up on Thursday, the day of the concert, it was as if Nuku'alofa had been painted Digicel red overnight. There were bright colorful billboards everywhere, something else that is not common in Tonga. There were new offices with bright red neon signs on them saying "Digicel" that were not there the night before. There were Digicel vehicles and a huge red bus with Digicel painted on it driving all over town. And there were people in the streets handing out flyers, promoting Digicel and the free concert that night. Almost every store, big and small, now had a red Digicel sign on it saying that you could buy your Digicel calling cards there. Even the bus terminal was painted with a bright shade of red. This all happened literally overnight. Tongans went to bed with Tonfon and woke up to Digicel. For most Americans, this might sound like simple marketing, but it is brand new in Tonga. I spent 23 years in television news, and I've never seen a company do such a masterful job of marketing and launching a product as Digicel did here in Tonga last week.

Thursday night, it was pouring rain, and I decided to skip the concert, but an estimated 10,000 Tongans showed up in the rain for the show. To put that in perspective, 10,000 people represents about 10% of the entire population of the Kingdom of Tonga and 15% of the population of Tongatapu, the island where the concert was held. Digicel handed out free backpacks, umbrellas, shirts, pens, etc. The next day, their new offices were packed, with lines literally out the door with people anxious to buy a new phone and sign up for their service.

When I flew back to Vava'u on Monday, I found a brand new Digicel office in downtown Neiafu and rode past a party sponsored by Digicel in a village where they had just installed a new tower.

On Tuesday, Digicel employees were going door to door in villages offering a brand new Nokia cell phone, a backpack, a SIM card and three dollars of credit for TOP$40. That's just over US$20. Three Digicel employees came into the bank where I work and sold about five phones to employees here, including me. It was a great deal. Until the Digicel launch, I had never seen a new phone in Tonga for less than TOP$100.

So you might ask, since TCC has known for months that Digicel was coming to Tonga, what did they do? As far as I could tell—nothing. They sat back and let it happen. As much as I respect the way Digicel came into the market, as a business volunteer who wants to help Tongan businesses, I wish I had been working with TCC to help them. From my perspective, there is a lot they could have done to minimize the impact of Digicel, but now it's too late. They are in a catch-up position. One of my fellow volunteers told me that TCC has discounted one of its phones to TOP$80, which is twice the price of the Digicel phone. There is some hope for TCC. Since cell phones are interchangeable between systems here, new customers could buy a cheap Digicel phone and then use it on the TCC network. Too bad TCC didn't think to offer to switch any Digicel phone back to TCC for free. Instead, they are selling new SIM cards for TOP$20. Not exactly a reason to switch back.

Completely Cut Off

The timing of the Digicel launch was perfect for me since my phone and many other items were stolen from the Friendly Islander Hotel. That included my passport, drivers license, a credit card and ATM cards for both my local bank account and the one I have in Florida. For two weeks now, I have had no ID, and I am not sure when I will get replacements. I am able to access my local bank account by going into the bank and asking to withdraw money. (They rarely ask for ID.) However, I can also only get money when the bank is open.

Since I've been in Tonga, I've been able to live on my small Peace Corps stipend without using money from home. However, psychologically, it does bother me a bit to be completely cut off right now from my money at home and to have no access to a credit card. While I haven't used either the home ATM card or credit card, there is a feeling of security knowing that if I needed money in an emergency, I could get it.

Without a passport, if I wanted to leave the country, I wouldn't be able to leave. I also have no visa that shows I am in Tonga legally. And even if I got out of the country, I wouldn't be able to drive anywhere since I don't have a license. (Peace Corps volunteers are not allowed to drive in their country of service.) Thankfully, I have a lot of confidence that in an emergency, Peace Corps would bail me out, at least temporarily. Hopefully the replacement IDs and cards will arrive soon.

Volunteer Changes

The make-up of our volunteers is changing again. The good news is that Jason, who was medically separated earlier this year, has been cleared to return to Tonga. Jason is a great volunteer, and we were all sorry to see him go. It's terrific that he is coming back.

However, John, another volunteer, decided that Peace Corps was not for him, and he ET'ed, which is Peace Corps speak for early termination. Since moving to Vava'u, I haven't seen much of John, but I hope he finds much happiness in his future endeavors.

With Jason's return and John's departure, we are holding at 29 volunteers out of my training group of 33 who are still here after seven and a half months in Tonga.

AN UNEXPECTED RESULT
Wednesday, May 21, 2008

I've been working this week with the owner of a *falekoloa* (small shop) who, like most Tongans, doesn't keep any records. I got involved after he ran up a substantial overdraft at one of the commercial banks. During my first visit, I discussed with him the importance of recordkeeping and showed him some simple ways to better track his sales and his cash. He immediately seemed to grasp what I was telling him.

Another problem that is very common in Tonga is that store owners take whatever stock they need for their personal use, and they don't account for it in any way. I explained to this particular business owner, that while it was ok to take stock for his own use, he needed to keep track of what he was taking and also what he was giving away to family members. I could tell he immediately understood why that was important.

On my next visit, I was thrilled to see that he had been recording every sale that he had made, had documented all of the *mo'ua* (credit) that he had extended to people and had started counting all of his cash. He told me that because he knew that I was coming back to check on him, it inspired him to keep good records. I told him I would keep checking on him.

Then something unexpected happened. He told me that he had been writing down everything that he was taking for his own use and for his family. He then said, "Once I realized how many cigarettes I was smoking every day, it made me cut back. I'm not smoking as much now." It never occurred to me that better recordkeeping would help someone cut back on smoking but it was a pleasant if unexpected result.

A Morning Feast

I had just finished eating breakfast at my house Wednesday morning and was sipping some coffee when I heard a woman in my yard calling my name. Outside, I saw a woman I work with at the bank, and she said, "Steve, I've come to take you to a feast." "A feast?" I asked. What time does it start? She said 8 a.m. It was now 7:55 a.m., and I hadn't showered or shaved, and I had an appointment with a client in one hour. Of course, I really wanted to go and wish that she had told me the day before, so I could have been ready and could have rescheduled my client visit. But like everything in Tonga, there is little planning, and she probably didn't even think about inviting me until she decided to drive by my house. I told her I couldn't go, and she promised to bring me food later.

I visited with my client, got back to the bank and there she was, with enough food to feed not only me, but every bank employee—with some to spare. There was fresh beef, which is a rarity in Tonga, and the usual pork, fish, chicken, etc. We went downstairs, and I was handed a plate and fork, but everyone else just dug in with their hands. The beef was delicious, like roast beef in the states.

Only in Tonga would there be a feast at 8 a.m. in the morning. I later learned that the feast was from a church conference that was going on all week.

Winter Arrives in Vava'u Tonga

There has been a noticeable change in the weather here in Vava'u. It's still hot, but I haven't felt any sweltering heat since I returned from Nuku'alofa early last week. At night, it is very breezy, and there is even a slight chill in the air. It's very pleasant and is starting to remind me of the beautiful weather we have in South Florida every winter. I've started sleeping with the windows closed, and I've only run the fan in my bedroom once in the past week.

Another indication that winter is approaching is the preparation for the season. In Vava'u, the season means whale watching and the arrival of the "yachties." Most of the businesses that were closed during the summer have now reopened, and a few new businesses have opened as well. The season will kick off in early June when 40 yachts from around the world are expected to sail into the harbor as part of an around-the-world yachting trip.

MEMORIAL DAY TONGA STYLE
Tuesday, May 27, 2008

There's no Memorial Day holiday for Peace Corps volunteers in Tonga, but the weekend was truly memorable. It started with a celebration of fellow volunteer Sarah's birthday and wrapped up with an all-day sail around Vava'u.

We started with an impromptu birthday party at my house with several of my fellow volunteers and other friends.

James made a cake for Sarah's birthday, but it wasn't just any cake; it was a Jell-O shot cake. What's that? It's Jell-O spiked with rum. It didn't look like much of a cake, but Sarah seemed to enjoy it.

Sarah LaRosa "scoops" her Jello birthday cake

We wrapped the weekend up with an all-day sail aboard the charter boat *Manuoku*. We realized within minutes of pushing back from the dock that our trip aboard the *Manuoku* might be different from past sails—mainly because there was no wind. At the helm was boat owner Steve, who graciously agreed to take us out. Steve has been sailing for years but has just opened his own charter business.

As a pretty inexperienced sailboat passenger, I wondered if we would spend the whole trip using the small outboard motor because of the lack of wind power. I had never felt a day so calm in Vava'u, and even the small pieces of ribbon on the boat were not moving as we pulled out of the Port of Refuge bound for the island of Mala.

As we sailed—well actually motored—out of the harbor, we noticed lots of logs, leaves and other debris just floating on the still water. Steve said that with no wind to make waves, the debris just sits there. We took turns watching for debris in the water as we slowly moved away from the main island.

Our first stop was Mala, an island resort. We didn't go ashore, but Steve did a great job of navigating through the coral heads. His tri-hull boat needs a depth of just three and a half feet. Mala is under renovation. From the looks of it, it will be a really neat place once the work is finished. You can see small fales scattered around the island with enough distance between them to provide some privacy. The beach looked amazing, as did the diving.

The new managers have invited us to come out, and I hope to go back soon.

After leaving Mala, the wind picked up and filled the sails. We cruised by 'Euakafa and then anchored off a very small island called Nuku. There was a reef here and some cool spots to snorkel.

Unfortunately, we are now getting into the yachting season in Vava'u, and we had to share the spot with four or five other boats. This was a first for me. On my past sails, we never saw any other boats. I'm sure as the season gets going, we'll see many more.

Thankfully, the people on the other boats seemed more interested in the beach than diving. That left us to enjoy the beautiful fish and coral formations. We even saw a stingray.

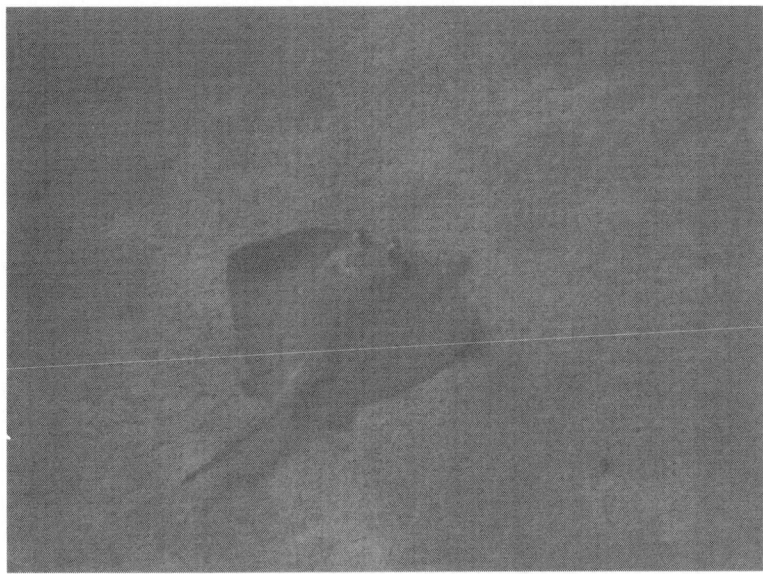

Stingray on the bottom of the ocean

Thanks to Stan for lending me his camera and underwater housing. I would have been really bummed if I hadn't been able to take some photos. I had my camera stolen from the Friendly Islander Hotel four weeks ago.

Heading to Ha'apai

I just found out that I am going to Ha'apai in two weeks on bank business. This means the only island group I will not have visited in Tonga is the Niua, which are north of Vava'u. I'm really looking forward to my visit, and I plan to stay over the weekend so that I have time to visit with my fellow Peace Corps volunteers who live there.

THE FAKALETI OF VAVA'U
Thursday, May 29, 2008

As the winter season starts to arrive in Vava'u, there are more and more events to entertain the tourists and the people who live here. Last week, one of the local bars began their weekly fakaleiti show. Fakaleiti literally translates to "like a lady," but make no mistake; these are not ladies, but men in drag. The bar was packed for the premiere of this year's show featuring three local fakaleiti. The highlight of the show, at least for the Peace Corps volunteers in attendance, was when Brian, one of the entertainers, came down off the stage and gave Justin a big peck on the cheek.

Justin and Brian

The photo pretty much says it all. It was also Jessie's birthday, and she got called up on stage by the owner, and we all sang "Happy Birthday" to her in English.

Farewell Amanda

Friday night, we all gathered to wish Amanda, our associate Peace Corps director, farewell. Amanda is the boss of all the volunteers and most of the staff at the Peace Corps office. She answers directly to the country director, who is the top person in Peace Corps Tonga. Amanda is leaving Tonga to accept a job as the training manager for Peace Corps in Costa Rica.

Sarah LaRosa and Amanda Rabinowitz

Amanda is the person on the right in the photo, next to Sarah. James and I played host for the event; we have the perfect spot for a gathering since we have two houses, two kitchens and two bathrooms between us. The theme was Mexican, and Rose, Alex and Justin all spent the afternoon cooking tacos and making salsa. (Thursday was the first time we have had fresh tomatoes in months, so we were thrilled to have fresh tomatoes for the salsa.)

Volunteers gather at Steve Hunsicker's house

At one point, I counted 18 people inside my house, including 13 of the 14 volunteers who live here in Vava'u.

A Surprise Visit

I had just finished eating dinner one night last week when I heard someone at my door calling my name. I saw a man I had never seen before who introduced himself. I recognized his name and knew he was the local manager for TCC, the Tonga Communications Company that supplies telephone, cell phone and Internet service.

He had heard that I could help him learn about inventory management and basic accounting. So he came in and I spent about 45 minutes with him. Another part of Tongan culture is that people just stop by when they want something, even the man who runs the telephone company. It wouldn't occur to most Tongans to call ahead. I was happy to help him and told him I would be glad to help him again in the future.

THE ISLAND OF KENUTU, VAVA'U
Tuesday, June 3, 2008

The Island Kingdom of Tonga is more than 100 islands, many of which are uninhabited. Some are very small, often just a giant rock with a few trees on it. Others are visible only at low tide. However, there are also some large islands where no one lives. Kenutu in Vava'u is one such island. It's located about a 45-minute boat ride from the main island. Last weekend, I joined 11 other Americans for a camping trip on Kenutu. We packed onto a small boat with probably more luggage than we needed and set off for a weekend adventure. The boat stopped in the water, not far from shore. There were no docks or other places to park a boat, so we walked in the water to get ashore. We made a human chain, passing each item of luggage from one person to the next until it made it to dry land. Then the boat left, leaving us as the only people on the island with no way to get off until the boat came back to retrieve us the next afternoon.

Kenutu, Vava'u

There is something refreshing about being all alone and knowing that you can't go anywhere. It was my first trip to this island, but it is a favorite of the Peace Corps volunteers, and they knew exactly where to go. We climbed up from the beach to a beautiful camping spot on the opposite side of the island. The camping site, covered in pine needles, sat on top of a tree-covered cliff with majestic views to the water below.

The Peace Corps campsite on Kenutu, Vava'u

We made camp and gathered firewood and then headed back to the beach. I donned my mask and snorkel and headed into the grassy waters where we had arrived. The snorkeling here was not spectacular, but I did see a few fish hiding in the grass as I swam by.

After watching a beautiful Tongan sunset, we made our way back to the campsite and started a fire. Dinner was hot dogs and pork and beans, and it tasted great. We ate as the light from the fire slowly overtook the light from the sky, creating a magical glow around our island for the night as we listened to the waves crashing into the cliffs below.

After dinner several of us went out to the bluff and looked at the stars. The stars were magnificent with no light pollution and no moon. We sat there stargazing before heading back to our tents to call it a night.

Sometime during the night, it started to rain. Pour would be a better adjective. Usually on our camping trips, we are all up in time to see the sun rise. This time, we all pretty much stayed in our tents until the rain stopped. Breakfast was oatmeal and cookies until Sarah brought out the eggs that we hard-boiled over the fire in Pacific Ocean water. It was a nice treat before the rain started again, and we went back to our tents.

Finally around 3 p.m., the rain stopped and we broke camp, heading back to the beach to meet our ride. While waiting, we took this photo of the survivors of a magnificent 30 hours on Kenutu.

Getting ready to leave Kenutu

The boat ride back was an adventure over the rough seas, but we made it—slightly wet but with great memories of camping on an uninhabited island.

Steve Hunsicker

TONGAN COOPERATION
Friday, June 13, 2008

Earlier this year, I was contacted by a woman who runs a website called AVO. Her site is all about markets around the world. She asked me if I would write a story about markets in Tonga. I did and she now has it posted on her website.

Here is the text of what I wrote for her:

The economy in Tonga is often described as a barter economy, but the word barter doesn't really explain the way things work in the Island Kingdom of Tonga. It might be better described as a "cooperative" economy, meaning that Tongans cooperate to get what they need. Usually, this cooperation is within family groups, but it extends to very large extended Tongan families, to neighbors and to friends. Most Tongans are given a piece of land on which to farm, often referred to as "the bush." The land is farmed by the family, but depending on where it is located, it may be owned (or controlled) by the nobles of a village or a member of the royal family. In exchange for the land, the Tongan family is expected to share the crops with the noble or royal family member who controls the land. Again, depending on who has control, the family may share on a regular basis or almost never.

The cooperative economy extends into all levels of Tongan society. Several members of the family may work in the bush, while others, usually women, may weave or make decorative cloth called tapa to sell at local markets. Another family member may work at what most Westerners would consider "a real job," and a grandmother, aunt or sister may help take care of the children. There is no typical arrangement except that the family unit is strong, and both the men and women cooperate to support their families.

And the roles are not always "full time." Some Tongan families will take their crops or their handicrafts to the market only when they need something. Others make their living by selling items every day. This culture can make a trip to the market exciting, but perhaps also a little frustrating. On any given day, at any market in Tonga, you will find the regulars but also the part-timers—those with an extra need that day. This can turn a trip to the market into a treasure hunt. And if you see something you like, you must grab it, because it may not be there the next day. It's also not uncommon to see a vegetable stand along the road or in front of someone's house. I once saw a man selling pineapple in what most people would consider the "middle of nowhere" on Vava'u. (The Vava'u pineapples are delicious, and if you visit during pineapple season, make sure you try them.)

If you want to try the usually delicious fruits and vegetables grown in Tonga, you will have to buy them either at a market or a roadside stand. The grocery stores don't sell fresh produce, except for the items that are imported like garlic and potatoes. This is because most Tongans either grow their own produce or get it from others.

On the main island of Tongatapu, there is one large market in downtown Nuku'alofa where you can buy everything from fresh vegetables to Tongan handicrafts to used clothes. On Saturdays, there is also a flea market located outside of town near the Tongan Cultural Center. In the village of Fanga, which is on the road from the airport to Nuku'alofa, you will almost always find many roadside vendors selling fruits and vegetables. On Vava'u, there is a market in downtown Neiafu and about two blocks away is a flea market, also open just on Saturday. For both the flea market on Tongatapu and the one on Vava'u, you have to get there very early. Tongans are early risers, and both markets are packed well before 8 a.m. If the vendor has made enough money for that day, he or she will just pack up and go home.

Tongans are very eager to please, especially palangi. Instead of a straight answer, they will often give you the answer they think you want to hear. In a craft store in Neiafu, one of my fellow Peace Corps volunteers asked the clerk if she could ship items to the United States. The clerk said yes because she assumed that was the answer he wanted. However, it turned out that the store doesn't ship and has never shipped. When it comes to price, Tongans will usually not negotiate on small items. However, sometimes they will throw in something extra. If you buy a pile of tomatoes and ask for a couple of chili peppers, you may get them free, or you may not. On larger items, price is negotiated but usually only because the Tongan has some expenses to cover. Perhaps school fees are due, and he or she doesn't have enough money to pay them. In that case, you can get a big discount. Other times, the vendor will hold firm on the price because they don't have anything they need at the moment. The concept of saving is not common in Tonga.

It also may help to put things in perspective. It can take a Tongan woman three weeks to a month to weave a mat. The profit from the mat is probably the only source of money she will have until the next mat is done. The money you are trying to save by negotiating will mean a lot more to the Tongan woman and her family than it will to you.

There is one caveat about buying Tongan handicrafts in a market or at a craft store. There are no fumigation chambers in Tonga to kill small insects that may be in the mats or carvings. Because of this, customs officials will sometimes not allow Tongan-made handicrafts into another country. This seems especially true for Australia and New Zealand. If you do decide to take something home with you, you might want to spray it thoroughly with bug spray so you can say that it was fumigated before leaving Tonga.

When Captain Cook first arrived in the Tongan Islands in 1773, he dubbed them "The Friendly Islands." The name is as relevant today as it was in Captain Cook's day. The Tongans are a friendly people who love to laugh and tell jokes. Whether you meet them in a market or while walking through a village, take some time to get to know the Tongans. You will almost always get a friendly response, and you might even get invited to their home for dinner. Sharing food with anyone is just another way that Tongans cooperate with each other and perfect strangers.

New Boat for Tonga

This is big news for those of us who live on Vava'u. Of course, I'm guessing it will be a while before we see the new boat. The *Olovaha* is one of two ships that bring all of our food and supplies to Vava'u from the capital city of Nuku'alofa each Wednesday.

> **Japanese Funding for New Inter-Island Ferry in Tonga**
> Posted at 17:50 on 08 June, 2008 UTC
>
> An agreement has been signed for a Japanese aid grant of 16 million US dollars for the construction of a new inter-island vessel for Tonga, replacing the 26-year-old passenger ferry, MV Olovaha.
> The Japanese government says the new vessel will be capable of carrying 400 passengers and 400 tonnes of cargo, at 53m long and 13.5m wide.
> It will be equipped with two, six-tonne cranes, a modern navigation system, radio apparatus and cargo-handling equipment such as eight reefer containers, 54 dry containers and two forklifts.

SEVEN DAYS IN HA'APAI, TONGA
Wednesday, June 18, 2008

I've often thought that visiting the Kingdom of Tonga is like taking a step back in time. If that's true, then visiting the Ha'apai Islands is like taking a LEAP back in time. The Ha'apai group of islands is located between the main island group of Tongatapu and the Vava'u Island Group where I live. A visit to Ha'apai provides a glimpse as to what life in Tonga was probably like before Tongatapu became an urban area and Vava'u a tourist destination.

Landing at the airport is your first clue that you are about to have a different experience. The runway stretches the entire width of the island and from the air; you can't help but wonder if the runway is really long enough to land the plane or if you will end up in the ocean. As we touched down, I noticed that the main road crosses the runway. Cars, and there are not a lot of them on Ha'apai, just sit at the edge of the runway until the planes land and then drive across to get to the other side. There is a gate to keep someone from driving across when a plane is on its final approach, but closing it means someone has to walk there to close it. It was closed when we landed, but I'm guessing it is sometimes left open, and it is up to the alert pilots to make sure there are no cars on the runway before they commit the aircraft to land.

The main village on Ha'apai is called Pangai. Notice I didn't say city. It's not big enough to really even be considered a town. There are two banks, the Tonga Development Bank where I work and Westpac Bank of Tonga, along with a few stores, a police station and one restaurant called Mariner's Cafe.

I came to Ha'apai on bank business. I never really expected that I would be taking business trips in the Peace Corps, at least not via a plane, but that is what I did. My job for the week was to help conduct some workshops for small business owners and also to do some staff training for the employees of the branch.

The bank is without question the most modern building in Ha'apai. It looks like any Western bank with a big lobby and teller stations. In the back is a large conference room and two bedrooms. I opted not to stay at the bank, giving up the comfortable looking double beds to stay with my friends Scot and Karen.

I pretty much worked all week, seeing Scot and Karen in the morning and then again in the evening after work. Friday after work, Scot, Karen and I headed over to Sami's house to celebrate her birthday. Sami is getting ready to finish her Peace Corps service, and it's the first chance I've had to spend time with her.

We were joined by Phil, a volunteer from my group, and several Japanese volunteers. We made tacos and finished the last of the tomatoes I had brought from Vava'u. Fresh veggies just don't exist in Ha'apai.

Biking in Ha'apai

Saturday, we headed out for a short bike ride to the southern end of the main island of Ha'apai. It's a nice spot where on a clear day you can see many of the other islands. Unfortunately, it wasn't clear, and we could only see three other islands from the point. Still, we had a nice time hanging out on the beach.

Volunteers Scot Fitzgerald and Phil Curtiss

The weather wasn't great and the bike I was riding was too small for my 6' 3" frame, so we headed back to Phil's house and spent the rest of the afternoon sipping wine and talking. Sunday everything shuts down in Tonga and Ha'apai is no exception. It was a nice lazy day.

Air Tonga Confusion

Getting out of Ha'apai on Monday was a true Tonga experience—the kind of thing that makes no sense but you just accept it for what it is. I was at the Peace Corps office in Ha'apai around noon when my phone rang and a Tongan woman from Airlines Tonga started the conversation by asking, "Is this Steve?" I said "Io," which is yes. She then asked me if I was still going to Vava'u today. I told her yes, and she told me that my 3 p.m. flight had been cancelled, and I now would have to be at the airport by 12:30 p.m. to fly to Tongatapu, which is in the opposite direction of Vava'u. After landing there, I would be taken to Vava'u. I said ok and immediately called the bank to see about getting a ride. I walked back to Scot and Karen's house, jumped into the waiting bank car and headed off to the airport and arrived by 12:20 p.m. or so. I then sat at the airport for about 45 minutes before anyone came to check in the flight.

While I was waiting, I was joined by David, who manages all of the Peace Corps business volunteers in Tonga, including me. He told me he had been bumped off an earlier Airlines Tonga flight at 8:30 a.m. when it was cancelled. We then waited until just before 2 p.m. to take off for Tongatapu. We landed, and there were four people on the plane going to Vava'u. We remained in our seats and the flight boarded. We soon realized that there were more people getting on the small 15-seat plane than there were seats. The last four people had no place to sit. A Tongan came on board and said the Vava'u passengers who came from Ha'apai had to get off the plane and take the next flight, which was at 5 p.m., about two and a half hours away.

After we got off the plane, they unloaded all of the baggage they had just put on the plane and asked us to pick out our bags. Then they reloaded the bags, and everyone except for the four people who were bumped flew away to Vava'u. David, who speaks fluent Tongan, asked the guy why we got bumped instead of someone else and was told that Ha'apai never called and told them that four passengers were going to Vava'u. You would think that since we had already been bumped and sent to a different city, we would have priority. It just doesn't work that way in Tonga.

The airport was very small, and I didn't really want to sit around, so I jumped in a cab and headed to Fua'amotu, which is the village near where the airport is located. I lived there when I first came to Tonga and decided to surprise my homestay family. I got out of the cab after seeing that the door to their house was open and saw the grandmother of the family. She was the only one home, but I soon saw a neighbor I knew and chatted with her for a while. It was a much better way to pass the time.

The grandmother became very concerned that I was going to walk back to the airport and started trying to find me a ride. This 80-plus-year-old woman was walking door to door to try to find someone with a car. I finally convinced her in my broken Tongan that I was going to walk. As I was walking, up drove Tau and his son Tevita, my homestay family. He was surprised to see me since he thought I was in Vava'u, but I jumped in the truck, and we visited on the way back to the airport. I waited awhile longer, and finally the plane came back from Vava'u and we were on our way.

I'll be returning to Ha'apai in October, again on bank business. However, my friends Scot and Karen won't be there. Peace Corps is transferring them to new jobs in Tongatapu. That's pretty unusual, but Scot's host organization never delivered on what it had promised Peace Corps. Scot and Karen are both actually very excited about the move because they both are now going to be in jobs that better suit their past experiences.

IT WAS LEGENDARY!
Monday, June 23, 2008

There is an old Tongan legend about a king who found out his wife was cheating on him. The legend says an enemy of the king seduced the woman, then tattooed her to show the king what he had done. When the king saw the tattoo, he took his wife to the island of 'Euakafa where she was beaten and buried.

Today, as you walk along the beach on this beautiful tropical island, you can still see where the gravestone was cut out of the rocks, and you can hike to the top of the island and see the remains of the grave.

It may sound like a creepy place to visit, but the island is beautiful. And today, the reef located just off shore is a real living legend. It's the best snorkeling spot I've found in Vava'u.

Sunday, I joined many of my fellow Peace Corps volunteers and several Japanese volunteers on a trek to the island of 'Euakafa. As we approached and dropped anchor, there was little indication of the beauty below. As I dove into the water, I found myself immersed in hundreds of small blue fish swimming all around me, making a beautiful contrast against the multi-colored coral spread out before me.

The current around the reef and the island is quite strong. I swam into some pretty shallow water and immediately realized my mistake as a wave slammed down on top of me, causing me to crash into some of the coral. I cut my knee but it was a minor cut. The more severe damage came to the coral that I accidentally broke. It takes years for this coral to grow, and while it was only a small fracture, I knew I would not be leaving these waters the way I had found them. Next time, I will not go into water that shallow.

I was swimming with my friend Justin. We both had cameras and had fun taking photos of each other underwater.

Volunteer Justin Smith

From the reef, Justin and I swam to the shore meeting up with others from our group who had come ashore in a dinghy. We walked along the sandy shore to the other side of the island from where we had been diving to the place where the ancient Tongans had somehow sliced a gravestone from the rock at the water's edge. From there, in our bare feet, we proceeded to climb 62 meters (203 feet) above sea level to see the remains of the grave and a spectacular view of the ocean below. Hiking back down, I was glad I was in bare feet as I needed the traction in the mud to keep from slipping.

A Return Visit to Two Caves

On the boat trip back we stopped at Mariner's Cave. This was my second trip to this cave that you can only enter by diving underwater and swimming to get inside. Unlike the first time I went, I had no qualms about going inside and easily made it. The only way you tell there is a cave from the outside is by the small yellow "X" that someone has painted just above the cave entrance. We also stopped at Swallows Cave, but only to look, as it was getting late and we needed to get back to Neiafu before it got dark. I previously visited Swallows Cave last November.

Swallow's Cave

'How I Met Your Mother'

If you have ever watched the CBS Television show *How I Met Your Mother*, you may have recognized the title of this post. I never watched the show in the USA, even though it aired on the TV station where I worked. One of the volunteers has the show, and it has quickly made the rounds of the Peace Corps volunteers here in Vava'u. The "It was legendary!" quote is used often by Barney, the main character. There is one episode in which Barney flashes back to his plans to join the Peace Corps. In another episode, he tries to impress a girl by telling her he is shipping out to join the Peace Corps the next day. It's a funny show and without the commercials, it only takes about 20 minutes to watch each episode.

Steve Hunsicker

THE PRINCESS AND THE FEAST
Friday, June 27, 2008

For many Tongans, life revolves around the church. And when the biggest church in Tonga has its annual conference, it's a BIG event. For the past two weeks, the Free Wesleyan Church of Tonga has been meeting in the capital city of Nuku'alofa. The church is a sister of the United Methodist Church, and its conference is international due to the large number of Tongans who live in New Zealand, Australia and the United States (mostly in California).

However, this annual conference is nothing like the annual conferences I used to attend as a child when my father was an active Methodist minister. This church conference is really a huge feast—not just one feast, but four feasts a day for two weeks. The first feast starts early in the morning, followed by a midday feast, a late afternoon feast and a supper feast at night. There are thousands of people at each feast, and there is no way anyone will leave hungry. In fact, most people take food home with them. The photo shows just one of probably 50 tables this size covered in food. The food is stacked in layers on the table, and it is some of the best food you can get. Depending on the day, you will find lobster, crab, octopus (my new favorite Tongan food) and always full pigs spread out snout to tail. Once the first group of guests finishes, more Tongans will sit down to eat the leftovers.

A Tongan feast

Wednesday, Tonga's Princess Pilolevu attended the conference, sitting at the head table being fanned by two young girls to keep her cool. While there were no security guards or fences to keep people away from the princess, Tonga is a very respectful society, and no one would approach the head table unless invited.

After the feast, I walked around with my friends Craig and Sione, taking photos and playing with the kids.

I was in Nuku'alofa on Wednesday to meet with someone from the US Embassy in Fiji who was visiting Tonga. I had to sign some papers to get my Peace Corps passport replaced. It, along with many other personal articles, was stolen from the (not so) Friendly Islander Hotel the last time I was in Nuku'alofa. The passport was the last item I needed to get replaced. I have now received the replacements for my other stolen items, and a check is on the way from my insurance company to reimburse me.

Special thanks to my parents, who shipped me all the replacement items, and also to the staff at Peace Corps Tonga, who helped navigate the package through Tongan Customs and then got it to me in Vava'u.

SOME GREAT PCVS (PEACE CORPS VOLUNTEERS)
Thursday, July 3, 2008

Perhaps it is only natural that when you have a small group of Americans living so far away from home that strong bonds and friendships will develop. However, I think there is more to these relationships than just geography. There are some pretty amazing volunteers here; people who you know have their hearts (and their heads) in the right place. I'm a bit prejudiced, but I think some of the best volunteers we have in Tonga are right here in Vava'u. I'm sure part of that is because I'm around these folks more than the other volunteers, but we've got a great bunch of 14 volunteers in Vava'u ranging in age from 23 to 59.

One of the things I like best about my fellow volunteers is the way they watch out for each other and help each other when necessary. And it is not just a matter of dealing with the usual issues like sickness, homesickness or relationships. It slips into work and every other part of our lives as Peace Corps volunteers.

Just recently, I had to be out of town when two important events took place at the bank where I work. The bank sent me to Ha'apai to do workshops and training there, but the week I was gone, two groups wanted some help on how to start a business. We found out about these groups from Shannon, one of my fellow volunteers, who knew that I worked with business people here in Vava'u. She is a teacher in the village of Tefisi. I spoke with the bank's branch manager, and we agreed we should not make these people wait until I got back from Ha'apai. So Shannon set up the meeting with the people from her village, and James, who is also an education volunteer and not a business volunteer, offered to go with the bank employees to assist with the training. Eight people showed up, and hopefully one or more of them will be starting their own business very soon.

Then, last week, we were scheduled to have a workshop on Tuesday in the main town of Neiafu. At the last minute, we had to move it to Wednesday. Unfortunately, I had an appointment with the US Embassy that day in Tongatapu and would not be able to attend. I went over to the Vava'u Youth Congress where Stan works, and he quickly agreed to help out with the workshop in my place. Stan is a business volunteer like me and also happens to have the same model of laptop as me, which includes a remote control for doing PowerPoint presentations. Stan helped set up the workshop, took pictures and assisted the bank staff during the session. Twenty-four people attended the workshop.

These are just two small examples of the kind of supportive atmosphere we have in Vava'u, but it not only extends to our fellow volunteers but also to the Tongans we work with every day.

INDEPENDENCE DAY IN TONGA
Monday, July 7, 2008

On July 4, 1776, the United States declared its independence from England. The US did this by proclaiming the country free of foreign rule, chasing the foreign military out and raising the American flag.

On July 4, 2008, exactly 232 years later, halfway around the world, a group of 10 Americans chose the island of Lotumu in Vava'u, Tonga, to follow in the footsteps of their forefathers.

Arriving on the island of Lotumu, once the home of the Tongan military, we scouted the island for soldiers. Finding only abandoned barracks and a watchtower, we proclaimed the island "the 51st state" and proudly raised the American flag while listening to the sounds of "America the Beautiful" and "God Bless America." Protected by two dogs and a fishing spear, we moved in, setting up camp and building a fire to let everyone know that America was here.

We proudly cooked hamburgers and freedom fries over an open fire while drinking American beer. We topped off our dinner with potato salad, pasta salad and chips. As the sun set over the blue Pacific Ocean, we listened to the sounds of the bars in nearby Neiafu, where the patrons had no idea that one of their Vava'u islands had just been conquered.

The next morning, we secured the dock where Tongan Navy ships had once docked and snorkeled around the bottom, observing the many tropical fish that now protect the coral below.

As the afternoon sun started to dip into the horizon, we basked in the realization that we were the first foreign power to ever rule an island in the Kingdom of Tonga. But then, we decided that it was time to give the island back to the Tongans. We sadly lowered the flag, picked up our litter and left, leaving no signs of our 24-hour invasion. However, we left with the memory of a great July 4th spent with fellow Americans.

DEEP-SEA FISHING IN TONGA
Sunday, July 13, 2008

I remember the first fish I ever caught. It's one of those life experiences you have as a young boy that you will always remember. In my case, I snagged my first fish when I was about eight years old while fishing with my father.

Since that first fishing experience, I have done some more fishing over the years. Most of it has been in lakes, off bridges or just standing on the beach. And while I've been deep-sea fishing in the Atlantic, I just had my first experience going deep-sea fishing in the Pacific.

Stan and I were the guests of Joe and his father-in-law, John, who were visiting Vava'u this week. Joe and his wife, Cory, are both members of my group and live on the main island of Tongatapu. Cory and her mom stayed behind at the Reef Resort, while we headed out to the open waters of the South Pacific. While I have done a bit of sailing since I've been in Vava'u, this was the first time I had left the protected waters of the Vava'u Island Group where the ocean is always calm. As we motored out, the waves got rougher, and soon we were holding on to keep from falling. Our captain put four lines in the water, and we were off. The further we got from land, the rougher the seas.

It was early in the morning and the first thing we saw were some whales on the horizon. They were too far away to capture with my camera, but we could see the distinctive tails jumping back into the water. We spent the next two hours in the open water without so much as a nibble. Finally, John caught the first fish of the day and a while later, caught the second fish, a barracuda. Stan then caught another barracuda, and I reeled in the last two fish of the day, also barracudas. We were on the water with lines out for almost seven hours, and all we had to show for it was five fish. We decided to call it a day and headed back to drop John and Joe off at the Reef Resort, while Stan and I headed back to Neiafu.

No one got sick and thankfully, even without taking any Dramamine, I made it. (The last time I went deep-sea fishing, which was in Florida, the water was a lot calmer and I did get sick). The boat captain kept the fish, but we headed home having fully enjoyed our day deep-sea fishing on the rough South Pacific.

POOR CUSTOMER SERVICE FROM TCC
Saturday, July 19, 2008

There are not a lot of businesses in Vava'u with big telecommunication needs. Most businesses have a phone line or two and perhaps an Internet connection. And while I don't have any hard data to support it, I believe that the Tonga Development Bank where I work is probably one of the larger customers of TCC, the local phone company. We spend more than a $1,000 a month with TCC for our data and voice services.

I recently put together a proposal to save the branch about $600 a month on its telecommunication costs by eliminating the expensive data lines and instead, using a secured Internet connection for data transfers. The proposal was approved by the head office in Nuku'alofa, and last week, I went with one of the bank employees to sign up for Internet service.

When we arrived at the TCC office, we filled out the forms and handed them in. We came armed with a signed purchase order and a request to have the Internet installed that afternoon. But when we turned in the paperwork, we were told that because we were an existing customer, they would have to do a credit check on us. They also said that they don't do credit checks on new clients. This seemed completely backwards to me. We then asked what was involved in the credit check and were told it was to see if we were paying our bills. I asked if they could just pull up our account and see if the bills were current. They replied that yes, they could do that, but their head office in Nuku'alofa was the one that did the credit checks. They refused to take our purchase order.

I then asked to speak to someone else and ended up talking with the person in charge of the Internet. He said it was no problem to take our purchase order, and he would be happy to come install the service later that afternoon. At that point, I thought we were done.

Then a lady came walking out of an office and said sorry, but no, they would not accept our payment and order until it was approved by their head office. We left and went back to the bank.

At the bank, we told the branch manager what had happened, and he immediately asked if we could go to Digicel, TCC's competitor, and get the service installed. I confirmed that we could do that, but I suggested that the branch manager first call the TCC branch manager to see if he could help. He did this, and in less than five minutes, we were on our way back to TCC to order our Internet service and schedule the installation. TCC said it would be done later that afternoon.

The next morning, after no one from TCC had shown up, we went back to their office. They told us that no one had shown up because we had not given them a check. Even though both TCC and TDB are government-owned organizations, TCC wouldn't accept a purchase order, and no one had told us that the day before. I did ask if we could just get our Internet charges added to our current bill and was told that would be no problem.

Finally, a few hours later, TCC showed up to install the Internet. Since the Internet here is from a WiMax system, all that is involved is putting up a receiver outside our office and running the wire inside. Because our internal network at the bank is wide open, I told the TCC guy not to install the Internet into our network, but instead to plug it into my laptop, which does have some security. When he plugged in the cable he had made into my laptop, there was no signal. I jiggled the connectors, and I could see the cable had a short and suggested he make another cable. Nope, instead he went out to his car, got his laptop, plugged the cable into it, jiggled the wires and it worked. He then proceeded to tell me that the problem was with the connection on my laptop. I didn't feel like arguing with him, so I let him set up the Internet. Once he left, I put the cable into my laptop, jiggled the connector and it started working.

However, just when you think this story might be over, there was one more "gotcha." I ran a speed test on the connection to make sure we were getting the bandwidth for which we had paid. Turns out, we were getting about a third of what we were supposed to get.

Two months ago, I wrote about how Digicel launched in Tonga with a big fanfare and a focus on customer service. At that time, I said that TCC acted like it didn't know what had hit them. You would have thought that by now, someone would have convinced TCC that it needed to change its ways. Apparently that hasn't happened. Perhaps a Peace Corps volunteer with a lot of sales and marketing experience should be assigned to their corporate office. Otherwise, I suspect that TCC will end up losing its customers, like it almost lost the business of the bank here in Vava'u.

The other possibility is that a company will buy out TCC and change it. Just this week, Westpac Bank acquired the assets of the Bank of Tonga from the government. They already owned a portion of the bank and now they own all of it. TCC seems like the next likely government entity to be sold, and already they are offering to sell a small portion of stock to interested buyers.

VAVA'U HAPPENINGS
Tuesday, July 22, 2008

Here are some of the things that have happened in Vava'u in the past few days.

Murder in Vava'u

For the most part, Tonga and especially Vava'u, is a pretty safe place, but we are not immune to crime. This past weekend, a Tongan man was killed on the waterfront. I don't know all the details, but apparently he got into a fight and ended up losing his life. A murder is very rare here.

Tonga Shark Attack on TV

The story of Tessa Horan, a Peace Corps volunteer who was killed by a shark two years ago, will be profiled on the Discovery Channel. Horan, who was living in Vava'u, was killed February 1, 2006. All the members of her group have now left Vava'u, but there is a library here that is named after her.

Tonga Peace Corps Group 74

The invitations are now going out to the next group of future Peace Corps volunteers in Tonga. We are starting to get e-mails from them, and some have posted comments on a website we built for them. That also means that we will soon be saying goodbye to many of the volunteers who are currently serving here. The members of Group 71 will start leaving next month, followed by the members of Group 72, who will start leaving in December.

That will leave just my group, Group 73, and Group 74. Group 74 is scheduled to start training on October 9th and swear in as volunteers in mid-December.

Camping at Port Maurelle, Vava'u

This past weekend I joined a group of my fellow volunteers in a combination camping and sailing trip. We left Friday afternoon aboard *Manu-o-ku*, a really great boat, and headed to a place called Port Maurelle. Once there we pitched our tents along the beach and camped for the night.

The next morning, we snorkeled and then spent a good part of the day sailing before heading back to Neiafu.

Swallows Cave

On the way back to Neiafu, we stopped at Swallows Cave. I had previously visited the cave, but never with fins and my camera. Inside you can see the bottom of the cave, some 80 feet below you.

PREPARING FOR THE CORONATION OF KING GEORGE TUPOU V
Tuesday, July 29, 2008

This week, Tonga is crowning a king. He's not a new king. In fact, he's been the king for almost two years, but is just now having the official coronation ceremony. Some newspaper accounts have estimated that 4,000 to 5,000 people may come to the country for the coronation. If that happens, it would be the most people ever to visit the Kingdom of Tonga at the same time. The activities are already underway throughout the kingdom, with most of the activity centered in the capital city of Nuku'alofa. The actual coronation takes place on Friday.

Millions of dollars have been spent on a new throne for the king, a coronation robe and all of the preparations. However, the government says the money is worth it because of the boost it will give the Tongan economy.

The Tongan prime minister's office is also now promoting the 60-year-old bachelor king as an architect of change who wants to make the Tongan government more open.

After the coronation, the king will be visiting all of the island groups, and each island has its own plans to welcome him. Here in Vava'u, there will be a huge kava ceremony, and many of the villages will be performing traditional Tongan dances for his Majesty King George Tupou V.

In Leimatu'a, which is the second largest village in Vava'u, the town officer's son has written a 10-minute song. The men of the village have spent just about every day rehearsing the dance to that song. The women will also do their own dance. My fellow Peace Corps volunteer Sarah lives in Leimatu'a and will be one of those dancing for the king when he comes to Vava'u in mid-August.

There are many rumors about who will be attending the coronation . . . everyone from Elton John to President George Bush. However, neither of those is listed on the official coronation website as attending.

I leave tomorrow (Wednesday) to fly to Nuku'alofa. Peace Corps has given outer island volunteers permission to attend the events without taking vacation time. I'm looking forward to attending. In my former career in TV news, I covered many events but never a coronation. This will be a first for me. I look forward to sharing my experiences with you after it is over.

NA'A' KU FEMAUAKENA
Friday, August 8, 2008

Na'a' ku Femauakena is Tongan for "I was busy." That's the best way I know to describe the incredible activities of the past week. The past seven days have probably been the busiest of my Peace Corps service but also perhaps the most fun I've had so far.

On Friday, Tonga officially crowned King George V. I was in Nuku'alofa staying with my friends Lara and Trent who live just steps from the palace. I woke up Friday to the sounds of a marching band, walked a few steps and joined hundreds of young girls from Queen Salote School who were sitting along the tapa-covered road waiting for the king to make the short trip from the palace to the church where the coronation would be held.

Steve Hunsicker waiting for the King

It was a regal affair, and even though there were dignitaries from all over the world, there was a refreshing lack of security. No guards with guns, no metal detectors and no security fences. I was less than three feet from the king when he passed by in his car with the windows open.

I was surprised at the lack of Tongans who attended the official ceremony. There were a bunch of media representatives and visitors hanging around outside the church, but very few Tongans. Inside were just invited guests. I snuck inside the church after the service to take a few photos of the throne and the church.

The throne where the King was crowned

A big surprise to many was that just days before the service, the king signed away many of his absolute powers, clearing the way for more rule by the people.

Probably the highlight of the day though was John McCain. No, not the Arizona senator who is running for president, but the *U. S. S. John McCain*, which is a Navy boat named after the senator's grandfather. The boat was in Tonga to represent the USA during the coronation. Friday evening, the U. S. Navy invited all the Peace Corps volunteers to come on board for food and cocktails. Quite simply, it was the best food I've had in 10 months. I ate shrimp, scallops wrapped in bacon, roast beef, fried cheese and chocolate chip cookies. There was an open bar with American beer and wine and real American soft drinks. It was as close to being back in the USA as you could ever hope to come in Tonga. It was great to act, eat, drink and talk like Americans again. I had to catch myself at the bar when I went to get a glass of wine because I started to say "thank you" in Tongan instead of English. I'm so used to saying malo now it almost seemed unnatural to say it in English.

The Navy also opened its ship to us. My friends Craig, Jessie and I wandered around the ship and eventually ran into a sailor named Eric Miller, who offered to show us around. We got a great tour, doing everything from sitting in the commanding officer's chair on the bridge to seeing the very cramped quarters where the men (there are only five women on this boat) sleep at night.

We probably spent close to two hours walking around the boat before rejoining the cocktail party on the helipad. It was a great treat.

Saturday, the village of Fua'amotu, where I lived when I first arrived in Tonga, danced for the newly crowned king and the king's sister, the princess. My homestay father Tau is the talking chief for Fua'amotu, so he led the entire village onto the palace grounds. My homestay mom Sia, who also danced, helped the princess get dressed for the event. After the performance, Tau came out and bowed to the king.

Sunday was a traditional day of rest across the kingdom.

On Monday, I started working on a video project for Peace Corps with my friend Scot. The video is being sent to Peace Corps Washington and also to the incoming volunteers of Group 74, who will arrive in October. It was like stepping back into television again after more than a year of absence. We shot interviews and some footage around Nuku'alofa and then headed out to talk with fellow volunteers Patrick and Bobby, who both live in smaller villages.

Monday night, we went to the home of the country director where he was hosting six former Tonga volunteers who had come back for the coronation. We got a chance to talk with them and learn about what life was like in the early years of Peace Corps. For a woman named Tina, this was her first visit to Tonga since she completed her service 37 years ago.

In 1976, a Peace Corps volunteer named Deb Garner was murdered in Tonga by another volunteer who never went to jail for the crime. Deb's boyfriend Emil was one of the former volunteers at the party, and I got a chance to talk with him about his involvement in the book *American Taboo*, which was written about the murder.

Tuesday, we did more shooting, including a trip to the head office of the Tonga Development Bank, where I worked before moving to the Vava'u branch in February. I was also able to have lunch with Sina, my homestay sister from Fua'amotu, at what may now be the nicest restaurant in Tonga, a place called Little Italy. It had just moved to a new location with a beautiful view of the water.

Wednesday, I flew to the island of 'Eua to interview Jason, Heather, Bria and Krystal, four volunteers from my group who live there. It was great to get back to 'Eua, even for just 24 hours and to see the homes and workplaces of the volunteers there. That afternoon, I joined the four 'Eua volunteers and three JICA (Japanese) volunteers for coffee and fresh fruit at Bria's house. For dinner, Jason cooked fresh octopus, one of my favorite Tongan foods.

That evening, Jason and I drank kava with the men in his village. Thursday, I got up at 6:30 a.m. and walked to the airport. When I got there, I was assigned the copilot seat on the plane. Yes, I was sitting in the empty seat next to the pilot. There is no copilot on the short, 10-minute flight back to Tongatapu. The plane only seats 10 people and it wasn't even full, which is another reason I was surprised to be sitting up front. When we went to take off, I had to sit sideways to keep my legs from bumping into the yoke as the pilot took us up.

After that, the rest of the day pretty much sucked. I landed at the airport around 9 a.m., and my flight was not scheduled to leave until 2 p.m. However, when I went to the Chatham Airlines counter, they told me there was room on a flight at 11 a.m., and they would put me on it if it was okayed by their head office. They called and got approval (there are no computers in the domestic terminal) and issued me a boarding pass. I even scored an exit row seat. I passed the time reading some *Newsweek* magazines. At exactly 11 a.m., the flight started boarding and I got in line. The woman from the counter came over and said, "Mr. Hunsicker, you can't take this flight. The pilot said it is too heavy." She said they had enough seats, but the plane was overweight, and since I was the last one to get a seat, I got bumped. Shortly after, I watched the plane take off.

I waited until 1:45 p.m. when we boarded my original flight. This time, I got on, but then they announced that the plane was going to stop in Ha'apai. Normally, the flight goes to Vava'u first then stops in Ha'apai on the way back. So we took off, landed in Ha'apai and waited there about 30 minutes to fly the rest of the way to Vava'u. I finally got home, and other than the usual frustrations of flying here, it was a great week.

Another item worth noting: I found out when I was in Nuku'alofa that the number of volunteers who will be coming in the next group has been cut due to budgetary reasons. Instead of 35 new trainees, we will be getting 24. Of those, 10 will be business and 14, education. We were also told that almost all of the new volunteers will be on outer islands and not on the main island of Tongatapu, which houses the most volunteers right now.

Steve Hunsicker

THERE GOES THE NEIGHBORHOOD
Sunday, August 17, 2008

My neighborhood has changed quite a bit in the past week. Actually not just my neighborhood but all of Vava'u. King George V arrives here today (Sunday) to celebrate his recent coronation. And Vava'u is definitely getting ready. I live across the street from the soldiers' barracks in Vava'u. There are normally just a handful of soldiers on duty, and they are a pretty quiet bunch. Last week, about 300 soldiers showed up, pitching tents in the field across from my house and moving in. Every morning around 5 a.m., they all get up and sing. So instead of being awakened each morning by the 5 a.m. church bells, I now wake up to the quite loud but beautiful voices of 300 men.

But that's just a small part of what is happening here. Everyone is cleaning up and decorating for the king's arrival. Litter, which is always prevalent around Vava'u, has disappeared. Every yard has been swept and the debris burned or carted away.

Perhaps the most visible change, however, are the arches that are posted across most of the major (and some of the minor) roads in Vava'u. These arches are called *matapa* in Tongan, which literally translates as "door" or "entrance way."

For the most part, each of the arches is built the same way. Four large coconut trees are put on each side of a road and then connected across the top. The two trees on each side are then joined together, and a small walkway is made over the road.

But beyond that, each arch is a work of art, and some people have spent as much as TOP$5,000, or about US$2,700, to build and decorate an arch. Some of the arches are pretty high tech, with fancy lights and professionally painted messages, while others are simpler.

Downtown Neiafu, which is the only town in the Vava'u Island Group, is also ready for the king. A large fence, which protects a construction site, has been painted just for the king's arrival, and there are balloons and Tongan flags lining many of the roads.

One thing that I have learned about the Tongan people in the past 10 months is that when they want to accomplish something, they find a way to do it. There is no question that the Tongans have accomplished a lot getting ready for the king.

However, the king's arrival is not without a bit of controversy. In Tonga, it is illegal to do almost anything on Sunday. The fact that the king is arriving on a Sunday when the airport is normally closed has caused some grumbling. Because of that, the king cancelled plans for a lavish arrival ceremony. Tonight, he is scheduled to attend a church service, but there are no official celebrations.

A Tongan "matapa" congratulating King George

The queen mother and the princess are both already in Vava'u. The princess was at the 10 a.m. church service this morning where the soldiers who are living in my neighborhood sang the "Hallelujah Chorus."

The Tongan military at church

The king is scheduled to be here through Wednesday.

AND THEN THERE WERE NINE!
Sunday, August 24, 2008

The number of Peace Corps volunteers assigned to Vava'u continues to drop as more and more of the members of Group 71 finish their service and head home. By this time next month, we will have just nine volunteers working here compared to the 16 we had at the beginning of the year. We won't get any new volunteers until mid-December, when the members of Group 74, who arrive in October, are sworn in as volunteers.

This past week, we've been busy with goodbye parties, camping trips and the wrap-up of the king's coronation.

A week ago, the choirs from each of the churches in Vava'u got together to sing for the king. The music was really spectacular, and even when the power went out in the middle of the service, the Tongans kept singing their hearts out. Unfortunately, the king was a no-show. The queen and princess were there, but the king's throne at the front of the church remained empty the entire evening. I thought it was a shame that these choirs had been rehearsing for weeks and then didn't get to sing for the king.

But many had another chance before the week was out. Sarah, my fellow volunteer, and her village were invited to the palace to perform for the queen. I came along to watch as she and the people of Leimatu'a danced and sang. Sarah did a great job, and except for the color of her skin, probably could have passed for a Tongan. On Tuesday, there was a formal kava ceremony with the king and invited guests. Everyone had to wear white. I was invited to sit behind where they were making kava, and I videotaped some of the ceremony. It's a long and very elaborate process to present the kava to the king, then prepare it and serve it to each of the men sitting in the circle. Wednesday was the coronation feast, and I was invited to go with Fuka, my supervisor at the bank. I've learned to limit my intake at these feasts but was happy to dine on a huge lobster and some fresh octopus. During the feast, several villages performed, including the village of Tefisi, whose members were dressed in traditional Tongan warrior costumes.

Not a lot of work got done last week in Vava'u until the king left on Thursday morning. Everyone, it seems, was busy catering to the king and the royal family.

Tongan boys perform a traditional dance

Thursday afternoon, the bank sent me to the island of Hunga to work with the owners of a fishing resort called Ika Lahi, which means "many fish." It was a truly amazing place in a beautiful setting on the Hunga Lagoon. It's probably one of the nicest resorts in all of Tonga. The owner, Steve, holds many records for big-game fishing, and Caroline, the other owner, is a great cook. I dined on fresh mahimahi and even had cheesecake for dinner—a real treat in Tonga.

I got back to the main island Saturday and within a few hours was back on another boat, this time heading to Kenutu with seven fellow Americans. We made camp on top of the cliffs, and it was very windy. Even though the water was hundreds of feet below, we could still feel the sea mist being blown up from the foot of the cliffs. We stayed on Kenutu until late in the afternoon on Sunday, before a boat picked us up and took us back to the main island.

Strong waves at Kenutu

But that wasn't the end of the weekend. A couple of hours later, we all went to Jason's house for sushi and to say goodbye to Amanda and Alex who are leaving Tuesday. One of the Japanese volunteers brought some sashimi she had made with onions. It was delicious. Jason, a fellow American who lives here, made traditional sushi rolls from fresh tuna along with miso soup.

Finally, I got home and slept in my own bed for the first time in four days.

LIFE IN VAVA'U
Saturday, August 30, 2008

The following was written by Joey 'Afitu Manfredo, who is the longest serving volunteer currently in Tonga. He is also our volunteer leader. He agreed to allow me to post this article about his recent visit to Vava'u.

Life in Vava'u

By Joey Manfredo

"My Friday afternoon shopping excursions to Neiafu are the equivalent of me riding the train two hours from Connecticut to New York City to buy a roll of toilet paper." -Sarah Kate Weaver

They are creative, inquisitive, welcoming and patriotic. They demonstrate perseverance in their work and support one another in their projects. After mixing in regular hilarity, the Peace Corps volunteers of Vava'u fully encapsulate their island's motto: Fatafata mafana.

Creative: Since the inception of foreign products to Tonga, PCVs have been facilitating trash pick-ups in Vava'u. Trash is always collected, but typically done half-heartedly and oftentimes the important messaging of proper disposal and recycling is lost. This was not the case at the Vava'u Faka'ofo'ofa Neiafu Clean-Up last month. PCVs Jessie Shepherd, Alex Crabtree, Jessica Bonthius and Sarah LaRosa developed a trash scavenger hunt in which individuals were given a certain number of points, depending on the type of trash they turned in, and were awarded prizes ranging from candy to Chinese cabbage seedlings. Cans that were collected were reused to pot the seedlings. Literature was distributed to parents. The Vava'u officers of the Ministries of Health, Environment, Labor and Tourism spoke to the crowd at the busy Saturday morning market. It was the most complete event of its nature that I've seen. Standing there that Saturday, taking in the program, I was proud to be a PCV.

Inquisitive: It's easy to read and ask questions about culture—but it takes a little more to get knee-deep in the stuff—especially in the dark, at 6 a.m., off the coast of 'Utungake. Jessica Bonthius is learning how to kupenga—net fish! Sorry to just burst forth with that, but it's too exciting to waste time with cutesy language. It's even more impressive because—except for fingota—fishing is a male-dominated field. It's a testament to Jessica's integration into her community, language skills, and overall Faka-Tonganess that she was taken under the kupenga fishermens' wings, er, fins.

Welcoming: Oftentimes, a PCVs house is his/her sanctuary. I enjoy conversing and visiting with neighbors, but freely admit that I have always tried to keep my actual home a fortress of solitude. So, I have great respect for volunteers who open their homes to neighbors. Sarah Kate Weaver goes beyond this and essentially has converted her living room into a playroom. During my visit to Hunga, kids were in and out, playing Go Fish, Uno and participating in "Skate's Great Candy

Exchange." Skate offers candy in return for fresh Hungan fruit. She even has a little resource library full of kids books and educational materials.

Patriotic: Instead of just eating hot dogs and lighting firecrackers to celebrate the Fourth of July, the Vava'u PCVs acted on the word's of Peace Corps' founding father, President John F. Kennedy—"Ask not what your country can do for you, but what you can do for your country"—and raised the flag on an uninhabited island, claiming it for America.

Perseverance: With Environment Week looming a few days on the horizon, the local Ministry of Environment rep reached out to PCVs Jessica Bonthius, James Barbour and Jessie Shepherd to help him put together a last-minute program, with no budget and no direction from the ministry in Tongatapu. Instead of telling the rep he was too late, they cleared their schedules and planned environment-focused events that included the introduction of a recycling bin to Vava'u Side School, along with a demo on its use.

Support: Senior PCV Alex Crabtree remarked to me how supportive the Vava'u volunteers are of one another. Without request, PCVs offer help to facilitate or just drop by nearly all events their fellow islanders are involved in. Regarding support, I have been most impressed with a simple happening at their monthly All-Vol. meeting. As the meeting came to a close, VAC-rep LaRosa asked if anyone had anything to add. Senoni took the opportunity to ask the more senior CE PCVs for advice on what activities she could do with her students during lulls in the school day. Around the meeting circle, people shared creative suggestions. It was so nice to see PCVs talking work with one another, sharing ideas and experiences.

Hilarity: Rose found herself in kid overload. In addition to teaching at Toula GPS, she runs the town library and helps kids with schoolwork from her house. At some point, everyone needs a break—but at this particular moment, tired from a long school day and longing for alone time, Rose couldn't think of a way out. Then it happened: DING. . . DING. . . DING. Rose politely asked the kids to leave her house so she could change for the weekday evening church service. To the delight of the Toula villagers, she found her respite in the halls of a village church.

All of the Vava'u PCVs are doing exceptional work. Here are just a few more tidbits:

• Amanda Strickler's morning exercise routine has inspired her neighbor, Lucy, to begin daily fakamalohisino and inspired local Internet guy Sione 4 to exclaim to partner Justin Smith that "Amanda is fitness."

• Stan Luker has turned the Vava'u Youth Congress Computer Lab free-for-all into an actual, functioning Internet cafe that is sustaining itself.

• I feel as though I should write this line about Amy in Tongan. She's already speaking more fluent Tongan than I speak English

• Though Steve was the last of Group 73 to arrive, he's already become the most well-known by advising nearly every business in town. He's also stumbled upon a seemingly inherent skill at fixing cash registers. Next time you're at Bounty in Vava'u, admire his work before checking out the view of the tahi.

- Justin continues to manage his time between IT advising at TCC with grassroots work maintaining the CPUs at the Leimatu'a computer center.

Steve Hunsicker

THE CASE FOR A MORE EFFECTIVE PEACE CORPS
Sunday, September 7, 2008

I have been closely following some of the debate over the future of Peace Corps and whether it is still an effective and necessary organization. *The Washington Post* recently reported on the cutbacks affecting Peace Corps, and several months ago, a former Peace Corps country director questioned the effectiveness of the organization in an op-ed piece in *The New York Times*. Both presidential candidates, John McCain and Barack Obama, have called for an expansion of the Peace Corps, and the National Peace Corps Association has just launched a campaign to double the size of the Peace Corps by 2011.

While I'm far removed from the politics of Washington, I do think it makes sense to increase the role of Peace Corps, but there are some important lessons that can be found right here in Tonga. Tonga is a beautiful place; it has the most fertile soil in the world, an educated population with a literacy rate higher than the United States and a rich culture. These are attributes that could make significant improvements to the Tongan economy if properly utilized.

One look around Tonga, and especially Vava'u, and you would think that such a wonderful place would attract a lot of tourists. There are islands where world-class resorts could be built, and certainly eco-tourism could flourish in a place like Tonga. There are not many places left in the world, and certainly not in the South Pacific, where the culture is as preserved as in Tonga.

Tonga would be a great spot for some multi-national company to locate a call center. The population speaks English, is naturally friendly and wages are very low. When it is 11 p.m. on the West Coast of the United States, it is 7 p.m. in the evening here (the next day).

Farming should be a no-brainer. The rich soil and abundant undeveloped land make the possibility of harvesting crops for export a real possibility. Tongans will tell you that "anything" will grow here, and for the most part, that is true.

So then, why with all these possibilities is Tonga a developing country whose top source of income is from foreign aid? It's not an easy answer.

Let's start with the amount of foreign aid that Tonga receives. It comes not just from foreign governments like the USA, Japan, Australia, New Zealand and China, but from individuals. In fact, there are more Tongans living abroad than there are in Tonga. Most of the overseas Tongans send money back to Tonga to support their families. Remittances from overseas are what make the Tonga economy go.

This is not a new phenomenon. Tongans have been living on handouts for years, and they see nothing wrong with it. Unfortunately, the free money can have an adverse effect on a Tongan's desire to work. Why work to develop a business when you know you will have everything you need to survive given to you for free?

However, that is just part of the dilemma. By law, all land is controlled by the king and the nobles, and only Tongans can own land. In exchange for being allowed to own the land, they have to share part of what they grow. A foreigner cannot own land, nor can a foreign company.

There are ways around this law. If you marry a Tongan, the land can be passed down to your kids. Land can also be leased to outsiders. Generally, a Tongan who owns land that he paid nothing for can make money by leasing it out if it is in the right location. It's another source of free cash. However, the government restricts the types of businesses that a non-Tongan can own. For example, it is illegal for an outsider to run a bakery, a grocery store or to be an electrician or plumber. The government allows exceptions for businesses that it deems Tongans do not have the skills to run. This includes most tourism-related businesses such as bars and restaurants. However, if you are an outsider and want to run one of these businesses, you will only be given a visa to operate it for two years. At the end of the two years, you have to reapply and hope you are given another two years. And depending on your business, your prices may be fixed by the government, so you can't sell any higher (or lower) than the set price. In other cases, you may only be allowed to mark up the price of the goods 15% above what you paid for them.

Ok, so if you can get past all of these hurdles and actually want to start a resort, a farm or a call center, you'll soon find yourself running into a brick wall.

Most of the "enabling" industries in Tonga are controlled by the government or run by Tongans, who have little incentive to invest and grow their businesses. The call center seems like a great idea until you realize that there is no fiber optic cable that connects Tonga to the rest of the world. What about using satellite? That exists, but the royal family sold most of the orbital slots to the Chinese government a few years ago. So if you want to use satellite, you have to use slots from another country.

What about building a resort for tourists? The only practical way to get people to Tonga is via airplane. That might be fine if you want to bring people to Tongatapu, which has regular international flights. However, the best destinations are on the outer islands, and the domestic airlines just don't measure up. Airlines Tonga, one of two airlines serving Tonga, just shut down for an "indefinite" period, stranding many passengers. Another problem for tourism businesses is that the airport, along with everything else in Tonga, shuts down on Sunday. So if a tourist wants to come for a week, he or she has to either leave on Saturday, cutting their vacation short by a day, or stay over until Monday just to get a flight. (Tourism businesses that offer lodging are allowed to be open on Sunday.)

That leaves the farm. There is plenty of land and ample rainfall. However, Tonga currently grows few crops that have any export value. The root crops that are the staple of the Tongan diet do not have a lot of demand outside of the South Pacific and are easily grown in other places. The exceptions are vanilla and perhaps pineapple. However, it takes a long time to grow vanilla, and so far, few Tongan farmers have embraced the crop. The price has also not been stable recently. Pineapple is widely grown but there are issues with exporting. Vava'u, where much of best pineapple is grown, has a ship just once a month to take crops outside of Tonga. And because Tonga has no fumigation equipment, many countries won't accept Tongan crops (and other products) for fear of bringing small insects into their country. Even if these obstacles could be overcome, pineapple is seasonal.

The challenge is that many Tongans and Tongan businesses don't have any experience in marketing their businesses and their country to the rest of the world. And not everyone thinks that making the changes necessary to attract foreign investors are worth it. If foreigners were allowed to own land, would they gobble up all the prime oceanfront land? Would they be responsible citizens or would the impact they have on Tonga change the culture and way of life forever? Would advances in farming and other industries end up putting Tongans out of work as technology replaces manual labor?

There are no easy answers, but I do think one way to start is by making some changes to the way Peace Corps works in Tonga and perhaps other parts of the world. Peace Corps is a grassroots organization, designed to work one-on-one with individuals in the host country to stimulate development and build capacity.

Why can't this same approach be taken to businesses and to the upper levels of government? Right now, Peace Corps is actively recruiting people who are over age 50 to serve worldwide. (I'm not quite in that group yet.) Imagine someone with real work experience who could sit down and work one-on-one with the leaders of business and government. Think of it as an "Executive" Peace Corps taking former business executives and former government leaders and pairing them with similar counterparts in Tonga.

Of course, that won't be easy either. Not only do you have to convince the business and government leaders of Tonga to accept Executive Peace Corps volunteers but also you have to recruit the experienced people to serve as volunteers. And Peace Corps will have to change too. Part of getting qualified volunteers into the key business and government jobs requires the Peace Corps in-country staff to be able to know well in advance the types of people who are coming to serve, so they can effectively find the proper position for each person. It makes no sense to convince the prime minister to take on a Peace Corps volunteer in his office if there is no volunteer qualified for that job in the pipeline. It also will take strong Peace Corps staff members with backgrounds in business in each country. These individuals will have to convince Tongan leaders of the benefits of working with experienced volunteers.

Right now, at least in Tonga, Peace Corps doesn't put volunteers in private businesses. To have an impact, that policy would have to change. Or, perhaps you assign a volunteer to three or four non-competitive businesses and another volunteer to the three or four competitors of those businesses.

I believe there will always be a place for the 20-something college graduates who make up the majority of Peace Corps volunteers. There are 24 new volunteers coming to Tonga next month. All but three are between the ages of 22 and 30. The other three, two men and a woman, are in their 60s. Of these, one is an education volunteer, one is a business volunteer and the other is in NGO development. It's good to see some older volunteers in the next group. (There are also two married couples arriving.) However, if Peace Corps is successful in bringing in more volunteers age 50+, hopefully there will also be new opportunities for their life and work experiences.

There are a lot of hurdles that would have to be overcome—not just in Tonga, but worldwide. Peace Corps has done a great job of teaching English and working with youth, but now I think it is time to take it to the next level. It won't be easy, but if done properly, it could change the way Americans are viewed in other countries and provide much needed assistance to those countries we serve.

BEAUTIFUL BRISBANE
Sunday, September 14, 2008

Before I left Tonga to come to Brisbane, I read the book, *In a Sunburnt Country*, by Bill Bryson. The book, which I thoroughly enjoyed, starts with the premise that most Americans don't know very much about Australia. It didn't take me long to realize that I was one of those Americans who didn't know much about this amazing country.

Brisbane is a beautiful, vibrant city—clean, modern with many outdoor activities. It's the capital of Queensland, and at least so far, the state has lived up to its nickname as "The Sunshine State." The city is built along the river, and it has many parks and outdoor cafes. It's a great town for walking.

The train system here is very efficient. You can get just about anywhere on a short train ride. Each day, I've tried to explore a different part of the city. The South Bank area has been my favorite so far. In addition to the manmade beach, there is a walk through a tropical rain forest and a good collection of museums and restaurants.

Today I'm downtown. I just went to Starbucks—my first visit in more than a year. The first day I was here, I went shopping at K-Mart. K-Mart has never been my favorite store, but I felt like a kid in a candy store with so much stuff I wanted to buy—things you just can't get in Tonga. I had a similar experience at the grocery store. I've also made it to Target but so far have avoided all of the typical American fast-food establishments like KFC, Subway and McDonalds.

One of the big attractions in downtown Brisbane is the Treasury Casino. It is in one of the oldest buildings in Brisbane and has been well preserved. The slots are mostly one- and two-cent machines, so you won't lose a lot without really trying.

The casino in Brisbane, Australia

My hotel room has a TV, which is also a treat. I've been without TV for the past year, and I've enjoyed watching not just the news but also the entertainment shows. Here in Australia, we have *60 Minutes, The Today Show, GMA, Meet the Press, Idol, Smarter Than a 5th Grader, Supermodel* and *Deal or No Deal*. The difference is that all of these shows are Australian versions of the ones we have in the USA. There are also a few shows from the USA like *NCIS* and *Beverly Hills 90210,* but most shows are pretty much targeted to the Australian audience.

Of course there are differences. I had to take a picture of this sign.

Billboard outside a Brisbane hospital

I saw it and had to wonder, what is a theatre nurse? Is that a nurse who acts? As it turns out, theatre is where a surgeon "performs" surgery. They don't call it an operating room or OR, it's called theatre. Hopefully, the surgeons all deliver outstanding performances.

I remarked to a friend of mine that I could live in Brisbane. I like it that much. However, I also have to remember that this is the first "real" city I've seen in a year. After living in a developing country for the past year, I wonder if I would have the same impression of Brisbane if I were fresh out of the USA. I think I would.

I've been particularly impressed with how eco-friendly this area is and how aware the residents are of the importance of preserving the environment. There is a campaign going on here now to urge residents to stop drinking bottled water and to drink the tap water instead. In taste tests, most Australians can't tell the difference between tap water and bottled water. (I've also been drinking the tap water, and it tastes fine.) According to the campaign, if you buy just one bottle of water, you could refill it every day for a year from the tap, come out ahead economically and help preserve the environment.

I'm only visiting Brisbane this trip, but I'm anxious to see more of Australia. Hopefully, next year I'll be able to make it back and see more of this country. While it is nice to be "down under" for a while, I'm also looking forward to getting back to Tonga.

SO LONG AUSTRALIA!
Tuesday, September 23, 2008

Hello from New Zealand. I'm on my way back to Tonga after just over two weeks in Brisbane, Australia. It's been quite a change from Tonga, but I'm ready to get back and resume my duties in the Peace Corps.

It's hard to explain the culture shock you experience going from a developing country like Tonga to a fully developed country like Australia. After almost a full year in Tonga, it is easy to forget what the rest of the world is like. When you spend every minute of your life surrounded by pigs running wild and roosters crowing at all hours, it's amazing how "silent" the sounds of a big city become. My first trip to the grocery store in Brisbane was like being in another world, and I guess I was. The produce section was so colorful with so many fruits and vegetables—some that I had forgotten even existed.

Once I got past the initial cultural issues, I found myself loving Brisbane. It's a great city, very clean and very environmentally friendly. I'll elaborate more on that in a minute, but first, I'll preface my comments by saying I haven't been in the USA for a year, so my frame of reference is a bit skewed. It's possible many of the same initiatives I saw in Australia are now underway back home as well.

Here's a small sampling of some of the cool things I saw related to the environment.

• The country just hosted a national "Walk to Work Day." Still to come is a "Leave Your Car at Home Day" when everyone will be encouraged to use mass transit. Both are efforts to get people out of their cars for both exercise and fuel efficiency.

• Many of the buildings have rainwater tanks attached to their gutters to collect rainwater. This is very common in Tonga, and rainwater is what I drink. But even in the downtown areas of Brisbane, you see the effort made to capture and conserve water. Every toilet is dual-flush, and most of the urinals are either no-flush or waterless. In parks, you see signs that say the city is watering plants with reclaimed water, and the parks also have tanks to gather the rainwater. (I've already mentioned the effort to get people to stop drinking bottled water.)

• The transit system is fast and well connected. It's easy to get a train to most locations and all stations are connected by buses and ferry service with free transfers. Even in off-peak times, you never have to wait more than 30 minutes for a train. Compare this to South Florida where Tri-Rail trains only run every two hours on the weekend (as of when I left for Peace Corps).

• Most of the cars are small. Not tiny, but sedan size and smaller. No huge SUVs. (Yep, I drove an SUV for probably 10 years.)

• The TV news stations do "green updates" during prime-time, talking about other efforts underway to be more eco-friendly.

There is a lot more to Australia than just the eco-friendly initiatives I've mentioned. However, the concern for the environment really made an impression on me.

I spent my last night in Brisbane eating a GREAT meal. I had some of the best lamb I've ever eaten and walked away from the restaurant stuffed like I haven't been in a long time.

My plane should start boarding soon. It's three hours late. Yes, clearly some things haven't changed during my year away. I'll be in Tonga for three more months before I venture out again. That's when I'm heading to Virginia and Florida for the Christmas holidays.

ONE YEAR IN TONGA
Monday, September 29, 2008

It was one year ago today that I walked out of my home in West Palm Beach, said goodbye to my friends and family and began the adventure of a lifetime.

Since that day, the people I associate and interact with on a daily basis are those I have known for just one year or less. It amazes me to think that I have seen no one I knew prior to September 30th, 2007 in the past year. However, I'm also amazed by the awesome friends I've made. While I may have only known my fellow volunteers for just a year, I've spent more time with many of them than with some of my long-time friends back home.

When I first met the people in my training group a year ago, it seemed the only thing we had in common was that we were all going to Tonga. For the most part, we were all strangers, even though some of us had been in contact with each other on blogs, Facebook and MySpace. We had 10 married people— something that was pretty unusual for Peace Corps at the time—12 single women and 11 single men. We were 33 people, and we would get to know each other very quickly. Today, one year later, we have 29 people from my group still here in Tonga. It's easy to understand why so many of us have stuck it out because even with all the problems, this is a pretty awesome place.

After spending two weeks in Australia, I found myself missing Tonga and my friends here. I think it took being away to realize how attached I have become. I received a great welcome back from the people at the bank where I work, and they even sent a car to pick me up at the airport. It was a great surprise to walk out of the Vava'u airport and immediately see a friendly face. Friday, I drove around to see several of my clients—people with whom I have worked in the past year. They also gave me a very warm welcome back. One woman told me she was afraid I wouldn't come back, which fits with the attitude of many Tongans who can't understand why a palangi would choose to live in Tonga when they could live in Australia, New Zealand or the USA.

Saturday afternoon, I joined most of my fellow volunteers and about 15 other Americans to watch the presidential debate, which was shown at one of the bars here. After the debate, I was talking with a couple of tourists from California who had watched the debate with us. As they were getting up to leave, they turned to us and thanked us for doing our part to serve our country and to help improve America's reputation abroad. I often receive thanks from Tongans for assisting them, but here were some fellow Americans thanking me. That really touched me.

I doubt the couple will ever know how much I appreciated their words, but it was a great way to close out my first year in Tonga and begin the second.

Malo aupito pae 'ofa atu (Thank you very much and love to you) for the support my family and friends have given me in the past year. I couldn't have done it without you.

THE OUTER ISLAND ADVENTURE
Thursday, October 2, 2008

By Peace Corp's definition, the island of Vava'u where I live is an outer island. That simply means that I don't live on the main island of Tongatapu. We have electricity, running water and cell phone service.

But my "outer island" experience is much different from that of the volunteers and Tongans who live in the villages on the small, really "outer" islands. They have no electricity, they take bucket baths with water they haul from a tank filled by rainwater and their choice of food is extremely limited. To go anywhere, you must take a boat.

On Thursday, I had the chance to visit six villages on three different outer islands in the Vava'u group. The bank is hosting a workshop for outer islanders next week, and my counterpart Kolokesa and I went to deliver invitation letters to participants.

The first stop was 'Otea, which is close enough to the main island that a good swimmer could probably swim across the channel. The proximity also means that you can still get cell phone service. We arrived in 'Otea around 7:30 a.m., and I immediately called my fellow volunteer Amy, who lives on the island. Seven-thirty in the morning may seem early by American standards, but I knew Amy would have been up for hours. It's a small village, and when she answered the phone, all she had to do was look out her door to see us. Amy, like most people who live on these islands, goes to bed when it gets dark and awakens when it gets light. The only illumination they have in their homes at night is from kerosene lanterns or candles.

While Kolokesa delivered the invitation letters, Amy showed me around her village and her house. She has a big house by Tongan standards, and we spent almost as much time looking at her house as we did seeing the village. After leaving Amy, we boarded the boat and headed to the village of Kapa. It's on the same island but too far to walk. Kapa is not on the water. We hiked quite a ways up a hill to find this village, which at first glance looked like it had been abandoned. Actually, even at second and third glance, it still looked abandoned. It reminded me of a hollow that you would find buried in the mountains of Appalachia.

Not only are there only a few people in this village, but they don't get many visitors. It's just not that easy to find. We finally found a person and asked him if there were any businesses here, like a small shop or a weaving hut. The answer, not surprisingly, was, "No."

From Kapa, we headed to another island and the village of Taunga. Taunga is an oceanfront village with big beautiful banyan trees along its beach. It was pouring rain, and we took refuge inside the house of a Tongan family. There was a small boy there who kept looking at me with wide eyes. I guessed that he probably hasn't seen many white people and may never have had one inside his home before. I reached in my pocket and handed him a fresh mango that I had picked up earlier. He devoured it, never taking his eyes off of me.

After waiting out the rain, we headed to our third island of the day and the village of Nuapapu. This village is also a hike from the dock, but you can see it from the water. It sits on a cliff overlooking the water, but you have to follow a trail to get there. It's beautiful walk, and there are fresh mangos everywhere, both on the ground and in all the trees. As we approached the village, there was a metal fence obviously designed to keep the pigs in the village and out of the forest. Once in the village, you could tell they had lots of pigs. I've never seen so much pig crap in all my life. It was everywhere, and to make matters worse, it had been raining, so the pig crap was mixed in with the mud and it ran over our sandals. It was pretty gross. As I was walking around, I was thinking that the village should be named Nui-poop-poo.

As soon as we got back to the water, I thoroughly washed my feet and shoes in the ocean before getting back in the boat. We then headed to Matamaka, which is on the same island. This village is now better known because there is a new beer being marketed in Tonga called Matamaka. Here there are no fences and the pigs wander right down to the water. However, it's a much cleaner village and probably the most active of any place we had visited so far. Our final stop of the day was in Falevai. It's on the other side of the island where 'Otea is located, and it is where we will be holding our workshop on Wednesday. As we walked through the village, we heard the familiar Tongan cry of "*Ha'u kai*," which simply means, "Come eat." Tongans almost always have food to share and share it generously. We went in, and there was a Tongan man who pulled out two pans, one with root crops in it and the other with pork. I looked for a piece of meat first, but it was all just pork fat. My counterpart was chowing down on the pork fat but noticed that I was not eating. He found me a piece with a little bit of meat on it, which I ate. I then reached into the pot of root crops and picked up a small piece of ufi, which is probably the most common of all Tongan foods. As I was putting it into my mouth, I noticed that there were teeth marks on this piece. That meant someone had eaten part of it and put it back in the pot. That's not unusual in Tonga. Food is shared and generally eaten with fingers, just as we were doing.

Vava'u Youth Congress

That wasn't the end of my day. Thursday evening, I joined my fellow volunteers at a fundraising dinner for the Vava'u Youth Congress, an NGO for the local youth. It was a charity auction and a Tongan feast. Most of the people attending were tourists or non-Tongans who live in Vava'u. The entire event was coordinated by my fellow volunteer Stan, who is the Peace Corps representative at the youth congress.

Stan did a great job coordinating everything. James and I even helped out a bit as guest auctioneers.

VAVA'U PEACE CORPS UPDATES
Wednesday, October 8, 2008

Since I've been a Peace Corps volunteer, we have never had every Vava'u volunteer in the same room at the same time. Generally, there are one or sometimes two people missing. Often it is because two of our volunteers live on outer islands, and we don't see them as often. Last Friday, to celebrate the one-year anniversary of Group 73, we ended up with every Vava'u volunteer in the Peace Corps office at the same time.

All of the Vava'u volunteers

The photo shows the people I associate with most often. From left to right are: Sarah Kate, Jessica, me, James, Sarah, Shannon, Stan, Amy and Janis. Our group will soon start to get even smaller as the members of Group 72 start to complete their service. They will be wrapping up just about the time the new group of volunteers will swear in and begin their service.

There should now be 24 new Peace Corps trainees in Tonga. I haven't met them yet. They were scheduled to arrive on the main island this morning. They are due to arrive in Vava'u next Wednesday and will train here for six weeks.

Solitia

There is a new member of my household here in Vava'u. His name is Solitia, which means "soldier" in Tongan.

Steve Hunsicker's dog "Solitia"

Solitia has spent the last two years with Justin, who just completed his Peace Corps service and has left the country. Solitia is a great dog, but she doesn't like to be left alone. The first few days he was at my house, Solitia climbed back up the hill to Justin's old house. Then last week, he followed me to work, and I had to walk him back home.

The most amazing moment was last Friday when I joined all of the other volunteers and about 25 other people to watch the vice presidential debate. We all gathered at a bar that is down on the water at the far end of town. To get there, you have to take the main road, walk down some steep steps, go past another bar and around several corners. Even for a person, it can be a hard place to find. About an hour into the debate, Solitia came walking into the bar. I have no idea how he found the place or even knew we were all there. I had no leash, so I coaxed him back up the stairs and to the Peace Corps office, which is nearby. From there, I found an old piece of wire and used it as a leash to get him back up the hill to my house.

I'm sure he is a bit confused still about where Justin is, but I was amazed he was able to find us.

Tapa for Cars?

I've been meaning to share this photo for a while and haven't gotten around to it. As you walk up the hill to my house, there is a car repair shop with a bunch of abandoned vehicles out front. The road to my house is also the same road you would take to get to the royal palace. During the coronation activities here in Vava'u in August, everyone cleaned up and there was no litter to be found. That presented a problem for the owners of the repair shop. Instead of moving the cars, they decided to cover them in tapa.

Junk car concealed with tapa

Tapa is the bark of a tree that has been pounded by hand and then stained. It's probably the most famous type of Tongan handicraft, and it takes many months to create a full-size piece of tapa. A tapa the size of these would sell for well over a thousand dollars. I found it funny that the owners would take something so valuable and use it to cover up junked cars. The day after the king left, the tapa was gone.

MY RETURN TO TELEVISION
Wednesday, October 15, 2008

It has been 16 months since I walked out of a TV newsroom for the last time. Since then, I haven't had anything to do with the content of television programs. That changes tonight when a program I put together will air on the local TV station here in Vava'u.

But this program is unlike anything I've ever done before, and by USA standards, I would be the first to say it sucks. However, by Tongan standards, it's a leap forward in local TV.

The TV station here has been on the air for just less than a year. The equipment is very basic, and they have no way to edit what they shoot. For a 30-minute program, they shoot 30 minutes of tape and then play it back the way it was shot. If there is something that must be edited out, they will dub the tape to a DVD, stop the tape, skip past the part that needs to come out and then start the DVD again. The station only broadcasts in the evenings unless there is a special event. It's most popular programs are those that it downlinks off of Sky TV (like DirecTV) and rebroadcasts, especially rugby matches. In the USA, of course, that would be illegal and copyright infringement. Here it is just the way they do things. (Tongans see no reason to pay for something they can get for free, which is why all the software and movies here are bootleg versions.)

The TV program I put together is about the Alonga program, which is a program for mentally and physically disabled Tongans. The group wanted to get something on TV and asked me if I would help. I said sure, not fully realizing what I was getting myself into. I did tell them that if I was going to edit it, I would prefer to shoot it myself, if they could get me a camera to use.

Last Thursday, the guy who runs the local TV station showed up at the Alonga class with his gear, which was a decent pro-consumer camera. He handed me the camera, tripod and microphones and left. As I was shooting, the battery died. I tried the second battery; it was dead, as was the third. I had about 10 minutes of raw footage at this point and no interviews—clearly not enough for a 30-minute program. One of the Alonga volunteers got in her car and tracked the guy down, who returned with a charger. However, as it turned out, the problem was with the camera. To get the batteries to work, you had to switch to play mode, back to record mode and then the batteries worked fine. (Of course, he didn't tell me this when he dropped off the gear.)

One of the Alonga teachers interviewed two parents who had children in the class, while I manned the camera. I then interviewed the teacher, asking my questions in English and having her respond in Tongan. Finally, I had about 50 minutes worth of tape and said I was done, even though I had only a vague idea of what the interviewees had said.

I packed up all of the gear, and the guy from the TV station asked for the tape I had just shot. I asked him if I could hold onto it until I got it transferred to my computer where I would edit it. At this point, he told me the program aired in a few hours and he would just air it the way it was shot. Clearly this would not work. It was not shot the way he was used to shooting. After a few minutes of discussion, we agreed that I would come to the TV station on Monday to dub the tape into my computer, and he would delay airing the program until tonight (Wednesday).

Once I had everything on my computer, I started editing. I had decided not to use a narrator but to use just video and interviews (sound bites) together to tell the story. With a narrator, I would have had to write a script, had it translated into Tongan, get it recorded and then edited. I simply didn't have the time to get that done by today.

Using a dictionary and my basic Tongan skills, I went to work on the video editing. It was a lot harder than I expected. It was especially hard to edit down the sound bites because my grammar is not good enough to know if the next word or phrase is relevant.

Now you might be wondering why I didn't have anyone from the Alonga program with me. Turns out, they were all in a conference and were not available, or they didn't speak Tongan either. I finally recruited my counterpart at the Tonga Development Bank to help me. I could not have done it without him.

So I got everything edited, and I was as happy as I could be with what I had, but it was only 22-minutes long, not the necessary 30. What to do? In the USA, I would have grabbed a camera and shot some more interviews and footage. But I didn't have a camera and had to make do with what I had. I decided to put together a basic music video at the end and edit the footage I had with some Tongan music. So I put together a four-minute music video and then inserted it twice into the end of the program. It was now 30 minutes.

In a million years, I would NEVER have done something like this in the USA. But I'm not in the USA, I'm in Tonga. As I said earlier, I might think it sucks, but an edited local program on TV is a first in Vava'u. And since the people here have only had TV for less than a year, it will probably look pretty good to them.

I have been teaching myself to edit. Even though I was in TV for 23 years, I did very little editing. However, since being in Peace Corps, I've been playing around with it. I put together two goodbye videos for fellow volunteers who were wrapping up their service. And my friend Scot and I have been working together on a video for Peace Corps, but Scot is doing the editing on that one.

Group 74 Arrives

They're here! The newest Peace Corps trainees arrived in Tonga last Thursday. These 24 folks make up Peace Corps Group 74.

Tonga group 74

After spending a few days on the main island of Tongatapu, the new group flew up here to Vava'u on Tuesday. They are very lucky that they got to fly. My group had to take a 22-hour boat trip to get here. However, the boat is out of service and being repaired in Fiji, so they missed out on that experience.

My fellow volunteers and I met the new group at the airport to briefly say hello as they left to meet their homestay families. They will be here in Vava'u for six weeks, and we are all looking forward to getting to know them better. I'll get to know the business volunteers as I'm helping out with their training.

Tonga Development Bank Workshop

Last week, we held an "Improving Your Business" workshop in the village of Falevai, which is located on an outer island. The workshop was designed to help Tongans learn important business skills, such as recordkeeping and money management. There was no electricity in the village and no tables and chairs. We rented a generator, so we could show our presentation on a screen to the participants who all sat on the floor.

ECONOMICS, EARTHQUAKES, PARTIES AND CASTRATION
Wednesday, October 22, 2008

OK, I admit, that's kind of a weird headline. But those are four things that have happened in the past week here in Tonga.

I'll talk about castration first, since that's probably the one that jumps out at you. As you may know, I recently adopted a dog, Solitia, that belonged to a Peace Corps volunteer who completed his service. Solitia is two years old, great with people but a bit aggressive towards other male dogs. He's never been fixed. Part of the reason is that there are no veterinarians in Vava'u and there is only one vet in the entire Kingdom of Tonga.

Last weekend, I heard that a vet from America and her husband were on a yacht visiting Vava'u. That's how the coconut wireless works. I met her husband on Saturday, and I can thank our unreliable electricity for the meeting. We've been without electricity several times recently; the longest was on Saturday when it was out for about five hours. It's gotten very hot again, and it was pretty miserable with no fan running in the house. I decided to head down to a local restaurant that is on the water to sip a few beers and enjoy the ocean breeze until the power came back.

That's where I bumped into Ben, the vet's husband, who told me his wife would probably be happy to fix my dog for me and already had plans to fix another dog next week. Today, I took Solitia to have it done and I watched. It's the first time I've watched an operation take place, and it was interesting to see Shawn, the vet, work. Solitia was knocked out the entire time. He's now recovering.

I first heard about the vet at a party at my house on Friday night. We gathered to say so long to Sarah Kate, the first member of Group 72 to complete her service.

Sarah Kate has spent the last two years living in Hunga, a small village on an outer island. She is the only American in her village, and it took a long boat ride for her to get into the main island here in Vava'u. While I think we all have different challenges in Peace Corps, I think Sarah Kate had more than most. It's not easy living in a place with no electricity, running water or easy communication to the outside world. However, she made the most of it, and I know her villagers are going to miss her, as will all of us.

Steve Hunsicker welcomes Tongan and American friends to his house

It was a big gathering, probably the most people I have ever had in my house, including a bunch of the Peace Corps staff who are here in Vava'u training the new group of volunteers.

I had a chance this week to meet with 10 of the new trainees. I worked with the trainees who will be in the Peace Corps business program on both Tuesday and Wednesday, and I am looking forward to getting to know them and the other members of their group.

During my first session with them, we discussed the Tongan economy and the way business gets done in Tonga. I gave them all an article I recently saw online that I thought did a good job of explaining some of the issues here in Tonga.

Finally, there was the earthquake on Sunday. It hit the main island of Nuku'alofa, and I happened to be on the phone with my friend Scot, who lives there, when it occurred.

I never felt much, but James was sitting in the yard with our landlord when it hit and said he could feel a slight vibration on the ground. We're about 150 miles north of Nuku'alofa, so it didn't have the same strength. I guess it made the news in the USA because my mom's cousins, Howard and Gloria, immediately sent me an e-mail to make sure I was okay. It's nice to have people checking on you. So now you know, it has been a week of economics, earthquakes, parties and castration. Now perhaps that headline doesn't seem so weird after all. It just reflects my life for the past seven days.

FISHING AND PHONE NUMBERS
Saturday, October 25, 2008

Fishing in Tonga

I went fishing Saturday with two Tongan friends. Both have a lot more experience fishing than I have, and I was keen to get out and enjoy the day. As it turned out, I caught the only fish of the day, a small grouper, which I landed shortly after we threw our lines in the water.

Steve Hunsicker with his "catch of the day"

However, the trip was a great Tongan experience. My two friends, like most Tongans, don't have rods and reels. They have fishing line, some fishhooks and some weights. My weight was a small piece of rebar with the hook tied about 12 inches above it. We used pieces of smaller fish as bait. I felt a tug on my line, but didn't really think I had a fish. However, when I pulled it up, there was the fish in the photo above. Six hours later and it was still the only fish we had caught, but we did do a great job of feeding the fish underneath us because they kept eating the bait.

The fish weren't the only ones eating. When we first got out on the water, my friends pulled out a big container of probably 20 sandwiches for the three of us. Then, once we got to the spot where we dropped anchor, out came more food—a big can of fatty meat and a huge bowl of root crops. Tongans love to eat and even when fishing, we had more food than the three of us could eat.

As we headed back to shore, we ran out of gas. We were near the shore, but still a good distance from where the car was parked. We ended up spending more than an hour swimming the boat back.

New Phone Number

I now have a new phone number. I had to switch after Digicel customers were shut off from being able to call TCC cell phones and landlines. Since most of the people I know have TCC, I finally made the switch. Digicel launched here in May with a huge fanfare and a great marketing campaign. Unfortunately, their service has not lived up to its hype.

Because of the problems, the Peace Corps has had to issue Digicel phones to its key staff. In the event of an emergency, we would be unable to call Peace Corps or even the police from our Digicel phones. There has also been another annoying problem here in Vava'u. If a Digicel customer sends a text message to a TCC customer, the TCC customer will get the message 25-30 times. I didn't really want to give up my phone number but finally realized it wasn't worth the hassle to keep the Digicel phone.

Now here's a funny story about my new phone number, compliments of my friend Alice, who also switched from Digicel to TCC. The last four digits of both our new phone numbers are 66. If you say the number 66 fast in Tongan, you are actually saying a slang term. So unless I'm careful, when I give out my new phone number, I'll be saying my number is "125 bend over."

Empty Shelves in Vava'u

It has been three weeks since a boat has brought supplies to Vava'u. All of our groceries, supplies, mail etc. come on one of two boats that usually arrive on Wednesday each week. Both boats have been out of service, and you can tell this by walking into any store in Vava'u. A small boat did show up on

Saturday with some chicken, other food and some mail, but there is still not a lot in the stores. But don't worry, we are not going hungry. Tongans grow a lot of their own crops, and there is still plenty to eat, just not the stuff (like chicken and milk) that is imported from New Zealand.

We are expecting a boat this week.

SAILING, SNORKELING AND SCARY STUFF
Sunday, November 2, 2008

It has been a busy few days in Tonga but also a lot of fun, especially the last weekend.

Halloween in Tonga

The weekend began on Friday night with Halloween. Halloween is not celebrated in Tonga, at least not in the way we do in the USA. But that didn't stop the Americans here in Vava'u from dressing up. Of course, there are no places to buy costumes in Vava'u, so we all had to improvise. I decided to be John McCain, while my friends Jason and Jessica dressed up as Joe the Plumber and Sarah Palin.

I put a lot of white powder in my hair and wore a t-shirt with the word "Maverick" on it. Our costumes weren't all that scary, but it was a lot of fun.

Sailing and Snorkeling

Saturday, we set off for a day of sailing and snorkeling aboard *Manuoku*, a really great sailboat that we have used before. In addition to the Vava'u volunteers, we were joined by Trent, Lara and Mikala, who are visiting from Tongatapu. We also had five Japanese volunteers with us.

There wasn't a lot of wind when we started, so we had to motor out of the Port of Refugee, but eventually, Captain Steve had enough wind to raise the sails. We headed to Port Maurelle for some snorkeling and sunbathing.

It is now summer here, and this is really a great time to get on the water in Vava'u. Most of the tourists are gone and the water is warm.

ELECTION DAY IN TONGA
Sunday, November 9, 2008

For the first time since I was 16 years old, I was not working on election night. Instead, I spent the afternoon at a local bar and restaurant called Mango, watching the results on CNN International with about 40 other Americans.

Mango sits directly over the water, and you can see the water beneath through the cracks in the floorboards. It's also one of the very few places here with satellite television.

We started gathering around 11 a.m. on Wednesday morning, which was 5 p.m. Tuesday night on the East Coast of the USA. By the time the first polls closed at 6 p.m. ET, we had a crowd of Peace Corps volunteers, Peace Corps trainees and an assortment of Americans who either live in Vava'u or are here visiting.

It was a pretty partisan crowd. With the exception of a couple of McCain supporters, almost everyone in the bar was supporting Obama.

When the election got called, there were huge cheers and even some tears as the Americans here united behind their new president. Later, when John McCain took to the air to give his concession speech, there was complete silence. No one moved or said a word as he spoke. Everyone was taking in every word he said. It was a much different story when Obama began his speech. Lots of cheering and more tears of joy.

After his speech, probably half the people left at Mangos decided to go for a swim in the Pacific, jumping off the deck and into the crystal blue water. Most of the Tongans looked at us like we were crazy.

I've had several questions about the election of Obama from Tongans. I would have to say the people here in Tonga are impressed that the US has elected a black president. They don't all understand it exactly, but they know that someone with dark skin has been selected. Many have the perception that all Americans are white and rich. Even in our group, we have a couple of African-American volunteers, and some Tongans think they are from Africa and not America.

A Mini-Reunion

There have been lots of Tonga Peace Corps volunteers visiting Vava'u in the past few weeks—volunteers we don't see very often. Two volunteers (Scot and Mikala) were sent here for work; several more (Casa, Lara, Phil) are here to assist with Peace Corps training; and a few more (Grant, Trent, Heather) are here for the VAC or Volunteer Advisory Committee meeting. It's been great to catch up with all of them.

Camping at Lotuma

We had planned to camp on Friday night on the island of Lotuma, which was the site of our Peace Corps July 4th celebration. However with the weather forecast predicting a 100% chance of rain, many decided not to go. I still went, along with six others, and we had a great time until the rain started. Unfortunately, as I got into my tent, I found out it was leaking, and I ended up spending the night sleeping in a big puddle of water. We called early Saturday morning for a boat to come get us to take us back to Neiafu. The rain didn't stop until Sunday morning.

Many of us went sailing together last weekend and had planned to take the Peace Corps trainees out on the water this weekend, but that didn't happen because of the weather. Hopefully, we will be able to reschedule that trip.

WATCH WHAT WE DO IN TONGA!
Wednesday, November 12, 2008

Another busy week here in Vava'u. I've actually had to start keeping a calendar to remember all of my appointments. Many have to do with the training of the new Peace Corps volunteers, but I have also been pretty busy at work at the Tonga Development Bank.

Peace Corps Tonga Video

Earlier this year, my friend Scot and I put together a video about life in Peace Corps Tonga. The country director asked us to do it to help explain Tonga to the incoming trainees and also to send to Peace Corps headquarters in Washington. Despite many issues with cameras, editing, audio, etc., we finally got it done. The video is online at:
http://www.vimeo.com/shunsicker/volunteers

Root Canal

I went to bed Monday night feeling fine. About an hour after I crawled in, I started having this pounding pain in my jaw and mouth. I could not sleep because it hurt so much. Tuesday morning, I called my friend Takako, who is a dentist and Japanese volunteer. After an exam and an x-ray, she told me I needed a root canal. I am so thankful that we have Takako here. I can't imagine what would have happened if I had had to rely on the Tongan health system. Thankfully, my mouth is much better. I go back to see her again on Friday to have the canal sealed.

The good news is that the part of the hospital where the dental clinic is located has been cleaned and painted since my last visit, when I thought it was a pretty scary place.

Tonga Development Bank Workshop

One of the things I regularly do here in Tonga is help put together workshops for business owners and potential owners to assist them in improving or starting their businesses. Wednesday, we conducted the last workshop of the year here in Vava'u. We had 36 people show up, our largest crowd to date. (In addition, we also had 10 Peace Corps trainees watching.)

I will be traveling to the Ha'apai group of islands in early December to conduct three additional workshops on outer islands.

HANGING WITH GROUP 74
Sunday, November 16, 2008

I got to spend Saturday hanging out on a boat with the Peace Corps trainees who are scheduled to become volunteers next month. They have been training here in Vava'u for the past month.

It was a big day for them. Just before the boat trip, they received their site assignments, meaning they now know where they will live for the next two years. We've all been wondering who will end up in Vava'u, and we got our answer on Saturday as well. (The newest members of Team Vava'u are Saskia, Scott, Bronzie, Jenny, Katie, Regina and Chad.)

We started our day with a visit to Mariner's Cave; this is the cave with the entrance that is below sea level. It's the third time I've been inside, but this was the first time I've done it at high tide. Several of the trainees came inside too.

After that, we went to Swallows Cave. Swallows is a big cave, large enough for our boat to get inside. (We were on a 40-person, whale-watching boat.)

This will be Sarah's last trip to the cave. She will complete her service in a few weeks. However, she decided to take a big leap for her last visit—climbing up and then jumping into the water below. The water is really deep, probably at least 50 feet, so even though she jumped a long way, there was plenty of water to cushion her jump. It's also a spectacular site because there is a second entrance to the cave at the bottom, which illuminates the ocean floor below.

YES, WE DO WORK IN PEACE CORPS!
Friday, November 21, 2008

I got an e-mail from a friend of mine in West Palm Beach last week who is a regular reader of my updates. He said he sometimes wonders if I'm on vacation here in Tonga. Then, after I posted some photos on Facebook of our sailing trip last week with the new Peace Corps trainees, one of the trainees' friends commented that Peace Corps looked like a big fraternity party.

I can fully understand why both of these people might have a bit of a distorted view of what my fellow volunteers and I are doing in Tonga. I tend to write about the fun things more than the work things because they are well . . . fun.

But just like working in the United States, we all have jobs to go to every day. In my case, I spend my days at the Tonga Development Bank either doing client visits or working at the bank office. Mostly, I help businesses here in Vava'u improve. I work with clients on recordkeeping and sometimes, on business plans. The details of my work often involve confidential client information that I don't share online. Right now, we are working with a Tongan business owner on a major expansion project. It will more than triple the size of his business. Once it is done, I'll certainly write about it because it is an exciting project.

I've also been building a website for a local motel. Because I want them to be able to update it easily after I'm gone, I'm using Blogger to build the site. That way, they can log in and easily edit the pages.

The main reason the site is not finished is because we have been without Internet service at the bank for almost a month. Our router died, and we shipped it back to our head office in Nuku'alofa. I won't bore you with the details of why it takes a month to get a router because truthfully, I don't really understand it either. We get a different story every few days. Even in a developing country like Tonga, there is frustration with the IT department.

My fellow volunteers also work at their jobs every day. James teaches at the Vava'u Side School, which is an all English-speaking primary school. The kids start speaking English at the first grade level.

Stan just got a new job. He had been working at the Vava'u Youth Congress, but that group has basically fallen apart due to organizational issues. He is still helping them, but now is working with a local college that is owned by the Church of Tonga. Amy, Shannon and Jessica all teach in government primary schools. Sarah works with a computer lab in her village, and Janis works with the Ministry of Education.

Those are the eight volunteers currently working here in Vava'u, but Sarah and Jessica will leave next month. We are getting six new volunteers in Vava'u in December. Four will be teachers and the other two will be business volunteers. One will be working with the Wesleyan Church School to develop a catering business, and the other will be on an outer island helping to start a clam farm. By January, we will have 12 American volunteers working here in Vava'u.

When you join Peace Corps, you are repeatedly told that you are considered a volunteer 24 hours a day. We represent the United States every time we interact with the people of Tonga, and the impressions they have of our country are shaped by what we do. Even a simple walk through town can make an impression.

Our escape from all of this is to get away where no one can see us. We call it *"palangi* time" (palangi, as you may recall, is the Tongan word for foreigner). When we take our palangi-time excursions, we can let our guard down a bit and not worry about the way we are conducting ourselves. For just a few hours every so often, we get to act like Americans.

As volunteers, we are given a living allowance of about US$350 a month. My friend who sent the e-mail also wondered how we could all afford these sailing, snorkeling and camping trips that I often write about. The answer is that we usually go with friends who own the boat and just chip in to help pay the gas or other expenses. We couldn't even begin to afford to pay the actual price to charter a sailboat. Other times, like this past weekend with the trainees, we get a special deal because we are in the off-season, and the boats are not being used.

We had 38 people on that boat (it holds 40), which brought the cost way down.

Camping and snorkeling are free. We just find a spot and go, or we take a local boat to the island where we plan to camp. The local boats are basically water taxis and generally serve a particular island or area. But just like a taxi, you can also ask them to drop you just about anywhere.

I've never outspent my monthly living allowance even though I also have to pay for a portion of my utilities out of my allowance—something many of my fellow volunteers do not have to pay. Yes, you do have to budget, but if you don't have enough money, you just do without. This is something I've learned from the Tongans.

Group 74 Training Update

The next group of Peace Corps volunteers here in Tonga have wrapped up the Vava'u portion of their training. Beginning Monday, the trainees will be attached to a current volunteer for a week. I'll be hosting a guy named Shawn who will be working in Nuku'alofa after he completes training. Then all the trainees will reconvene on the main island for a couple more weeks before they officially become volunteers.

There are now 22 trainees left out of the original 24 who came here in mid-October. Two of their group have already gone home.

THANKSGIVING TONGA STYLE
Friday, November 28, 2008

I am thankful that I live in a wonderful place surrounded by people I really like, and I'm doing something that I enjoy. On Thanksgiving Day, I joined 20 fellow Americans to celebrate Tonga style.

We had been planning the day for more than a month. In Vava'u, it's not easy to get all the ingredients you need to prepare a traditional Thanksgiving meal. But thanks to our party organizer and my fellow volunteer Sarah, we had a great meal with turkey and all the trimmings.

Sarah was able to get a local restaurant to give us their kitchen and their dining room for the day at no charge. They closed and we took over. It's summertime and the off-season here, so they probably would not have had a lot of customers anyway. In fact, they may have made more off of our bar tab than they would have with paying customers.

Peace Corps volunteers and trainees celebrate at Mana'ia restaurant

The Mana'ia Restaurant is located right at the edge of the water. It's one of the nicest restaurant settings in all of Vava'u, and we were all thrilled to be back for the second year in a row.

The addition of cinnamon pie to the dessert menu was a special treat for me this year. Cinnamon pie is a Hunsicker-family recipe that goes back generations. My mom sent me the recipe, and a couple of the volunteers made it. While not quite as delicious as the original, it was still good and a great way to remember my family back in the United States.

After dinner, it was time to enjoy the great atmosphere at Mana'ia as we took off our shoes and savored the company and awesome views.

Our group included the eight volunteers who live here in Vava'u, six Peace Corps trainees who are attached to us and some American friends who live here full-time.

Dancing the Night Away

After cleaning up and closing up Mana'ia, our next stop was the Kaila Bar. The Kalia Bar is right in downtown Neiafu. When we entered, the only other people in the bar were the bartender and the disc jockey. From the main street, you can see right inside the bar, and it didn't take long for us to draw a crowd. Before long we had a large group of Tongans all watching the crazy Americans dancing the night away.

Saskia, Shawn and Amy do a Thanksgiving dance

We eventually drew such a large crowd that the bar started charging a five-dollar cover. Since the bar happens to be one of my clients, I was thrilled to see them doing this. It was smart business, especially for a Thursday night in the off-season.

Mt. Talau

The area where I live in Vava'u is called Mt. Talau. The main town of Neiafu sits at the base of the hill. I live about a fifth of the way up the hill. But until this week, I had never climbed to the top, although I had talked about it several times and had made it part of the way up to where a national park begins. That changed on Monday.

Stan also now lives on Mt. Talau. We both have had Peace Corps trainees attached to us this week. Shawn, who is from Minnesota, is staying with me, and Scott, from New Hampshire, is staying with Stan. The four of us climbed Mt. Talau, and the views from the top were great.

Trainees Scott Yurcheshen and Shawn Hobbs with Volunteers Stan Luker and Steve Hunsicker

Scott, who is on the left, will be living on one of the outer islands here in Vava'u, while Shawn, who is next to Scott, heads for the main island of Tongatapu.

Water Woes

It has been a lot of fun having Shawn stay with me this week, but unfortunately, I have been without water every day for about the past 10 days. It will come on and work occasionally for about four hours a day or so. But you never know when it will work and when it won't.

Today, even though I knew it was a futile endeavor, I went to the water board to find out what was happening. The woman behind the desk told me in English, "Maybe the machine is broken." OK, maybe? I didn't push it, but instead I asked when it might be fixed. Her reply was, "Maybe this weekend." I then left. It's possible she had no idea, or it's possible she was giving me the full story. Until it is fixed, I'll be filling buckets from the rainwater tank outside my house and taking bucket baths.

Special Thanks

Being a Peace Corps volunteer takes a lot of support from family and friends. It would be very difficult for me to be here if I didn't have a very supportive family and an awesome group of friends back in the United States. Thank you so much to all of you for the way you have helped me out when I needed something and for the e-mails and occasional phone calls. It's really great to hear from you and I thank you for it.

A TONGAN WEDDING
Wednesday, December 3, 2008

If you were going to select a time to get married, most Americans wouldn't even consider getting hitched in a church wedding at 10 a.m. on a Tuesday. However, that's a great time for Tongans to get married.

The tradition of weekday marriages stems back to an ancient belief that some days (like Saturday) are unlucky. Consequently, you won't find many Tongans getting married on the weekend.

And even a "traditional" church wedding is not traditional by USA standards. This week, I had a chance to observe my first wedding in Tonga. It was the marriage of my landlord's daughter, whose name is Na'a.

While the Tongans may be superstitious about the day on which to get married, they don't have any superstitions about the groom and the bride seeing each other before the ceremony. In fact, it would be impossible for the couple not to see each other.

The wedding begins when the bride and groom go to the courthouse to get their marriage license. That is done just before the church service.

The signing of the wedding documents

Only a few people are allowed inside the courtroom when the marriage documents are signed. But family and friends wait outside and then join a procession of tapa-covered cars headed to the church. Once at the church, the bride and groom enter together along with their family members.

After the procession, the groom goes to one side of the church and the bride to the other.

However, like an American wedding, emotions run high as you can see in this photo of the proud parents, my landlords Kepu and Save.

Proud parents Save and Kepu Tupou

Eventually the bride and groom are brought together, rings are exchanged and they are pronounced husband and wife.

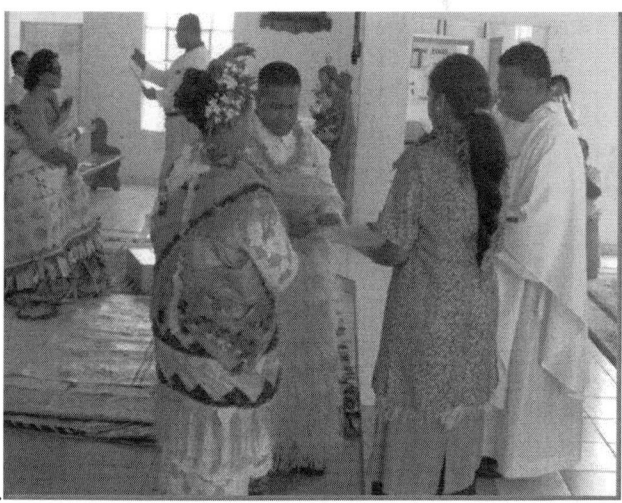

The bride and groom

But because this is conservative Tonga, there is no kiss—only a brief Tongan hug. After the service, everyone comes outside to congratulate the couple and take photos. Interestingly, in most of the photos, the bride and groom are not standing next to each other. In Tonga, you will almost never see any display of affection between men and women in public. Even in church, the men and women do not sit together, so it was no surprise that the couple didn't hold hands or even stand next to each other.

After the service it was back to the house and time to eat. James and I didn't attend the feast as we had a going-away lunch for our fellow volunteer Sarah.

Goodbye Sarah

My good friend Sarah is about to complete her service. Sarah was actually the very first person I ever communicated with in Tonga, long before I met any of my other fellow volunteers. I found her e-mail address online, and we started corresponding. I had no idea back then that I would end up living in Vava'u and that we would become such great friends.

The lunch was pretty low-key. The other volunteers will still see her again, but because I'm leaving to go on a bank trip to Ha'apai, this was my chance to say goodbye.

Sarah has been our activity planner in Vava'u. She's the one responsible for organizing many of the camping and sailing trips, along with get-togethers and volunteer meetings. She will certainly be missed. She's also very involved in her village and has been a really engaged volunteer.

Ha'apai and USA Bound

As mentioned above, I am leaving for the Ha'apai Island Group in about an hour. I'll be spending the next nine days conducting workshops on three outer islands. These are some of the most remote islands in Tonga and depending on the weather, it may take us 12-14 hours each way by boat to get to one of them.

From Ha'apai, I'm heading to the main island of Tongatapu. I'll be going to Fua'amotu to spend a weekend with my first homestay family. Then on December 16th, I'm heading to the United States for the holidays. I'll be spending 10 days in Northern Virginia with my family and then 10 days in South Florida at my house. It will be my first trip back to the states since I left 15 months ago. I return to Tonga on January 8th, 2009, to begin my second year of volunteer service.

INTERESTING PEOPLE AND PLACES
Thursday, December 11, 2008

I've had a chance in the past week to meet some really fascinating people and go to some interesting places. I was in the Ha'apai Island Group in the Kingdom of Tonga. Ha'apai is located about halfway between the main island group of Tongatapu and the Vava'u Island Group where I live. As part of my job, I come to Ha'apai twice a year to work with businesses and conduct business-training workshops. This visit, I spent all my time on small outer islands (and a lot of time in boats).

The Island of Ha'ano

It takes about an hour via boat to get to Ha'ano, but it is well worth the trip. This small outer island is one of the cleanest places I've seen in Tonga. With friendly people and a beautiful setting, it's also an island of surprises. The village of about 120 people has underground electric and city water service. At night, there are even streetlights to illuminate the paths through the town. I never expected to find such "luxuries" on a small island. The power is provided by generators, but it only runs for eight hours a day, generally from about 6 p.m. until 2 a.m. Every drop of diesel fuel is brought to the island in small cans. The cans are filled up on the main island, carried to the dock and then transported by boat to Ha'ano, where they are emptied into the generator and then returned via boat for another fill-up.

Of course, not all the modern conveniences are great. During our workshop, we had one participant whose cell phone rang at least 20, if not 30, times. It rang so many times that even some of the Tongans started snickering every time it rang. I later learned that the reason no one said anything to her was because she was married to the town officer.

One of my fellow Peace Corps volunteers, Grant, lives on this island; however, we actually were not on the island at the same time. As I was arriving on Friday morning, he was just leaving in a boat to the main island. We quickly shouted across the water that we would get together for dinner that night on the main island.

Patti

I first met Patti on my last trip to Ha'apai in June. She was building a resort on a nearby island. I told her if I could do anything to help, to let me know. So a few weeks ago, I heard from her. She wanted to know if I was available to come out and work with her. After a few phone calls, we agreed that I would come out Saturday and return on Sunday. I also asked Patti if my Peace

Corps friends Grant and Phil could join me on the trip to her resort, which is on the island of 'Uholeva.

None of us had ever been to the resort before and didn't know what to expect. We packed as if we were going camping; however, we quickly realized that none of our preparations had been necessary.

As we stepped off the boat, we could not help but be impressed with what Patti has created on this island. She has a piece of property that stretches from one side of the island to the other, and she has constructed small fales on both sides to host her guests. There are 11 buildings, each constructed in Indonesia and shipped to Tonga. Five are for sleeping.

The main fale' (building) at Serenity Beaches

While this might not seem like a big feat, let me tell you a little bit more about Patti. She retired from the Four Seasons in Hawaii where she was a massage therapist. During a sailing trip, she found the property where her resort is now located. She made an offer on the spot to lease it and then began the process of figuring out how to get it built. She moved to Ha'apai by herself, not knowing anyone and with little business background. She has now created a really amazing place, which I find remarkable for a woman who is just a few years younger than my own mother.

Jimmy

If you want to get to Patti's island from the main island, you will need to go by boat. We were lucky enough to get Jimmy and his boat to take us. Jimmy is quite a colorful character, and he kept us entertained during the two hours we spent with him (one hour each way). He told us stories about his youth and about funny things that have happened to him. He bragged about how he has been smoking heavily since 1965. If you ever happen to be in Ha'apai and need a boat, ask for Jimmy.

Xavier

I've heard a lot of jokes from my friends and family comparing living in Tonga to the CBS Network show *Survivor*. It's really not the same thing. However, this week I met a man from French-speaking Switzerland who is living the true *Survivor* experience. His name is Xavier, and he is spending 10 months alone on the island of Tofua. Tofua is an active volcano and for the most part uninhabited. Xavier decided to go there with no more than a knife and some very basic camping equipment to live life away from what he calls the trappings of modern society.

He's also shooting a documentary about his adventure. He has been on the island for three months and just made his first trip back to the main island. He could no longer charge his video equipment and came to town to try to get that resolved.

As a Peace Corps volunteer, we are not allowed to travel to Tofua because some former volunteers got stuck out there and had to be rescued by Peace Corps. So until the rules change, I'll have to wait for Xavier's documentary to see what it is like.

The Island of Mango

Monday morning, we left the main island of Ha'apai and traveled six hours south by boat across open water under the starlit skies to the island of Mango. We got up at 2:30 a.m. to begin our journey. My friend Grant decided at the last minute to join my Tongan counterpart Kololesa and I for the trip. We were also joined by Paula (a man), who is a loan officer at the Ha'apai branch of the bank. Grant and I slept for most of the trip. Finally, I heard the boat's 60-horsepower motor slow, and I peeked out from below deck to see the lush tropical island of Mango. It may be one of the most inviting places I've ever seen. Even before stepping on shore, you knew you were somewhere special: Perhaps it was the nicely planted flowers along the water that marked the path to the village or the lovely sandy beach. Once on shore, the first impressions held as we wandered around the island and were warmly greeted by the people.

A couple of kids quickly adopted Grant and I to show us around the village. However, because I was not feeling well, I ducked out and found a small Tongan hut on the beach and lay down on the mat inside. The people of the village quickly realized I was not feeling great, and a little boy showed up at the hut and asked me if I wanted some *otai*, which is a drink made from fresh fruit and coconut juice. A while later, someone brought out a bottle of

Pepto Bismal and then another told me he had some pills that could help me feel better. I declined both offers.

I wasn't actually feeling that bad, but the people of the island seemed so concerned about me, it was really touching.

We stopped in Mango because their one link to the outside world, a radio telephone, had stopped working. We had brought a replacement on the boat, but unfortunately it didn't work either, so when we left, the people of this island still had no communication with the outside world.

The Island of Nomuka

For the past two years, there have been two Peace Corps volunteers living on Nomuka. Both just completed their service. I don't know either volunteer very well having met Ada just once and Janelle, twice. Nomuka is really in the middle of nowhere. I had hoped that both volunteers would still be there when we arrived so that I could get to know them better, but they had just left, although we were told that Ada would be returning.

Even though I don't know the Nomuka volunteers well, I have a newfound appreciation for them after spending 24 hours on the island. It's a dirty little island and the people are not that friendly. In short, it is everything that Mango is not. Its one redeeming quality is the beautiful lake that sits in the middle of the island. The four of us spent the night in a kava hall, and while Grant and I did do some exploring, for the most part that was where we spent our time.

We also held our bank workshop at the kava hall. We had arranged to hire a small portable generator for the three-hour workshop so that we could power our computer and projector for the PowerPoint presentation. However, about five minutes before the workshop, we were told that they only had enough petrol to give us one hour of power. I quickly changed the presentation and we made it work.

The Island of 'Uiha

After our workshop, we got back in the boat and made the four-hour boat trip to U'iha. We arrived just before sunset and couldn't help but be impressed with this village that looks west into the setting sun. I've always been fascinated by sunsets. Watching a sunset is a relaxing way to end the day and a beautiful way to usher in the evening. It was a great welcome to U'iha. We spent two nights on 'Uiha and quickly became big fans of the island and its people. The town put us up in an empty house and provided us with mats for sleeping and even pillows. Everywhere we went, we were welcomed warmly and the scenery was really great.

Details of a Tongan Business Trip

During my TV career, I often took business trips, usually staying in nice hotels and eating at great restaurants and flying in either business or first class. This business trip could not have been more different from those trips. I slept on the floor most nights with just a sheet over me. There was only one restaurant in the entire Ha'apai Island Group, and it was located on the main island. Meals ranged from traditional Tongan—fried fish and root crops—to cold cans of spaghetti eaten on crackers. Our travel was aboard a 38-foot, handmade Tongan boat with a single 60-horsepower outboard motor. By comparison, it was a really nice Tongan boat—one of the best I've used.

THE TONGAN PARADOX
Thursday, December 18, 2008

For the past several months, I've been corresponding with some business students at the University of Colorado about Tonga and Peace Corps. They were assigned to me by their professor. The students have just completed a case study, which is below.

They fictionalized some of the details (like my name, former job, etc.), but I think they did a good job of capturing some of the issues in Tonga.

I hope you enjoy reading their work, which has been lightly edited.

The Tongan Paradox

Disclaimer: Sam Battan and Andrew Venclovas prepared this case study under the direction of instructor Francy Milner, as the basis for discussion and training, not to illustrate either effective or ineffective approaches to a problem or project.

Introduction

It was five o'clock in the evening when Edward finally got the call from the Peace Corps' South Pacific placement officer. After a multitude of headaches from the application process had been resolved, it was finally time to tell his boss that he would soon be leaving his long-time position at a major consulting firm to go spend time as a Peace Corps volunteer (PCV), assisting with business development in the Kingdom of Tonga. On the long commute over the bridge into New Jersey, Edward couldn't help but be overwhelmed by all of the uncertainty that he would soon be facing. Once finally home, Edward had to express his excitement, "I can't wait for the opportunity to help a developing country realize its potential!"

At the very same time, 8,000 miles away in a small village on the island of Vava'u, Tonga, Mele was preparing lunch for her six children in their humble island cottage. Mele's family didn't make enough money to save any, but still lived a very happy and well-nourished life. Mele and her husband were educated through the twelfth grade, and their kids attended a respectable public school. They never went hungry because they ate what they produced on their two-acre farm. What material possessions they couldn't afford were usually given to them by family or neighbors in the village, or sent from Mele's uncle, who lived and worked in New Zealand. However, Mele's village had recently been living without some of the main food staples such as bread and milk, because the local general store had not gotten a shipment of supplies from Tongatapu, the kingdom's capital, for almost two weeks. For some reason, the boat that usually dropped off supplies just hadn't appeared. Mele was a rational thinker, and she pondered, "What if I could open up a general store of my own? More stores on this island ought to make the chance of this happening again much less." Although this was just a thought, months later Mele and a then-unknown PCV named Edward would realize this goal.

Background

The Kingdom of Tonga is an archipelago located in the South Pacific Ocean consisting of 176 islands, 36 of which are inhabited. There are approximately 101,901 people living in Tonga, with about two-thirds of that population inhabiting the main island of Tongatapu. Estimates show that the nation has been inhabited for over 3,000 years, with vast cultural shifts attributed to foreign interaction. As part of a subtropical climate, Tonga experiences warm temperatures from December to May, cooler temperatures from May to December and has extremely rich, fertile soil, which accounts for its abundance of crops including coconuts, vanilla beans and bananas.

The Kingdom of Tonga is a constitutional monarchy and is the only island nation in the region to formally avoid colonization. Tonga is a quiet nation that is relatively isolated, with a political structure divided among the king, the nobles and the commoners. Recently, there has been increasing pressure on Tonga from Australia and New Zealand to Westernize and abandon the deeply entrenched Tongan culture. Some fear that this interference will break down cultural traditions and deep extended families.

Tonga's economy depends in large part on the remittances from other nations where Tongan nationals reside. Most of the inflow of foreign aid comes from Australia, New Zealand and the United States, which accommodates over half the registered citizens of Tonga. Rural natives primarily rely on agriculture, which makes up 30% of total GDP. The remaining portions of the GDP include various services and industries like telecommunications, most of which are owned by the Tongan government. In fact, the government operates seventeen different state-owned enterprises (SOEs) that accounted for 45% of total GDP in 2007. Some critics believe that the "large, underperforming public sector is holding back the growth of the economy both directly and indirectly."

Tonga's isolated island culture creates an overwhelming need for sound family structure and values. Most homes have several generations living under the same roof. Reunions are also regular because if a Tongan isn't familiar with his or her family tree, there is a good chance undesirable dating may occur. There are hierarchical ranks within each family, which are not universal, and range from where a member sits at the dinner table to household chores.

The world recognizes Tonga as "The Friendly Islands," and almost all Tongans are extremely welcoming to foreigners and treat guests as members of the family. However, gender is a strong determining factor in one's role as a Tongan, and certain tasks are associated exclusively with males or females. For example, Tongan families are seemingly patriarchal in nature, while the women actually make most important decisions inside the home. Tonga's government also has a mandatory education system for young people up to the age of 14 years. Thus, literacy rates are the highest in the Pacific and are at about 99% for 15-24-year-olds.

The Peace Corps has had an extensive presence in Tonga since the first volunteers arrived in October of 1967. Since that time, over 1000 volunteers have served willingly, primarily as teachers. Presently, a new micro-enterprise development team has sprung up to help natives create income-generating businesses for their families domestically, rather than overseas. The volunteers aim to train and motivate communities, and teach basic business skills.

A Whole New World

"Toto, I have a feeling we're not in Kansas anymore," Edward chuckled to himself as he lay in bed reflecting on his first day's experience in this new, unchartered territory of Tongatapu. Since the moment he stepped off the plane, Edward was bombarded by culture shocks. As he was going through the Tongan version of customs, the friendly man dressed in traditional military garb stopped him for some questions. "How long are you going to be living in the lovely Kingdom of Tonga?" asked the man in scattered but impressive English. "Two years," Edward said while holding up his middle and index finger. Much to his chagrin, Edward's assigned Peace Corps trainer explained to him that he had just told the customs officer to 'F' off. Cultural differences, Edward would find, not only caused such social faux pas, but also resulted in a significant limitation to free enterprise as a means for economic growth.

After his weeklong training, Edward was boated to the island where he would be spending the next two years. Vava'u was second in population to the main island, Tongatapu. His reaction after the first couple of days was that the island teetered on the "edge of modernity;" it had paved roads and a reasonably sized retail district complete with two banks and a few stores, but most of the population sustained a living off their small-acre farms.

Edward was lucky enough to receive a luxurious housing arrangement (compared to other Peace Corps volunteers). His had running water, a full kitchen and electricity. It was provided by the bank that Edward partnered with, the Tonga Development Bank. Nonetheless, Edward's experience was far removed from his life in the States. The power went out in Edward's house four times in the first week, and the cell phone graciously given to him by one of his colleagues had about a 50% success rate for placing or receiving a call—on a good day. The Internet connection, when it was working, downloaded data at 32K, just a little more than half of the speed of a dial-up modem in the United States. Although these were just mild inconveniences to Edward, there were also infrastructure issues that created problems in Edward's line of work—developing the skills of the business owners in his local community.

About three months into his stay in Vava'u, Edward was able to go into villages and help business owners on an individual basis. "Here is where I can do the most help; this is what I know best," Edward thought en route on his first community excursion. On his return from the village, Edward's ego was long gone; he still had a lot to learn before he could actually help private enterprise prosper in Vava'u.

Once, when Edward first walked into a small general store, he was amazed to find the shelves almost bare and no one in the shop except the man who owned it.

"Where are all of your goods?" Edward asked with curiosity. "Still in Tongatapu, waiting to be shipped to me!" the man said with a genuine smile and no concern whatsoever.

"So, you are waiting on supplies to be shipped over from the main island?"

"Yes, my friend Edward. The boats usually come every Monday and Wednesday, but for the past two weeks have not showed up."

"Why?" was the only thing Edward could think of saying.

"It is a mystery to me. There really is no reason to worry though, it is pineapple season, and the kids and wife are eating as heartily as ever."

Edward concluded later that the infrastructure was definitely not in a place to sustain a competitive market of any sort. He pondered, "How are these business owners supposed to keep a steady supply chain?" and "Why is the government not investing in the proper transportation and commercial channels? These were puzzling questions for Edward, but not as puzzling as the main question in his mind: "Why aren't Tongans doing anything about it?" It seemed that he still had some things to learn about Tongan culture.

The Dirty "M" Word

Soon after Edward's first encounter with a Tongan business owner, he met Mele. Her husband came into the bank where Edward was working and inquired about starting a small grocery store in their village, 10 miles away. In these situations, Edward learned, men were the ones who made public appearances and asked the questions, but it was actually the women who kept the books and made the business decisions. Accordingly, Edward asked Mele's husband to bring Mele in for a group discussion on how to start up a grocery store. Once all three were behind closed doors, Edward dove right into questioning.

"Why do you want to start a grocery store?" Edward asked.

"To provide for our family and friends," Mele's husband replied.

"Why not do it to make a profit and save some money?"

"We have been experiencing some food shortages, and our only concern is the well-being of our family and community."

"But wouldn't money make you happy? If you ran your store correctly, you could have extra income to spend on whatever you wanted."

"Money doesn't make us happy, Edward. Having food, shelter and a good family is what makes us happy. For the necessities we cannot produce ourselves, we rely on the money sent to us by Mele's relatives and mine," Mele's husband concluded.

It was now apparent to Edward that the Tongans' motivation was what confused him the most. Mele and her husband had no clear idea of what "profit" even meant; all they wanted to do was provide for their friends and family and make sure no one went hungry. Those values were engrained in Tongan culture just as much as self-preservation was engrained in the American culture; remittances and handouts were the only way of life. "Where are the incentives for Tongans to start a business for profit when they get money sent to them for doing nothing?" Edward pondered.

The Argument for Free Enterprise

Edward made a lot of progress with Mele as well as multiple other small business owners. Throughout the course of a year, Edward championed a multitude of small victories, including:
• Helping Mele and her husband start their general store.
• Teaching over 10 small business owners proper bookkeeping methods.
• Developing a website for a small Tongan business owner.
• Training Tongan bank staff in underwriting of loans.
• Assisting in IT problems throughout the island of Vava'u.

Still, he was having trouble finding a large-scale solution to promote free enterprise and ultimately, promote economic growth. Edward believed the government's regulation of business, as well as the culture and lack of infrastructure, was hindering economic growth. In his opinion, helping small business owners with their business skills was a very small-scale solution; there was still little hope for a nation-wide privatization of the economy. The Tongan SOEs, coupled with strict property laws, decreased demand for foreign direct private investment and greatly increased the barriers of entry to all industries. Edward found hope when a private company came to Tonga and took the mobile phone market by storm. Prior to this, there were only two cell phone companies in the whole kingdom. The largest, UCall, is owned by the public telephone SOE, and in distant second for size and revenues is Tonfon, a company owned by the king and other government officials. Digicel, a global cell phone giant, bought out Tonfon in early 2007. The process took months, and for about a year, Digicel operated Tonfon as it had always been run. When Digicel started promoting a free concert by American reggae star Shaggy, everything changed drastically. No one knew what Digicel was, and there was no explanation as to why the company was sponsoring a concert, only that it was free and everyone was invited. The night of the concert was met with heavy rains, but despite that, over 10% of the whole population ended up attending the concert. After the show, Edward went to bed without seeing a single Digicel sign or advertisement. When he woke up, Digicel banners and billboards were almost everywhere in town and, according to Edward, the town had been "painted Digicel Red overnight." Along with all of the new marketing ads, Digicel representatives were traveling door-to-door selling phones and two months of service for US$20. Edward had never seen a company do as masterful a job of marketing and launching as what he had witnessed Digicel accomplish. Although this was a rare case of free enterprise thriving, it gave Edward hope that it could happen again in the future.

After witnessing Digicel's success, Edward returned to Vava'u to work with small business owners, still trying to help free enterprise prosper in the great Kingdom of Tonga. He felt good about helping Tongan small business owners, but he was still looking to implement a solution to provide Tonga with sustainable growth. It wasn't for a lack of ideas; Edward believed the national economy could benefit greatly from its beautiful geography and fertile soil, as well as its educated population. Tonga could attract ecotourists, support multinational call centers and export crops if the infrastructure and institutions were in place. But what could the Peace Corps do to help make these ideas a reality? As Edward's stay in Tonga was winding down, he had a perspective-changing realization. There will always be a use for the 20-something college graduates who enter the Peace Corps, but what countries like Tonga need are older, more experienced PCVs to work on an individual basis with the upper levels of government. In order to modify the current milieu in which the Tongan government operates, Edward believed the Peace Corps must work harder to actively recruit older adults with "real-world" experience. Only then will significant progress be made in repairing the gaps in Tonga's economic infrastructure.

On the 17-hour plane ride back to the United States, Edward was optimistic about the future of Peace Corps in Tonga. As long as the right volunteers were working in the right places, there would be significant progress made on the most pressing of issues, including:
• Improving infrastructure.
• Disaggregating the large and underperforming public sector.
• Incentivizing individual entrepreneurs.
• Promoting foreign direct investment.

Lingering Questions

What else could Edward have done to promote a large-scale solution? Are there any ways to address the lack of infrastructure and unfavorable regulatory environments and promote capitalism without damaging the rich culture? What will it take for Tongans to stop relying so heavily on remittances and take initiative themselves for economic growth?

BIG FIRE IN VAVA'U
Friday, December 26, 2008

A big fire in Neiafu destroyed a number of businesses last week.

I know many of the people who owned these businesses and have done work for two of them during my time in Peace Corps.

Neiafu fire photos, courtesy Viliami Muna.

I'm in the United States and not Tonga at the moment. Here is the way the fire was reported in Matangitonga.to:

> A SECOND big fire to hit Neiafu within a month destroyed a block of the central shopping area of the small town this afternoon.
>
> Fanned by a breeze the fire spread rapidly through at least eight small businesses on the seaward side of the main street. It is thought that the fire started outside of the buildings on the seafront area.
>
> The Neiafu fire brigade received the call at 3:18 pm and confirmed that the fire gutted all the buildings from the Teta Tours and Airlines Tonga offices, including the Bounty Bar all the way to the O. G. Sanft Building, but stopped short of the Tonga Development Bank's cement building and a new development next to it that had a cement fire wall in place.
>
> Ketiola Lolohea, of the Neiafu Western Union Office, said that fanned by the wind the fire spread rapidly through the roofs of the old timber buildings and threatened to spread across the road to the new ANZ Bank and her offices but the fire brigade bulldozed a small building on the corner to stop the fire from spreading further.
>
> She said that the O. G. Sanft Building – one of the oldest commercial buildings in Neiafu, as well as an auto parts store, the Guttenbeil handicrafts shop and nightclub, the Friendly Islands Bookshop, Kelly's Store, Lita Store, the Bounty Bar, Airlines Tonga, and Samiu Vaipulu's offices were destroyed.
>
> Other businesses destroyed were Arnotts wine and Digicel cards store, Grey's Bottle Store, Salesi Paea's bar as well as the Kalia Bar and the Otu Moi Plumbing Store.
>
> "The police got everyone out of the buildings so no-one was hurt," said Ketiola.
>
> The fire appeared to have spread from the direction of the O. G. Sanft Bldg. and Guttenbeils' shops.
>
> Earlier, on November 13, a fire destroyed the administration and entertainment block of Neiafu's Paradise Hotel.

BREAKING A TONGAN TABOO
Monday, December 29, 2008

The Ha'apai Island Group is a quiet place and perhaps one of the more traditional places in Tonga. It's a place where families are strong and the values are traditional. On the main island, there is just one restaurant, one bank and a few shops.

Even during the middle of the "work week," you can walk down the main street and never see a car and only pass a few people.

That changes on most Saturdays. Saturday morning is time for people to gather at the small market on the edge of town. It's not just a place for buying and selling but a place to hang out and be entertained with traditional Tongan songs and dances.

Like most places in Tonga, you won't see men and women dancing together, and even families tend to segregate themselves by sex as they browse the market and converse with each other.

Tongan men perform at the city market on Ha'apai

I'm guessing this way of life has existed for many years. On a recent Saturday in late December, that all changed thanks to the appearance of six of my fellow Peace Corps volunteers at the market.

The volunteers were traveling around Tonga in an effort to educate Tongans about AIDS. Since talking about sex in mixed company is a big

Tongan taboo, just imagine how hard it must have been to discuss something like AIDS and other sexually transmitted diseases to a mixed group of mothers and fathers, sisters and brothers, grandparents and infants.

To educate the Tongans, the volunteers, who all live on the main island of Tongatapu, decided to write a skit and then lip-synch it in Tongan. By USA standards, this skit would be rated G. Nothing in it would be considered inappropriate for even the youngest Americans.

But this isn't America, and as I watched and listened to the skit being performed, I was almost as interested in the reactions of the Tongans as I was in the performance.

At first, you could see that Tongans were just being polite, paying attention to the volunteers who were putting on a skit for them. But the crowd quickly turned quiet once the full impact of what was being discussed sunk in. I'm not sure if it was because they were paying such close attention or because they were in shock. I have to think this was probably the first time most of these people had ever heard a topic like AIDS discussed in public.

It was also interesting to notice that NO ONE moved during the performance. Everyone just watched with poker faces.

At the end, there was polite applause, and the crowd quickly went back to normal. The entire presentation was done in a very culturally sensitive way, but the topic itself was certainly not culturally appropriate for the crowd. I think this is one of the challenges that Peace Corps volunteers can face, especially when talking about something like AIDS. It's important to be sensitive to the culture, but sometimes, you have to break down traditional taboos in order to get the message across. I really commend Alexis, Andrew, Emily, Enrique, Bobby and Alicia for their efforts to increase AIDS awareness in Tonga. They did a great job putting this together and hopefully their efforts will help.

There are a couple of side notes to this topic. No one really knows how big of an issue AIDS is in Tonga. There have been a handful of documented AIDS cases but testing doesn't exist and when someone dies, the cause of death is usually just listed as "sick." There really is no accurate way of knowing how many people have AIDS.

Another interesting note: When the "AIDS Roadshow" volunteers arrived in Ha'apai, they went to check out the supply of condoms at the local health office. They were all old and expired.

The volunteers have different versions of their skit, some geared to all-female audiences and others to all-male audiences. While I didn't see those, I'm guessing they are a little bit easier than the performance they gave at the market in Ha'apai.

A TALE OF TWO FLIGHTS
Wednesday, January 14, 2009

Just over 15 months ago, I was sitting in the Los Angeles Airport waiting to board my first flight to the Kingdom of Tonga. Today, I'm in the same terminal getting ready to get on the same Air New Zealand flight after spending almost a month in the United States.

Sitting here brings back lots of memories of that first trip and the excitement that I and my fellow volunteers all felt as we started our Tonga Peace Corps adventures. That night, as we sat and waited to board our flight, we all wondered what Tonga would be like, what we would learn, where we would be living and how long it would be before we talked again with our families and friends.

Tonight I know the answers to those questions, but I'm still excited. I'm looking forward to seeing my friends and getting back to Vava'u. I've missed being there.

That doesn't mean I haven't enjoyed my trip to the United States. In fact, it's been a great trip, and it was a lot of fun to catch up with my family and friends. I didn't experience the huge culture shock I was expecting. I think part of that is because I went to Australia in September, so it hadn't been that long since I was out of Tonga. A couple of things did hit me.

I first flew to Virginia, and when I arrived, it was below freezing. That's the coldest weather I've felt in two years. At my sister's house, I walked into her kitchen and saw an open bag of chips on the counter. My first thought was that I should close it immediately so the ants wouldn't get in the bag. Then I remembered, I was in Virginia, in the middle of winter, and I didn't have to worry about the ants. In Vava'u, you never leave food out because the ants will be all over it.

Arriving at my home in West Palm Beach was also a bit strange. I was vacationing in my own home. The house was just as I left it, but it still seemed a bit foreign after being gone for 15 months and much different than my house in Vava'u. One night, I met some friends at the Gansevoort, a South Florida club. I went to the bar and ordered two drinks . . . just two regular vodka drinks. The price was $30! Talk about culture shock. Fifteen dollars per drink and that didn't include the tip! I can live in Vava'u for a week on what those drinks cost. Today on the plane, there was a write-up about the Gansevoort in the in-flight magazine. It failed to mention the price of the drinks.

My stay in Florida ended up being a week longer than expected. I had to have a root canal done, and after consulting with the Peace Corps medical office, they agreed that I should stay and have it done in the United States. I was happy with that and got to enjoy an extra week of "sick leave" in South Florida during the best time of the year to be there.

As you might expect, I got a lot of questions from my family and friends about my Peace Corps experience. The most common questions were: "What are you going to do when you get done with Peace Corps?" and "Are you going to extend your stay in Tonga?" Others wanted to know details of the Tongan culture and more about my work and personal life in Tonga. It was great to answer the questions, and more than a few people told me that given the economy in the United States, I picked a great time to be in Peace Corps.

I couldn't agree more, and as I get ready to board my flight, I know I am ready to go back. And unlike that first flight, I now know what to expect, where I am living and that I am going to have an awesome second year.

My second year will begin, like my first year, with training on the main island. Because my group is at the midpoint of our service, we will all be gathering in the main city of Nuku'alofa for our MST or mid-service training conference. That means I'll be staying in Nuku'alofa until the end of next week before I finally get to fly home to Vava'u!

THIS IS TONGA
Friday, January 23, 2009

There is a new volunteer here in Tonga named Peter. He's a retired airline pilot and lives on the main island of Tongatapu. When something happens that defies logic or that seems strange compared to the United States, Peter simply explains it by saying, "This is Tonga."

So in honor of Peter, I thought I would share a couple of "This is Tonga" moments that have happened to me during the past week.

My first tale is set at a local Indian restaurant. It's a new place and small. I went there for dinner with about 12 other volunteers. We were the only customers. I think we all ordered curry—most of us asked for fish curry, but there were a few orders for vegetable curry and an order for chicken curry.

After about 20 minutes, the first two plates came out. Twenty minutes later, another plate came out and then about 15 minutes later, two more plates came out. We realized that we were getting our dinners in the order that they were placed. And it was pretty obvious that each plate was being cooked one at a time. Now since there were probably seven or eight orders just for fish curry, you would think they would cook all of them together, but that didn't happen. Just under three hours after we entered the restaurant, the last two volunteers got their food. And we were still the only customers. Why did each plate of food get cooked individually instead of together? "This is Tonga."

The second "This is Tonga" story is from the same night. The restaurant doesn't serve beer and after several of us had finished our dinners and everyone else was still waiting, we went out to a corner store to buy a few beers. It was raining really hard, and the store is about a block away from the restaurant. As we were walking back, we stopped under a small roof that was outside another restaurant, and we started drinking our beers. Yes, we were standing on the street with open containers in the middle of town drinking beer. Not only that, we were loitering outside another restaurant that we weren't patronizing. In the United States, several things would have happened. The cops might have been called or the restaurant owners might have chased us away. Neither of those things happened. Instead, the women in the restaurant grabbed chairs from inside and brought them outside to us so we had a place to sit. "This is Tonga."

Peace Corps requires that each volunteer have a physical at the midpoint of his or her service. I arrived at the clinic and waited about 90 minutes before the nurse called me. As I was waiting in the exam room, I heard the doctor say that he wanted to retest the last two patients who had had their blood sugar checked because he thought the machine was bad and giving inaccurate readings. Not long after that, the nurse came into the room where

I was waiting and took my blood pressure using what looked like a home blood pressure machine. The machine said my blood pressure was extremely high. I've never had high blood pressure in my life, so I asked the nurse if she could either recheck it using a different machine or do it manually. She took it manually and guess what, she proclaimed that my blood pressure was fine. So clearly this clinic was using machines that either needed to be repaired or replaced. A couple of days later, some other volunteers went to the same clinic and also had blood pressure tests. The clinic was still using the same machine that had given me the bad reading. Yes, "this is Tonga."

Biking to the Beach

Even though I lived on the main island of Tongatapu for several months, I never got a chance to explore it by bicycle. On Sunday, I joined my friends, Peter, Shawn and Alicia on a ride to a remote beach located not far from the house where the king lives. (He doesn't live in the palace.)

Alicia and Shawn play with a Tongan girl

It was a really easy ride because unlike Vava'u, where I live, Tongatapu is very flat. Once we got off the main road, we made our way through bush land, under some beautiful canopy trees, past horses and cows and down a dirt road to the ocean.

I had expected to find an empty beach since technically swimming (and probably bicycling) are illegal on Sunday. Instead, there were about 40 Tongans of all ages hanging out on the beach and in the water, enjoying the big waves. Some were Tongans from New Zealand, but others were locals who live here all the time. The four of us were the only palangi at the beach.

MY PEACE CORPS EXPERIENCE IS HALF OVER
Wednesday, January 28, 2009

It's hard for me to imagine that I have less than 11 months remaining as a Peace Corps volunteer. When I first arrived on October 1, 2007, I didn't expect the time to go by so quickly. Now 15 months later, I've completed three months of training and just over one year of service.

My group just completed its mid-service training (MST), and the next time we all get together will be for our close of service conference (COS).

I hadn't thought a lot about reaching this point until I got an e-mail from a reporter for the *South Florida Sun-Sentinel* who was working on a story about the number of Floridians who were joining the Peace Corps. He asked me if I would share my thoughts about being in Peace Corps and explain why I joined. Here is how I replied to him:

I've been here for 15 months now, and joining the Peace Corps has been an amazing experience. As to why I joined, the easy answer is that Peace Corps was something that I had always wanted to do, but kept putting off. But there is actually a bit more to it than that. It's not easy to walk away from a well-paying, 23-year career. I loved TV news for most of my career, but I found that I was enjoying it less and less. What I always enjoyed the most was being involved in the stories that really affected people's lives and really helped them. When all of the thank-you notes started showing up in the WPEC newsroom after Hurricane Frances hit South Florida, that was really rewarding because I knew we had done something that was meaningful and appreciated.

I think joining Peace Corps was a personal quest to find something that would help people in a positive way.

It was not a quick decision. It took seven months from the time I first filled out my application to the Peace Corps until I finally received the invitation to serve in Tonga.

I have no regrets at all about joining Peace Corps. Are there frustrating days? Of course, but the good days far outweigh the bad ones. I spend my time working with small business owners either helping them start or improve their businesses. I have one client who had run up a TOP$20,000 (about US$10,000) overdraft at a local bank and was on the verge of having to close his business. He has now paid that down, his business is doing much better, and he is expanding by adding a taxi-cab service. Not all of the people I work with have that much success, but even seeing someone taking a small baby step forward is rewarding.

The Tongans are a wonderful people and very friendly. Getting to know them and their culture has been an amazing experience. It has been a bit of a struggle for me to learn the Tongan language, but most people here speak English so I'm able to communicate easily. I also wear a skirt and short sleeve shirt to work every day. That's the traditional Tongan business attire. Never did I think I would wear a skirt, much less enjoy it. However it is quite comfortable in the heat. And it's quite different from the coat and tie I used to wear to work at WPEC every day.

The climate here is similar to South Florida, except our seasons are reversed. We are in the middle of summer right now, and there is currently a tropical depression over the Kingdom of Tonga. Last night, I nailed all of my windows shut while my neighbor climbed the breadfruit tree next to my house, so the winds didn't send breadfruit through my windows. (Breadfruit is about the size of a coconut.)

A Tongan breadfruit tree

It looks like my comments didn't make the *South Florida Sun-Sentinel* story, which was headlined, "Peace Corps says more Floridians joined in 2008." However, it gave me a good chance to reflect on the past 15 months.

WARDROBE MALFUNCTION
Monday, February 2, 2009

It should come as no surprise that Tonga is a conservative country. For the most part, men hang out with men and women with women. Even in church, you will rarely see a married couple sitting together.

Friday night, all 11 volunteers here in Vava'u gathered for a meeting. After the meeting, in true Tongan fashion, the "boys" went to Mermaid, a local bar, while the "girls" stayed at the office. Eventually, the women joined us at Mermaid. The place was packed, mostly with Tongans.

On any Friday night, Mermaid is really "the" place to go in Vava'u (even more so now that two other bars burned down in December). It's a good place to people watch, and even Tongans who don't drink will show up and just hang out.

As the night progressed, the dance floor started to get crowded, and in typical Tonga tradition, the floor was primarily filled with women dancing with other women. I was sitting with my back to the dance floor looking out into the harbor when one of my fellow volunteers asked, "Did you see that?" I asked, "What?" and didn't get an answer. The next thing I heard was another volunteer saying, "I never thought I would see that in Tonga." That was enough to make me turn around, but all I saw were the people on the dance floor.

Then I heard that while dancing, one of the Tongans, a thin woman around 30, had suffered a wardrobe malfunction in Janet Jackson style. And as with Janet, there was a question as to whether it was intentional or accidental.

Now, you are probably wondering why I'm telling this story right? Well that wasn't the last we saw of her. Not long after the wardrobe malfunction, I was sitting in my chair when this same woman came over and grabbed me and planted a kiss right on my lips. To say I was shocked is an understatement. I mean, this is Tonga. I've never seen a Tongan kiss a member of the opposite sex in public, and here I was getting kissed by some strange woman I had never seen before. I wish someone had taken a picture because I would love to have seen the look on my face.

As you might imagine, my fellow volunteers were laughing like crazy. Well apparently, the woman noticed the laughter and my shock, so a few minutes later, she came back and kissed me again.

That was the last I saw of her. But it just goes to show that even in a place as conservative as Tonga, the unexpected can happen.

Goodbye Jessica

My friend Jessica is on her way to the United States as I write this. Jessica is the last member of Group 72 to leave Vava'u. She is certainly going to be missed. Jessica always had such positive energy and was always a pleasure to be around.

We gathered at my house last night to say our goodbyes and took our "mandatory" group photo, which we take at just about every gathering. (And yes, that is my dog's butt in the front of the photo.)

Steve Hunsicker with his dog "Solitia" surrounded by his fellow vounteers and friends at his house in Vava'u

It was a Mexican-themed dinner. We made tortillas and added some meat, rice and fresh guacamole for a great meal. The avocados are in season now and are delicious.

Vava'u Fire Update

I mentioned the fire above and thought I would give you a quick update. Nothing has been cleaned up. The remains of all the buildings that were destroyed are still there. The bookstore and the general store have both reopened in new locations, and one of the bars has set up a tent on the waterfront and is selling beer from there.

The fire was started by three young boys, around age eight. They are being charged. They were apparently trying to burn out some wasps, and the fire spread.

DID I DENGUE OR DID I NOT?
Monday, February 9, 2009

It's the rainy summer season in Tonga, and that means not only lots of heat and rain, but also lots of mosquitoes. Recently the Peace Corps advised all of the volunteers to be especially careful because of an increase in the number of cases of dengue fever in Tonga.

In case you don't know, dengue is a tropical illness that causes a high fever and a rash. It is transmitted by mosquitoes and is nicknamed "break-bone fever" because when you have it, you feel like every bone in your body is breaking. (See Wikipedia for more information.)

I also heard that if you think you have dengue, you probably don't. If you think you are going to die, then you probably have dengue. There is no treatment for dengue, other than to treat the symptoms. It will usually run its course in a week to 10 days.

A week ago today, I started to feel sick. At first, I thought I might just be tired from staying out too late on Monday night saying goodbye to Jessica. I left work early on Tuesday and slept from 1 p.m. until 7 a.m. the next morning. I had no energy and ate only a few bites. By Wednesday, I knew something was wrong. I had a fever, my joints were killing me and I had no appetite. I was also constantly thirsty and drinking lots of water. I contacted our Peace Corps medical staff on the main island who advised that I had the early symptoms of dengue fever.

By Thursday, my fever was at 100.2 degrees and my joint aches only got worse. In addition to the fever, I was having chills. I did not eat at all on Thursday. I spent Thursday night alternating between taking cold showers to cool down and putting on a warm-up suit and burying myself under layers of blankets to stay warm. On Friday, with the exception of having really sore eye sockets, I felt better, and Friday afternoon, I actually got out of bed and sat on the sofa to watch a movie. I was feeling better and thought the worst was over. Apparently this is one of the "tricks" of dengue. It makes you think you are better, then it kicks you down again. That's exactly what happened.

I went to bed Friday night and was shaking so badly that I felt like I was having convulsions. I was barely able to stand and debated whether I should go to the hospital or not. However, knowing Tongan medical care, I decided that all they would do is give me some Panadol (Tylenol) and send me home, so I opted not to go. Probably less than an hour later, I was sweating so badly, I had to go take another cold shower.

By Saturday afternoon, my fever had broken and I was starting to feel better. On Sunday, I started eating again and Sunday afternoon, I walked out the door of my house for the first time in more than four days, feeling like my old self.

So did I have dengue? I actually don't think so. I never got a rash, which is a classic sign of dengue, and the duration of my sickness was a lot shorter than most people experience with dengue. If I did have dengue, it means I can't get it again, or at least not the same strain.

I think it is more likely that I caught some other kind of tropical fever. There is a blood test you can take to see if you have been exposed to dengue, but that seems like a moot point now. And a special thanks to James, who stayed with me and took care of me while I was sick. It's great to have good friends like him and the other volunteers who called to check on me.

SWIMMING WITH JELLYFISH!
Sunday, February 15, 2009

I've often thought that the unexpected experiences are often life's best—the things you never anticipate that turn into unforgettable adventures. I never anticipated I would swim with jellyfish this past weekend, and even if I had, I probably would have imagined a painful experience involving getting stung by this misunderstood sea creature.

Friday afternoon, we set sail aboard *Manuoku*, one of our favorite sailboats in Vava'u. Less than an hour after leaving the harbor, we spotted thousands of jellyfish swimming beside the boat—more than I've ever seen anywhere. The jellyfish, in all shapes and sizes, seemed oblivious to our presence as we passed. Steve, our captain, told us that these jellyfish don't sting and that some Tongans eat them.

As we neared our camping spot, we saw another school of jellyfish. These looked a bit different, but Steve assured us that we wouldn't get stung if we jumped in the water and swam with them.

That's exactly what we did. I can't even begin to describe the feeling of plunging off the side of the boat wearing my mask and snorkel and descending in the crystal clear Pacific surrounded in all directions by these translucent creatures. It almost felt like a science fiction movie.

Not long after being in the water, my hand brushed against one of the jellyfish. I immediately recoiled, my mind still remembering my last encounter with a jellyfish in the Florida Keys. That time I got stung, but not this time. Then another brushed against my leg, and this time, I still flinched a bit, but was growing more accustomed to the touch of the "jelly" on my skin.

Before long, I was holding the jellyfish in my hands and playing with them as if I belonged in their underwater realm.

I took a lot of video while in the water, but none of it comes close to capturing this experience. Everywhere I looked, I was surrounded. It's an adventure I won't soon forget.

Camping (Kind of) on an Uninhabited Island

I have a friend whose idea of camping is to pull up in his RV, plug in and camp. There weren't any RVs on the island we visited this weekend, but the style of camping was a lot closer to that of my friend in the RV than to the style of primitive camping I usually enjoy here in Tonga.

Camping in style

The 11 Peace Corps volunteers who live here in Vava'u, two of the Japanese volunteers, an Australian volunteer and a few other folks were all the guests of our friends Ben, Lisa and Jason.

They own the island, and while it is uninhabited, it had more luxuries than some of my fellow volunteers have in their Peace Corps houses. Our amenities included a gas grill, chairs, tarps and even a generator to power lights at night. Even when the rain started falling, we stayed dry under the tarps and didn't need to retreat to our tents.

Their island is really amazing. It's a beautiful spot not far from the old harbor of Neiafu. (We left from the new harbor, which is about a three-hour boat trip since you have to sail around the main island to get to the other side.)

Sailing the South Pacific

After a night of camping, it was time for a day of sailing. Some of the volunteers decided to stay on the island a while longer, but most of us climbed back aboard *Manuoku* and spent the rest of the day sailing and snorkeling. While we did see a few jellyfish during our sail, it was nothing like the experience of the day before.

Fire Follow-up

The area of Neiafu that was destroyed by fire in December is finally being cleaned up. Last week, a group of Mormons removed most of the debris from the fire area.

There is now also a fence along the sidewalk so that someone doesn't accidentally fall off the edge.

Goodbye Enrique

Another member of my training group left the Peace Corps last week. Enrique is now back in the United States. Enrique is the first person from our group to leave since last April. Out of our original group of 33, there are now 28 of us left. There are 21 volunteers from the group that swore in as volunteers in December, and we have three volunteers who extended from earlier groups. That gives us a volunteer population of 52 throughout the kingdom.

CHANGES IN PEACE CORPS TONGA
Tuesday, February 24, 2009

It has been a sad week in Tonga as four volunteers—all of whom live on the main island of Tongatapu—have ended their service. Alexis, Cassie, Trent and Lara are all now gone. With the departure of Enrique last week, five volunteers from the main island have left in less than two weeks.

Each has their own reason for leaving, but I am particularly saddened by the loss of Trent and Lara, a married couple from Hawaii. I've been good friends with the two of them almost since my first day in Tonga. I've stayed with them during my visits to Nuku'alofa, and they have been here to Vava'u and have stayed with me. Trent and Lara were model volunteers, taking time not only to respect the Tongan culture, but also to make strong ties with the local people. Both were dedicated to their jobs, and Lara, who worked with geographic information systems (GIS), was doing some really great things.

The really sad part is that neither wanted to leave Tonga or the Peace Corps, but circumstances at home required them to return. I completely agree with and understand their decision, but will miss them a lot. I was fortunate to be able to briefly say goodbye to them in person on Monday when I was passing through Nuku'alofa, the capital city on the main island where they lived.

More Changes Coming Soon

Right now in Tonga, Peace Corps has two programs for volunteers. One is education and the other is business. For the most part, the education volunteers teach English to Tongan children while the business volunteers do a wide range of projects dealing not just with business, but also with government agencies and NGO's (non-government organizations).

As a business volunteer, I might be a bit biased, but I really think there is tremendous potential for volunteers in the business program to have a big impact on Tonga. There are not a lot of Tongans with business experience. I have yet to walk into a Tongan business, and I've been in a lot of them, where they didn't need help with basic business principals.

In an ideal world, Tonga would continue to have both programs, but if given a choice of only having one program, I would pick the business program.

Unfortunately, Peace Corps has decided to eliminate the business program in Tonga. The current business volunteers will be the last to serve. Beginning this fall, Peace Corps will only be sending education volunteers to Tonga.

The current plan, though not final yet, will have all volunteers working under the Tongan Ministry of Education. The good part of the plan is that instead of just teaching English, Peace Corps will be looking for volunteers who can teach science, math and industrial arts as well. There will also be five volunteers in each group who will be classified as business, but will work in the schools teaching computer or business skills. There are no plans to attach any volunteers to other ministries or organizations except the Ministry of Education.

The change is happening because of a survey that Peace Corps did to review its current programs. It will also give Peace Corps one point of contact, the Ministry of Education, to deal with volunteer site selections.

I get that this change will be easier for Peace Corps, but am disappointed to see the business program go away.

Last September, I wrote about the many opportunities that could exist here for business volunteers. Those opportunities are still here.

The change won't affect any of the current volunteers, as we will be allowed to finish our projects.

UNDERWATER RECOVERY
Friday, February 27, 2009

Last November, I went snorkeling in Swallows Cave with a group of volunteers who were still in training here in Vava'u. I let a friend borrow my mask and snorkel in the cave, and the snorkel came loose and ended up at the bottom of the cave, some 60-80 feet below. That was the last I saw of the snorkel but my mask survived.

Since the loss of my snorkel, I have been using one that was left by a former Peace Corps volunteer. I don't like it as much as the one I had, but it works.

Several weeks ago, I was talking with my friend Riki, who owns Riki Tiki Tours, a dive shop here in Vava'u. I briefly mentioned to him that I had lost my snorkel in Swallows Cave. Monday, I was sitting at Aquarium Cafe when Riki comes walking up with my snorkel in hand. He had taken some people diving in the cave and found it on the bottom.

I was amazed, not just that Riki had remembered that I had lost my snorkel, but that he found it four months after I lost it and that it was still there. It's in great shape and I look forward to using it again. Thank you, Riki!

A Great Week in 'Eua

I just got back from spending a great week on the island of 'Eua. The bank sent me there to assist with a workshop and to train the staff at the branch. I also met with some clients during my visit. But the real fun started Thursday night when my friends Shawn and Peter arrived from Tongatapu. We started our long weekend together by meeting up with the 'Eua Peace Corps volunteers at the only place in 'Eua that sells beer—The Hideaway.

On Friday, Shawn and I, along with my bank counterpart, Folau, got to see a lot of the island thanks to a guy from the bank who offered to show us around.

Steve and Folau at the natural land bridge on 'Eua

One of our first stops was at the edge of a giant cliff. We drove right up to the edge . . . too close for comfort, before we stopped.

But the real scare came when it was time to leave. The driver popped the clutch, and we lurched forward slightly before going into reverse. Shawn and I just looked at each other briefly, both with looks of panic, when the car went forward. Thankfully, we had a good driver, and we didn't end up at the bottom of the cliff.

Next stop was a natural land bridge. It's a giant bridge carved out by the ocean.

Shawn Hobbs at the natural land bridge

We saw a lot of other great sites before we met up with Peter and Jason, who lives on 'Eua. From there, we headed to the north end of the island for a beautiful hike.

Saturday, the four guys were joined by Ashley, Heather and Jenny for a hike to a place called Smoker's Cave, which is a giant waterfall. You cannot see the bottom.

We also made it to the two lookouts on the east side of the island. From there we went to a place called Rat's Cave. This was my second visit to Rat's Cave. I came a year ago with my friend Craig, who has now completed his service.

To get inside Rat's Cave, you crawl on your belly through a cave to a small opening. You then have to drop down inside the chamber below. But because you are at the edge of a cliff, it looks like if you slip, you will go down the side of the cliff. It can be a bit intimidating, but once you have done it once, it is pretty easy the second time. The guys all camped Saturday night, while the women went back to town. Peter and Jason put hammocks up on the lookout and slept under the stars, while Shawn and I stayed in a tent nearby.

It was a great trip, and I highly recommend 'Eua for anyone who really wants to get away. There are only two places to stay, and both are pretty modest, but the scenery and seclusion are well worth it. From the time we started our hike on Saturday until we returned to the main road on Sunday, we did not see another person.

There are numerous caves, some which have never been explored. It is the only Tongan island to have parrots, and it also has species of plants found nowhere else in Tonga.

PEACE CORPS WAGES AND BENEFITS
Thursday, March 5, 2009

By definition, the word "volunteer" implies that you are doing something for free and are not paid for the work you provide. Dictionary.com defines a volunteer as "a person who performs a service willingly and without pay."

As a Peace Corps volunteer, I am prohibited from accepting money for any services that I provide, but it would not be true to say that I work for free.

While I don't receive a salary, my basic needs are met. I am provided with a house and enough money to buy food and other necessities. The stipend I receive is supposed to allow me to live at approximately the same level as a typical host country national, and I live comfortably, though certainly not at the level to which most Americans are accustomed.

Since I just finished doing my taxes and since I'm often asked, "How much money do you get?" I thought I would detail exactly what I do get. I've converted all amounts to US dollars.

Housing Arrangements

In Tonga, each organization that hosts a Peace Corps volunteer is responsible for providing a house for that volunteer. The house must have locking doors and windows, a bed, a table with at least two chairs, and fresh water must be available within a reasonable distance of the house.

Sometimes, this means the volunteer will live on a school campus or in a house owned by the organization or by someone who works for the organization. In my case, the Tonga Development Bank pays to rent a house for me (and by Peace Corps standards, I have a really nice house). The bank pays my landlord $177 per month for my house. Since December, the bank also is paying $97 a month for my utilities. Previously, I was paying those bills myself. That means the bank pays about $3,200 a year to have me work for them.

Living Stipend

In addition to having my housing provided, Peace Corps pays me a monthly stipend of $310 to cover all of my expenses. That works out to just over $10 a day for all my food and other needs. If you are counting, that means I get about $3,700 a year from the US government for my volunteer service. That total also includes $24 a month that is classified as a vacation-leave allowance. We get $12 a day for each of the 24 days of vacation we are allowed each year. That amount is fixed by Peace Corps headquarters for all volunteers worldwide. The amount of the stipend varies in each Peace Corps country.

The vacation-leave allowance and a portion of our stipend are considered taxable income. For all of 2008, my taxable income for my work as a volunteer was about $800.

Readjustment Allowance

For each month you serve as a volunteer, you also earn $225 that is held by Peace Corps and then paid to you in a lump sum when you complete your service. This amount is 100% taxable. In 2008, just like every other Peace Corps volunteer in the world, I earned a readjustment allowance of $2700.

The Bottom Line

I had earned taxable income of approximately $3500 from Peace Corps in 2008. And this year it came with an extra surprise. I was not eligible for the stimulus program last year when I was still working for a good portion of the year, but I found out that I can get it this year. That means I'll be getting a tax credit of $300.

Since I've been in Tonga, I've been able to live on my stipend. I have not tapped into any money from home to use in Tonga, even though I have ordered a few things and had them shipped to me. And certainly my stipend didn't pay for my trip to the United States at Christmas. Vava'u, the island where I live, is the most expensive in all of Tonga. We pay more for everything here than anywhere else in Tonga. To be fair, we also don't have the same choices or temptations as the volunteers on the main island. But part of being a volunteer is living with and like the Tongans. That means if you don't have something or you can't afford something, you just do without it.

Peace Corps Volunteers Meet the King

Six Peace Corps volunteers who live on the main island of Tongatapu had a chance to meet and talk with the king of Tonga this week. You might think that in a country the size of Tonga, meeting the king would not be uncommon. However, the king is well, a king, and he can pretty much pick and choose which individuals he wants to visit with. The occasion was a visit by the new US ambassador to Fiji, who is also responsible for Tonga.

A WHOLE NEW (UNDERWATER) WORLD
Sunday, March 15, 2009

There are more dive shops in Vava'u than there are gas stations or bakeries. It's not hard to figure out why since divers from all over the world come here to enjoy the warm crystal blue Pacific and the colorful coral and marine life that live beneath the surface.

And because not a lot of divers make it here, the coral is pretty much undamaged from human contact, and the different species of fish are amazing.

Since I have been in Tonga, I've been snorkeling a number of times and have immensely enjoyed the view from the surface, but I finally decided I wanted to go a bit deeper, so I've been taking classes to get my PADI open water scuba certification.

Saturday, I took my last class, and I walked away with my certificate and a lot of great memories of life underwater.

I look the class with my fellow volunteer Stan and an Australian friend named Emma. Riki, our instructor, who runs the Riki Tiki dive shop, snapped this photo of us underwater.

Stan Luker, Emma Shepardson and Steve Hunsicker take diving lessons

I have to confess I was nervous about taking diving lessons. There are no decompression chambers in Tonga, and it can be scary to think about being so far underwater and running out of air.

However, Riki is a great teacher and always made us feel at ease. As part of our training, he had to turn off our air underwater and make us share air with a buddy. We also had to take off our masks and air supplies while underwater. At every step, Riki first explained at the surface what was going to happen and then once underwater, he demonstrated what we were supposed to do before he asked us to do the exercise. It was a great confidence builder, and none of us ever felt uncomfortable doing anything we were asked.

That doesn't mean there weren't some problems. (Perhaps challenges would be a better word.) I had trouble getting equalized to the underwater pressure a couple of times and learned that I needed to dive down a little slower than my friends.

I also struggled a bit learning to take off my weight belt on the ocean floor and then putting it back on the correct way. For the record, I always got it back on, but it took me a while to be as graceful doing it as Riki wanted.

I feel very fortunate to have found an instructor as skilled as Riki here in Vava'u. I had to miss our very first class because I was sick, and Riki was great about giving me a private make-up lesson so that I could catch back up.

Now that I'm certified, I am already looking forward to my next dive. There are so many great places to go here; the hardest part will be figuring out which one to explore first.

In case you were wondering, there are four dives shops in Vava'u, three bakeries and two gas stations.

VOLCANOES AND EARTHQUAKES
Friday, March 20, 2009

If you pay attention to news about Tonga, you probably know by now that a volcano has erupted not far from the main island of Tongatapu, and we have felt a number of earthquakes because of the eruption.

The volcano is on Hunga Tonga, which is located about 150 miles or so away from me in Vava'u.

Some of the first photos of the eruption were taken by Leta Havea Kami, who is the deputy managing director of the Tonga Development Bank where I work. She was on her way here to Vava'u when she snapped photos from the plane.

Photo of the volcano taken by Leta Havea Kami

I felt the earthquake early this morning. It lasted for a while, but didn't rattle the dishes and didn't have any noticeable impact other than the normal shaking.

A tsunami warning was issued for all of Tonga after the quake. Peace Corps put us under a "code white," which is the lowest level of emergency activation that they issue. It simply means to pay attention to the radio and be alert. Once the warning was cancelled, so was our code white.

Steve Hunsicker

A SPEECH WORTH READING
Thursday, March 26, 2009

The following is a portion of a speech made on the Senate floor this week by Senator Johnny Isakson of Georgia. He was speaking in support of the National Service Act.

I thought his speech was worth sharing.

> This past Saturday, I attended one of the most moving ceremonies of my life—moving in a sad way but also in an uplifting way.
>
> Unfortunately, a wonderful young lady, 24 years old, from Cumming, GA, Kate Puzey, was killed in Benin, Africa, on March 11. She was a Peace Corps worker who graduated first in her class in high school, was an honors graduate from William and Mary, and she studied French in Paris to learn the language that led her to be able to go to this part of the world and teach this poor African nation about agriculture and other skills. She served since July of 2007 and was in the last 2 months of her service in Benin.
>
> I went to this service because I felt moved. I am ranking member of the African subcommittee on foreign relations. Paul Coverdell, who served in the seat I now hold, was a director of the Peace Corps. I felt moved that morning when I got to go to the service and sit in the back of the room and pay my respects to a great American. I left having listened to 12 eulogies by young people whose lives were changed by Kate. The acting director of the Peace Corps, Ms. Jody Olsen, delivered a beautiful eulogy.
>
> I realized how much voluntarism means to the United States, not just on our shores but in Africa and on continents around the world. I commend people such as Senator Dodd who have given time in the Peace Corps. I ask the Senate to give its unanimous support to this legislation. I dedicate this speech in honor of Kate Puzey, to her life, and what she did as a Georgian and as a volunteer. She joined the Peace Corps and changed the plight, the lives, the hopes, and in fact the future of children in that small country on the west coast of Africa.
>
> God bless the Peace Corps and the life of Kate Puzey. And thanks to those who have volunteered and to the committee that has brought this National Service Act reauthorization to the floor of the Senate.

I have found volunteering in the Peace Corps to be a wonderful experience for me. I hope that many more Americans in the future have the opportunity to serve both at home and abroad.

A TONGAN FUNERAL (AND KISSING THE DEAD)
Monday, March 30, 2009

It was a sad week at the Vava'u branch of the Tongan Development Bank. Last week, two of the men I worked with each lost their mother. The first woman was buried on Saturday and the other, on Monday.

Monday's funeral was for the mother of 'Ofa. 'Ofa and his wife, Hangale, have always been great to me. On my first day at the bank, 'Ofa was one of the first to come in just to talk and to introduce himself. He always seems to have a smile on his face and enjoys a great laugh.

The other funeral was for Fakava's real mother. He was raised by adopted parents, which is very common in Tonga. I was not able to attend the funeral on Saturday, but I did go to the funeral on Monday. It was the first Tongan funeral I've attended, which is surprising since I've been here for 18 months.

In Tonga, there are no funeral parlors. When someone dies, they are loaded into a vehicle and put in a freezer at the hospital where the body is kept frozen until it is time for the funeral. There are no embalming facilities in Vava'u, and the families are responsible for preparing their loved one's body for the public viewing.

Because there are many Tongans overseas and on other islands, it is not uncommon for a funeral to be a week or longer after a person dies. That was the case with 'Ofa's mother. She passed away last Tuesday and the funeral was six days later on Monday.

On the day of the funeral, the body was taken to the family house where hundreds of people gathered to mourn with the family. When there is a *putu* (funeral), the bakeries will often sell out of bread and the stores will end up with empty shelves because it is the job of the family to feed all of the people who gather to spend the day with them.

As we arrived at 'Ofa and Hangale's home on Monday, the first thing I noticed were all the people sitting around. As is tradition, the men were sitting together drinking kava while the woman sang and congregated on mats in the shade around the house.

It is traditional to present a gift to the family in honor of the deceased. The bank presented 'Ofa and Hangale with cash, a mat, a Tongan tapa and numerous other gifts. Before entering the house, we lined up in a fashion similar to the women in the photo below.

Once we had our gifts in hand, we paraded single file into the house.

Taking gifts to the family

Once inside we laid down our gifts then walked forward to see the body of 'Ofa's mother.

Kissing the Dead

It is tradition that each person kisses the deceased on the forehead to pay his or her respects. I knew about this tradition and had lots of time to think about it before the funeral. I knew it would be expected for me to kiss the corpse, and I was prepared for it. Or at least I thought I was. As I gently pressed my lips to her forehead, I was not appalled or even bothered by it. What I hadn't been prepared for was how cold she would be. It made sense that she would be cold since she had been on ice for almost a full week, but the cold was a surprise.

Steve Hunsicker kisses the body of his friend's mother

As I was leaving the house, I was then presented with a beautiful piece of silk. This is another Tongan tradition. When you come to pay your respects, a family member gives you a gift from the many gifts that have been accumulated. Unfortunately, the grieving family never comes out ahead because they end up giving away more than they receive. I tried to give the silk back to 'Ofa but he refused saying it was the Tongan way.

It was sad to see 'Ofa so clearly upset by the loss of his mother. He is a really wonderful man.

The good news is that he and Hangale are about to have a baby, which I'm sure will bring a smile back to his face.

A BAD YEAR FOR BANKING IN TONGA
Monday, April 6, 2009

It's been said that when America sneezes, the rest of the world gets a cold. That may not be as true today as it was 25 years ago, but the current economic crisis in the United States is having an impact in places as far away as the Kingdom of Tonga.

There are three commercial banks in Tonga plus one development bank. Last year, Westpac Bank of Tonga lost TOP$6 million or about US$3 million. ANZ, another commercial bank, lost about US$1 million. The third commercial bank, which is Malaysian-based MBF, has not reported its year-end numbers as of the end of March.

The Tonga Development Bank is owned 100% by the government. It was able to make a small profit of about US$450,000 last year, but that was down from previous years. (The Tonga Development Bank is one of just three enterprises owned by the Tongan government that turns a profit. The majority of government-owned enterprises in Tonga are in the red.)

Some of the reasons for the bad turn in the Tongan banking industry are the same as in the United States, especially bad loans. But another problem that is just starting to show up is a reduction in the amount of remittances that Tongans receive from families overseas.

The number one source of income for Tonga is overseas remittances, followed by foreign aid. As Tongans in the United States, Australia and New Zealand suffer financial hardships, it is having a trickle-down effect on the Tongans here. That means that many Tongans who were paying back loans with remittances from families overseas are now unable to fulfill their obligations.

The Tonga Development Bank recently asked me to help it put on a workshop to address the problems being faced by the banks in Tonga and to help come up with new ways of doing business. For three days, we huddled in a room on the third floor of the bank with all of the banks employees participating. The goal was to be able to "manage at a higher level."

Steve Hunsicker and his co-workers at the Tonga Development Bank

We even worked on a Saturday. In the photo above are all of the people I work with on a daily basis except for 'Ofa and Hangale, who were absent because 'Ofa's mother had just died.

The bank organized similar workshops at each branch and in each department at the head office in Nuku'alofa. I give the bank a lot of credit for having the foresight to realize that it can't continue to operate the way it always has. And unlike American banks, the Tongan banks have many additional cultural barriers to overcome as well.

The workshop was not always easy, and it was tough on many of the Tongan staff to learn that more is going to be expected of them in the coming year.

At the end of the workshop, everyone got a Snickers bar. (OK, I know that doesn't sound very Tongan, and actually the Snickers bars were my idea.) It's very rare for us to have American chocolate here, and I thought it would be a nice treat.

The bank employees were also given a little over US$7 for working on a Saturday. Hopefully, some of what we did over the three-day workshop will help the bank have a better year next year.

Steve Hunsicker

PEACE CORPS SURPRISES
Monday, April 13, 2009

When I signed up for the Peace Corps, I thought I had a pretty good idea of what I could expect from my experience. I did lots of research, asked lots of questions and got a lot of good information reading the blogs of current and past volunteers.

But no matter how prepared you think you may be, it is unlikely that your Peace Corps service will be anything like you expect. For some volunteers, that is a bad thing, and they end up going home early. Others do the best they can with the unexpected, and some find that their experience is very different but perhaps better than they ever expected.

As I wrap up 18 months in Tonga, I find that I'm in that latter category. I came here with very few expectations and have found joining Peace Corps to be one of the best decisions I've ever made.

When I signed up, I was prepared to live on a small island, perhaps with no electricity. I certainly didn't expect to have access to the Internet daily. I imagined I would be working with just one or probably just a couple of businesses helping them in my role as a business advisor. When I thought about the friends I would make, I always thought in terms of the nationals in the country where I would be serving. I never really thought much about getting to know my fellow volunteers. I figured I would be living in a small village and would know everyone by name, and they would probably know me. I also thought I would be alone most of the time and that I would probably read more books than I ever imagined. I thought I might read those books by candlelight or a small kerosene lantern.

My friends had a different idea of what my Peace Corps experience would be like. One told me of his experience living in a Peace Corps house with armed guards and another friend wanted to know if I would be digging ditches, which is kind of the Peace Corps cliché. Others joked that I would be living like Tom Hanks in the movie *Castaway*, and another thought my work would be like that of a missionary. In reality, none of my expectations nor the predictions of my friends turned out to be reality.

My "surprises" have for the most part been positive. I've made many friends, but it hasn't just been with the Tongans. It has been with my fellow volunteers and also with many of the people who live here . . . the so called "ex-pats" from the United States, New Zealand and Australia who run many of the tourism-related businesses.

Instead of working with just one or two businesses, I've worked with many businesses through my job at the Tonga Development Bank. The bank's goal for me has been to assist any business that needs help, including businesses that don't work with the bank.

I live in a pretty nice house by Peace Corps standards, and I have electricity and running water almost all the time. Tonga is still a developing country, so those services are not always reliable. I have slow, but daily access to the Internet, so I have been able to keep in contact with my friends and family. Clearly my standard of living is nowhere close to what I was accustomed to in the United States, but I'm doing just fine.

I live in a town. It's not large, but it's certainly not a village. I know a lot of people and certainly a lot more people know me. I'm still surprised when strangers come up to me and call me Steve. The town is big enough that I still meet new people on a regular basis, which is nice.

I never imagined I would be taking business trips in Tonga, but I've been to most of the outer islands in Vava'u and to some of the Ha'apai Islands as well. I've made three trips to 'Eua, and I am scheduled to do a lot more traveling this year before the end of my service.

But to be fair, not all of the surprises have been pleasant.

I've been really sick just once and had a bizarre case of fish poisoning that caused me to temporarily lose 80% of my left arm and hand use. I have learned which Tongan foods will "give me the runs" and which ones won't. I've also eaten many things I never thought I would eat, and I've had cravings for "real" American food more times than I can count.

I was robbed while staying at the Friendly Islander Hotel, and I have had to say goodbye to friends who have either completed their service or who have left early.

When I look back at the past 18 months, I can't believe how quickly the time has passed. My good days have far outweighed the bad days, and as I write this, there has never been a day when I felt like quitting.

Very soon, a new group of Americans will be getting invitations to come serve their country in Tonga. These will be the people who will replace my group once we come home in December. Tonga is not for everyone. There are times when you wonder why you are here and even why Peace Corps is here. Some volunteers have had really unfortunate things happen during their service . . . things a lot worse than anything that has happened to me. And some people come here with very unrealistic expectations either about Peace Corps or about what they think they can accomplish. However, I can't imagine that I would have been as happy serving anywhere other than Tonga.

I look forward to my remaining months of service, but I also look forward to going home. I know that while my real home is in the United States, Tonga will always be a part of me.

STEVE AND STAN'S NEW ZEALAND ADVENTURE
Wednesday, April 22, 2009

One of the perks of being in Peace Corps is being able to travel to other places near your area of service. For those of us in Tonga, it is often other South Pacific Islands or Australia and New Zealand.

I've just completed an almost three-week stay in Kiwi Country with my friend and fellow volunteer Stan. Early in the trip, I remarked to Stan that I had never figured I would go on vacation with someone half my age. He answered by saying he never thought he would go on vacation with someone twice his age. Touché' Stan! He turned out to be a great travel companion.

The trip was a first for both of us. While I had spent a few hours at the Auckland Airport on my way back from Australia last year, this was the first time I got to see this remarkable country.

North Island New Zealand

We decided before we left that we would spend most of our time in New Zealand on the South Island. We spent a night in Auckland, a night in Rotorua and two nights in Wellington before taking a three-hour ferry ride to the South Island.

We both thoroughly enjoyed Wellington, which is a vibrant city reminiscent of a Greek island with houses built into the hills along the coast. The city is active and has a very positive energy. Before arriving in Wellington, we visited Waiotapu, which is a geothermal site on the North Island.

It was fascinating to see boiling hot water bubble from the ground and steam rise from mud pools as we hiked around the area. There is also a small geyser that is "started" every morning when they dump soap into it.

The best meal I had during my entire vacation was on the North Island and happened quite by chance. We decided to take the back roads from Auckland to see more of the countryside. Not far outside of Auckland, we stopped at a small market to get some sandwiches. The market did not make sandwiches, but the proprietor suggested we try a place just down a small side road called Margaret's Garden. I ordered mussels in a cream sauce with pasta and a nice glass of wine. My food was simply spectacular, while Stan judged his good.

South Island New Zealand

It is fall in New Zealand and the further south we traveled, the more brilliant the colors became. Our first stop was Nelson, which is near many of the region's wineries. We stayed there from Monday to Wednesday, and there was not much going on in the town. We did meet up with our Peace Corps friends Scot and Karen who were visiting from Tonga as well. The highlight of our stay there was a hike along the coast track at the Abel Tasman National Park. The water levels between high tide and low tide are dramatic, and a boat that floats at high tide will be completely aground at low tide.

Venturing further south, we stopped in Kaikoura. We ate some fresh crayfish from a roadside stand and visited a seal colony south of town. Unfortunately, we didn't see any seals. It snowed while we were sleeping, and we awoke the next morning to snow-capped mountains all around us.

We spent four nights in Christchurch with our friend and former Peace Corps volunteer Justin. He moved to New Zealand after completing his service and now works there. We caught a movie there and did some rock climbing. We also had a fun night on the town, with Justin showing us many of the hot spots. We went to a place called Boogie Nights, which was an 80s-themed disco complete with a lighted dance floor. I may have been the only person in the place who actually remembered going to places like this in the 80s.

At Mt. Cook, the views were spectacular on the day we arrived, but we left early because the next day it rained. That was really the only day that the weather didn't cooperate with us during the trip.

Queenstown is great. It was one of the best places we visited on the trip and also where we decided to jump out of a perfectly good airplane from 15,000 feet above the ground below. It was a spectacular adventure that included a 60-second free fall.

The night before the jump we met probably the most "colorful" character of the trip. We went into a small place called The Minibar. Inside were just the bartender and one customer. The customer looked like a homeless person and was mumbling. As we were talking with him, he went to a corner of the bar to get his chainsaw and fishing pole! What? That's right, this guy was in a bar in Queenstown with a chainsaw and a fishing pole. We later saw him walking down the street carrying his accoutrements. We don't remember his name, but for the rest of the trip we laughed about our Queenstown encounter with "Chainsaw Man" and wondered why we hadn't taken a photo.

There are a number of fiords on the South Island, with Milford Sound being the best known. We skipped Milford and opted to go further south to a lesser known place called Doubtful Sound. The area only gets sunshine one out of every three days and getting to the sound is an adventure all by itself. We first took a one-hour boat ride across a lake. From there, we took a 45-minute bus ride to the sound and then a three-hour boat tour of the fiord. While we didn't experience much rain, it was still overcast. We did get to see some seals where the sound empties into the Tasman Sea.

Doubtful Sound got its name from James Cook, the famous explorer who was the first European to visit both New Zealand and Tonga. While mapping the area, he wrote on his charts that it was a "doubtful harbor" and the name stuck.

One of the best places we stayed during our trip was at a small backpacker's accommodation in Manapouri, which is where you catch the first boat to get to Doubtful Sound. The place is called Freestone Backpackers. We shared a cabin with some German tourists. We all had our own bedrooms, and the common area had nice leather couches, a pot belly stove with plenty of firewood and a very nice shared kitchen. You could look out and see the lake from the front of our cabin.

Probably the highlight of the entire trip was our last Saturday in New Zealand. We debated whether we wanted to stay in Queenstown for a fourth night, go back to Mt. Cook and hope the weather would be better or go visit the glaciers. The glaciers were a long drive, but we eventually decided to head that way.

Franz Josef Glacier is on the west coast of New Zealand and a long way from anywhere. As we were driving north toward the glacier, we saw a sign that said, "Last Gas for 120KM" and promptly filled up, not wanting to run out of gas in the middle of nowhere.

To get close to the glacier, you have to wade across "glacier cold" water, but the chill on your feet is worth it. We walked as far as we could past several great waterfalls until we reached a rope running up an incline. A sign warned that only experienced climbers and guided tours should proceed. We decided to go forward, and what an adventure it was. We used ropes to pull us up steep slopes, and we waded through creek beds just to get to the glacier. But that was nothing compared to the hike back. We accidently stumbled upon the end of an adventure trail and took it back. Here, we pulled ourselves up on rocks using chains that we anchored into the rocks. We found ladders for the really steep climbs and lots of scary terrain. However, it was all worth it. We got some great views of the glaciers and had a hike that normally you would have to pay for to enjoy.

Recommendations If You Are Coming to New Zealand

- Until my trip to New Zealand, I had never stayed at a hostel or backpackers' kind of accommodation. I was surprised to find that you could get a pretty nice private room at these places. In addition to Freestone Backpackers mentioned previously, another of our favorite places was the YHA Wellington, where our twin room even had a French press with free ground coffee. We would also highly recommend Freeman's Bed and Breakfast in Auckland. We spent our last night there but left for the airport at 5 a.m., so we didn't get to sample the breakfast.

- There are a lot of New Zealand beers. We tried many different kinds, often sampling different beers every night. My favorites were the Mac's Brewjolais and the Montiefs Celtic.
- We had several good meals and would recommend Margaret's Garden, mentioned before, and Harborside Seafood in Auckland. There is also an Indian restaurant in Queenstown at the top of the street across from the McCafe that was quite good.
- We had a good experience with our rental car company, EZi Rentals, and would use them again. We made several changes during our trip, and they were very accommodating. Plus, all of the staff we met were friendly. Our first car was a Nissan March, and it didn't have a lot of power on the mountains. But our other two cars were both Hyundai Getz, and we liked both of them.
- We used the Lonely Planet New Zealand travel guide extensively. It was published in September, and most of the information was up to date. We found it much better than the Fodor's guide, which we also had.

Two Places to Avoid Staying if You Are Heading to New Zealand.

- The first is Cactus Jack's in Rotorua, which is a Western-themed hostel. The room was clean, but very small and the atmosphere was very weird. We were also disappointed with our stay at the YHA Hostel in Franz Josef. The facility was not very clean, there was no water pressure in the showers, and the hot water ran out quickly.
- Our worst meal of the trip was in Queenstown at The Fishbone Grill. This place is a top pick in the Lonely Planet guidebook, but we thought it was really bad. We decided to give it a try because there was a sign out front that said "Bluff oysters." We had eaten raw Bluff oysters earlier in the trip, so we decided to go there. When we sat down, the waitress told us they were out of Bluff oysters. We suggested they take down the sign out front. A while later, we heard a table near us also asking for Bluff oysters. The sign was still outside. Stan's food was tasteless, and mine, the local salmon, was extremely greasy . . . so much so that I couldn't eat it. We never saw our waitress again after she took our order; some other people delivered the food. We finally got tired of waiting and went up to the front counter to get our bill. I would not go back here.

Other Notes from the Trip

- We both were impressed with New Zealand's commitment to self-sufficiency. They use geothermal, solar and hydroelectric sources to generate most of their power. Everywhere we stayed there were signs asking us to turn off the lights when we left to save power, and the heaters were generally on a timer.

• Prices were pretty good, as the dollar is strong right now. We never paid more than US$60 a night for a room, and we paid just US$13 each to stay at the Freestone Backpackers mentioned above. The price of a beer in a bar ranged from about US$2 to US$4.

• We would often travel for many kilometers with no radio, especially in the mountains. When a station clicked in, no matter the format, we would listen to it. We didn't have an FM modulator for an iPod and no CDs. While memorable, the worst song we heard—and thankfully we only heard it once— was a song that repeated the same lines over and over again. It went:

> *We're just ordinary people*
> *We don't know which way to go*
> *Because we're ordinary people*
> *Maybe we should take it slow*

THIS AND THAT
Wednesday, April 29, 2009

Here are some recent happenings in Vava'u that I thought were worth sharing:

Murder in Vava'u

Tonga may be the "Friendly Islands" and guns may be illegal, but that doesn't mean violent crimes don't happen. While I was in New Zealand, a 47-year-old man was killed here in Vava'u. According to the local scuttlebutt, a 22-year-old man started harassing the victim at a local bar, asking him to pay for beers. A fight started and the 22-year-old hit the victim in the head with a car jack. He is now in jail. A similar murder happened last year in Vava'u.

While it is uncommon to have a murder in Vava'u, it is extremely rare to have a murder on the small outer islands. Earlier this month, a 22-year-old woman was killed on the small island of 'Uiha in the Ha'apai Island Group. 'Uiha, which I visited last December, has about 750 residents. The suspect, a 30-year-old man, is now in jail.

There have been two other murders in the kingdom this year. Both of those took place on the main island of Tongatapu, where the majority of the Tongan population lives.

Sailing, Camping and Snorkeling

I joined a group of Australians, Japanese and Americans this weekend for a sailing and camping trip aboard *Manuoku*. Our first stop was Swallows Cave, where we climbed the walls and jumped into the very deep water below.

After leaving Swallows Cave, we sailed around before setting up camp at Port Maurelle, which is pronounced MORE-el. One of the Aussies had a guitar, and as we were sitting around the campfire, we tried to write a song. We only finished four lines before we gave up.

> *Here we are at Post Maurelle*
> *Watching the sea swell*
> *Sipping on our tasty drinks*
> *Sharing our cross-cultural links*

It's not exactly a great song, but it was great to get together with people from different cultures and realize how much we have in common.

Cruise Ship Visitors

A large number of the tourists who come to Tonga each year arrive on cruise ships. They generally arrive in the morning and depart in the late afternoon. Both the main island of Tongatapu and the Vava'u Islands where I live are regular cruise stops. On Friday, a ship with 1,900 passengers stopped in Vava'u. To say that the visitors changed the town is an understatement. Instead of Tongans, everywhere you looked you saw white people carrying cameras. While I realize the ships help the local economy, I had to wonder how many of these people, if any, would leave here with even a small understanding of what a wonderful place Tonga is.

During the middle of the tourist invasion, I was walking down the street with my friends Chad and Katie when two of the tourists spotted the West Virginia University shirt I was wearing and wanted to know if we were Americans. They were surprised to learn that there were Peace Corps volunteers in Tonga and then mentioned that their daughter had served in the Peace Corps and now works for the Peace Corps in Atlanta.

They asked if they could take our picture and repeatedly thanked us for our service.

Facts About Tonga

I found a web page with some updated information about Tonga. Here are a few quick facts I picked up from the site:

- Location: 170 islands in the southwestern Pacific Ocean
- Population: 101,991 (189th)
- Density: 352.9 people per square mile
- Capital city: Nuku'alofa (population 23,438)
- Foreign tourist visitors per year: 39,451*
- Adult literacy rate: 99.2% (m 99.1%/f 99.3%)
- Average number of children per mother: 3.8
- Average life expectancy (m/f): 73/69

*The number of foreign visitors shown above includes those that arrive on cruise ships.

A Final Note

I grew up in Lexington, Virginia, where our local newspaper was *The News Gazette*. Each week, the paper carried a column called "This and That." I have no idea if the column still exists, but the column would run stories about how "the parents of Joe Smith of Lexington are visiting this week from North

Carolina," or "Mike Jones and his family just returned from a vacation in Virginia Beach."

As I was writing this, I somehow remembered that column and decided to do a "This and That" style post this week. I hope it is at least a little more interesting than the column I used to read in the paper.

One other note about *The News Gazette*: I used to sell the newspaper when I was around 13 or 14. I would buy the papers for 10 cents and sell them for 15 cents. My profit was the nickel I made on each paper. Most people would give me a quarter for the paper, so I actually made 15 cents on most papers. I sold about 40 or 50 papers a week.

WORK SLOWS DOWN
Saturday, May 9, 2009

Things at my work at the Tonga Development Bank have slowed to a snail's pace. My counterpart was promoted in January to branch manager in 'Eua. He is not being replaced in Vava'u. In addition, the bank is talking about cutting back on additional positions due to a slowdown in the banking business and a drop in the number of people applying for loans. Because I have so little to do at work right now, I have proposed that the bank allow me to put together a video highlighting the bank's services and success stories. They have agreed to let me do this, and I've written the first draft of a script. Once approved, I'll shoot the video and edit it together. I will need someone to help me with the translation, as I plan to do it all in Tongan. The bank plans to air it on Tongan TV and also perhaps play it on a TV set in the lobby of the branches.

I'm excited about this project because it will give me something constructive to do that can be used even after I finish my Peace Corps service. It's also a lot better doing this than sitting around all day at work with little to do. Most of the bank's employees are in the same position as me. If you walk in, you will see the employees just sitting around and drinking tea. Our daily tea break can now stretch to two hours because of the lack of business.

We are less than a month from the start of the traditional tourism season here in Vava'u. Everyone is hoping that the season will give the economy a much needed boost.

Vacation Plans

I have 11 days of vacation left, and I plan to make a return trip to Australia. But this time instead of visiting Brisbane, I plan to head further south to Sydney and Melbourne. I'm planning to go in early September, returning just in time for my COS or close of service conference on September 15th. Even though we don't officially complete our service until December, this will be the last time that my group will be together. Right now, I plan to leave Tonga in early December, travel for a few weeks and then be back in the United States in time to spend Christmas with my family.

Steve Hunsicker

A DAY AT THE OFFICE
Wednesday, May 13, 2009

My workload at the Tonga Development Bank has slowed down, and there have been a few days recently when I have not had much to do. Last week, I was walking to work thinking about how I only had one appointment at 9:30 a.m. I had a feeling that my client might cancel, leaving me with nothing on the agenda for the day. I had been at work for less than a minute, when the phone rang, and it was my client saying she couldn't make 9:30 a.m. and wanted to reschedule for 2 p.m. I agreed and sat down to read my mail. A few minutes later, the phone rang again, and it was the same client telling me she was going to go look at a boat she was thinking about purchasing and asked if I wanted to go with her. Since I had nothing else to do, I said sure, and we agreed to meet a little later.

I got to the dock and saw my friend Riki, who owns a dive shop. Turns out we were going in his boat and while we were out, he was going to replace the chain on two boat moorings. I told him I would be glad to help, so he told me to go grab dive gear and an air tank out of his shop, and before long, we were on the water heading out.

After a nice 45-minute boat ride, we got to the moorings; I suited up and went diving for 45 minutes. It was my first dive since getting my certification. I helped Riki a little but mostly just dove around on the ocean floor.

After surfacing, we went and checked out the boat with my client and then rode back to the dock. We got back late, but I was still happy to spend some time helping my client with her books. What I thought would be a boring day ended up being great.

How often do you go to a bank to work and end up diving in the Pacific? Just a "day at the office" in Peace Corps Tonga.

Goodbye Stan

Wednesday afternoon at 3 p.m.: Most of the Vava'u Peace Corps volunteers were gathered at The Aquarium Cafe. There were tears and hugs as we started to say goodbye to our friend and fellow volunteer Stan. On the radio, an old Beatles song was playing.

> *There are places I remember all my life,*
> *Though some have changed*
> *Some forever, not for better*
> *Some have gone and some remain.*
> *All these places have their moments*
> *Of lovers and friends I still can recall*

Some are dead and some are living
In my life, I loved them all.

The song, while random, seemed appropriate for the occasion because for all of us, The Aquarium Cafe and Vava'u will always be places we remember. And those memories will include Stan, who has been part of our Peace Corps adventure for the past 20 months. Stan is on his way back to the United States, and he'll certainly be missed here in Vava'u. Even though his Peace Corps service is over, I'm confident the friendships he has developed will be long-lasting. I'm going to miss having him around but look forward to seeing him once I return to the States.

BISCUITS AND GRAVY
Monday, May 18, 2009

I've never been much of a cook. I know how to do the basics, and back in the United States, I could do a pretty mean steak on the grill, and I make decent gravy. However, the whole idea of baking is a pretty foreign concept to me, unless you count microwaving as baking.

In Tonga, there are very few pre-made food items available. It's pretty much the basics like sugar, flour, salt, etc. And even those items can disappear at times. A few weeks ago, there was no flour in most of the stores for a few days until the boat came with a new supply.

The bottom line is that if you want a cake or pizza dough, you make it from scratch. Sunday morning, I woke up with a craving for one of my favorite breakfast meals: biscuits and gravy! I knew I could make the gravy, but wasn't sure about the biscuits. I found the recipe book that Peace Corps gives to each volunteer. I have to confess, it was the first time I had opened it. Inside was a recipe for biscuits. I didn't have all the ingredients, but I figured I would substitute and leave out some things. Amazingly, the biscuits came out great. They weren't anywhere near as good as Bojangles' biscuits but were pretty tasty.

Climbing Mt. Talau

I live on Mt. Talau, which at 430 feet is the highest point on the main island of Vava'u. I live a lot closer to the bottom than I do to the top, and while I may say I climb Mt. Talau every day, I don't climb all the way to the top.

Twice in the past two weeks, I've ventured all the way to the top—first, last week with my friend Chad, and then again, on Friday with Chad and Katie.

Legend has it that Mt. Talau used to be the tallest mountain in Tonga. Many years ago, however, some evil spirits from Samoa tried to steal the top of the mountain but only got a short distance away before they dropped it into the Pacific, forming what is now the island of Lotuma. Lotuma later served as a Tongan military base and was the site of our American July 4th celebration last year.

PEACE CORPS TONGA TOP 25
Wednesday, May 27, 2009

My friend Sarah, who completed her service here in Vava'u in December, has put together a list of the "25 Reasons You Know You've Volunteered in Tonga." I think it is a great list and my personal favorite is:

7. You have friends named Loketi (rocket), Telefoni (telephone), Vai (liquid), Feiloaki (introduce yourself), Venitaleita (ventilator), Puke (sick), Makoni (telegram) and Vaka Puna (airplane).

New Baby

My friend's 'Ofa and Hangale just had a new baby daughter. This photo was taken at the hospital just two days after she was born.

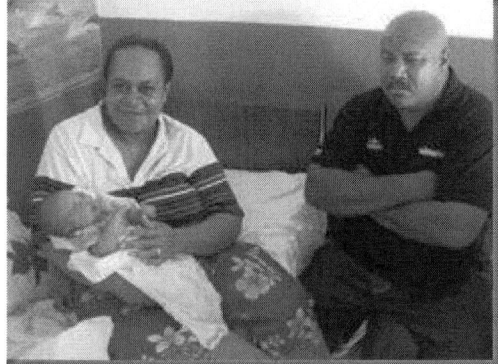

'Ofa and Hangale with their new baby

Religious Recruiting?

The Church of Scientology has come to Tonga. The picture below is from downtown Neiafu.

Church of Scientology recruiting tent

Officially, the church says it is here to target drug and alcohol abuse in the South Pacific. Of course, I'm guessing they are also hoping to educate Tongans about their church and perhaps even do a little recruiting.

Religious recruiting is a big business in Tonga, and the Mormons have pumped lots of money into the kingdom to bolster its ranks in this region.

It's Diving Friday!

I got a chance to get back in the water on Friday. This photo was taken at about 30 feet when I decided to take my mask off to pose for a picture.

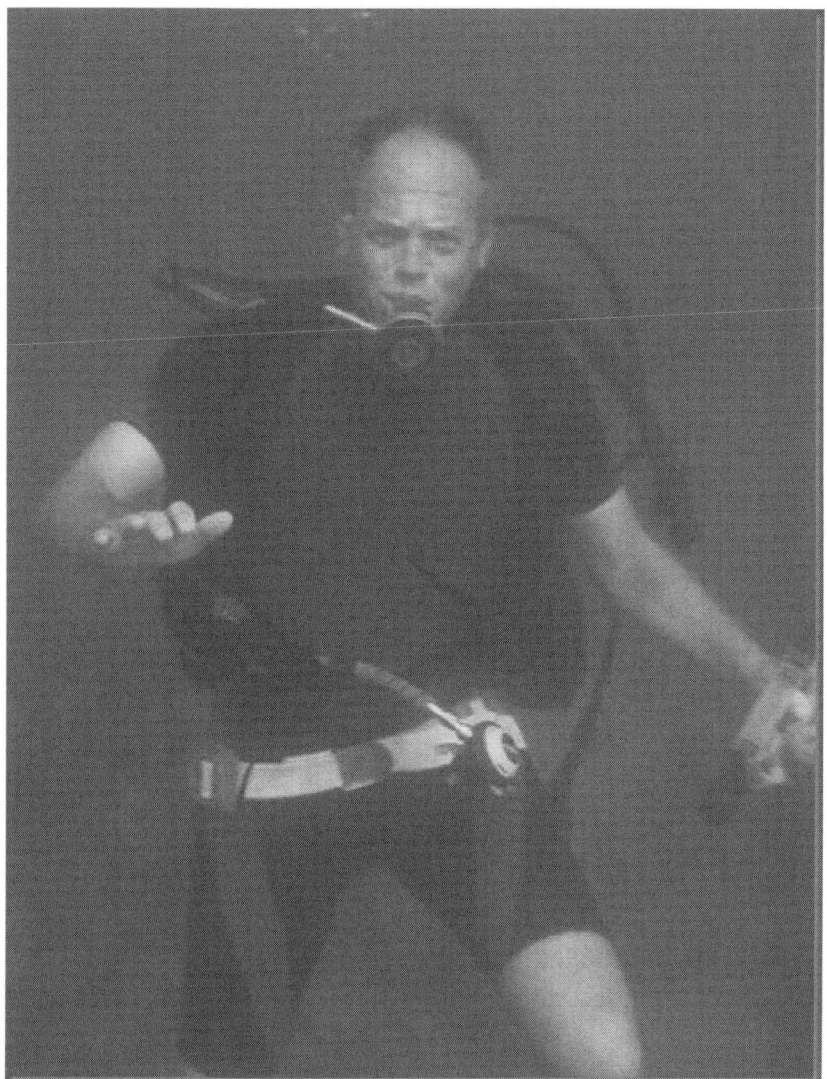

Steve Hunsicker on the bottom of the Pacific Ocean

We dove in the harbor, which was a bit murky, but it was still great to gain more experience underwater. It's the second dive I've done since getting my open-water certification.

Peace Corps Tonga Group 75

From my perspective, the most important thing that Peace Corps does each year is to develop sites for new volunteers. That process started this week for the members of Peace Corps Tonga Group 75 who will arrive here in October.

The first step is meeting with schools who are interested in hosting a volunteer. (Only schools will be hosting volunteers beginning this year since the business program has been eliminated.) Volunteers will either teach English or business as their primary volunteer project.

Here in Vava'u, I was asked by Peace Corps to attend the meeting and do part of the presentation for new potential sites.

Puke Esau, our Peace Corps staff member here in Vava'u, put together the presentation. I thought he did a great job outlining what is required of potential site locations and describing the benefits of the program.

Group 75 will start its training in October and will become volunteers in December, replacing all the members of my group (Group 73) when we complete our Peace Corps service.

LOTS OF WORK TO DO!
Thursday, June 4, 2009

A big part of my job at the Tonga Development Bank has been assisting with workshops for Tongans who either want to start or expand their businesses. We average about 25 people per workshop, and we conduct the workshops in all parts of Tonga. To date, I've been at 14 workshops.

This year, I designed a completely new curriculum for the workshops, including new PowerPoint presentations and training exercises. I did the work in English, and then a bank employee at our head office in Nuku'alofa translated everything into Tongan.

We conducted our first workshop using all the new materials in the village of Tefisi. We got a wonderful response. Of the 23 people who attended, 22 of them requested that we come back for a follow-up visit at each of their places of business. That will take a lot of time for me to accomplish, but it is the best response we've ever gotten at a workshop.

Tonga Development Bank workshop

I've also proposed putting together a video that can be shown at workshops after I complete my service. I am waiting on approval from the head office before I start on that project.

I am very happy to have so many new people to go visit. My workload at the bank has been very slow since I returned from New Zealand, so it is great to be busy again. We have another workshop next Wednesday.

Radio Days

I made a brief return to USA radio last weekend. My former station, WVAQ, had a "Class Reunion Weekend," bringing back on-air staffers from previous years. I was able to listen to part of the weekend because it was streamed live online. I was interviewed on the morning show about what I had been doing since I left the station in 1984, and they had a lot of questions about Peace Corps and my experiences in Tonga. My first full time job was doing news for WVAQ and its sister station, WAJR. I had lost touch with everyone I worked with in those days, but thanks to Facebook and the reunion weekend, I've gotten to reconnect with many of my former colleagues.

Tongan Scholarships

Last week, I accompanied my boss, Fuka, to the local Wesleyan (Methodist) school where he presented scholarships from the Tonga Development Bank to three Tongan boys.

Fuka Kupu awards a scholarship to a Tongan student

The money will be used to pay for their school fees. The bank gives out scholarships every year all over Tonga as part of its effort to help the country.

SIX MONTHS REMAINING IN TONGA
Thursday, June 11, 2009

Exactly six months from today I will officially finish my Peace Corps service in Tonga. For my group, Tonga Group 73, it means the end of our time together as volunteers. We became volunteers on December 12, 2007 after completing two and a half months of training. Our official end date is December 12, 2009. However, many of us may actually start leaving in November. According to the Peace Corps rules, any volunteer can leave 30 days early with the permission of the country director. That permission is almost always given and especially in the case of our group since we close out our service so close to the holidays.

My group started with 33 people. As of today, we have lost exactly one third of the volunteers who started with me through either early terminations ("ET" in Peace Corps speak) or medical separations. This week, two more of my friends, a married couple, decided to leave. They were one of five married couples in my group, and they are the fourth to have left early. In raw numbers, eight married people and four single people have left early for a total of 12 departures.

Three months from now, in mid-September, the remaining volunteers in my group will get together for the last time at our close of service conference. While we will certainly still see the people who live in our island groups, it will be the last time we will see some of our fellow volunteers. The COS will be held on the main island of Tongatapu.

I'm looking forward to my last six months here. The time has really gone by quickly, and I'm happy that I am still happy being here. It's been a great experience, and I expect the last six months will be as well.

The Third Annual Lu Cook-Off

One of the most traditional foods in Tonga is called lu. The leaves of taro plants are filled with meat, coconut cream and onions and then roasted in an outdoor oven. I eat lu almost every Sunday, and the types of meat range from canned beef to chicken to sipi, which is also known as mutton chops.

For the past three years, the volunteers in Vava'u have hosted a lu cook-off to see who can make the best and most creative lu. This year, the event was held at my house, and I won . . . but not without a bit of controversy.

The rules for the cook-off state that you must use either coconut cream or onions or both in your lu. I decided to make a dish called "apple lu-icious" as in delicious. I planned to take apples, cinnamon, sugar, butter and coconut cream and wrap them in taro leaves. The key word here is planned. I asked my landlord if he would husk a coconut for me and make the coconut cream. He said he would. Friday afternoon, as we were getting ready for our feast, I saw my landlord get in his car and leave, never to return that night. He forgot to make the coconut cream, so instead of following the rules, I left it out. The judge (a local restaurant owner) decided I still had the best tasting lu, and I got the trophy.

It was a pretty fun night. We drank wine and pigged out on each other's creations. We had Thai lu, stuffed pepper lu, lu dolmades and lemon custard lu.

In case you are wondering why there are no pictures of the lu . . . no one took any. We were all too hungry and forgot about it until it was all gone.

THIS ALL HAPPENED IN ONE AMAZING DAY!
Sunday, June 14, 2009

The winter season has arrived in Vava'u. This is the time of year when tourists start to visit, the harbor fills up with yachts and all the businesses that were closed during the off-season are reopened.

For those of us who are volunteers, it gives us a chance to enjoy some of the things that the tourists do when they come for a visit. That was certainly the case on Friday, when I had a pretty amazing day.

The timing couldn't have been better. I had a long but busy week at work, and Friday turned out to be the perfect ending to the week.

The Shark Encounter

For the first time since getting my dive certification, I headed out to a couple of the really cool dive spots in Vava'u. The conditions were perfect . . . even at more than 60 feet below the surface, the water was crystal clear.

We dived at two places—one called Split Rock and the other called Fingers. Split Rock is exactly what it sounds like—a huge rock that fell to the ocean floor and split, allowing you to dive around and through it. The rock sits on a beautiful colorful coral reef with many species of fish swimming around.

Diving in the South Pacific

There is also a cave near here. It's actually more of a large cavern, but it is pitch black inside unless you use a light.

Inside, we had hoped to see a couple of reef sharks, which are known to hang out in the cave, and that is exactly what we saw.

It was my first encounter with sharks in the water, and it was really amazing to see these whitetip reef sharks swimming just a few feet in front of us. Since I'm not that experienced at diving, I would never have entered the cave on my own, but my friend Lori was with us for the dive. She works for PADI, the organization that does scuba certification, and she is an instructor of PADI instructors. That's the highest level of diving certification that you can achieve. Having her along was great and really made me relax. I figured if I got into any trouble, there couldn't be a better person to have with me.

We dove to almost 70 feet below the surface. We took this photo at about 45 feet down. Al, who owns Dolphin Pacific Diving, took the photo for us.

From left to right are Steve, Emma, Amanda, Lori, Jason and James.

The second dive spot, Fingers, is named because of the five small tunnels or crevices (similar to human fingers) that you swim through to get around. As you are diving through, you realize that you can't go straight up and surface even if you wanted to do that. Some of the openings are pretty tight, and you have to remember that you are a lot wider than normal because of the air tank on your back.

Without a doubt, it was the best day I've had diving, and I can't wait to get back out again. (And if you are coming to Vava'u, be sure to look up Al and the staff at Dolphin Pacific Diving.)

Watching the NBA and a Yacht Race (Kind of)

Every Friday during the winter season, there is a yacht race when both local boat owners and those who are visiting race their boats around the harbor. This past Friday was the second race of the season. After getting back from diving, I joined my friends Chad and Katie at Mango Cafe, which is right on the water. It's one of the few places with satellite TV, and we had planned to watch the end of the NBA Finals Game 4 and also the yacht race.

While we got to do both, the real entertainment came from the staff at Mango. They were all rehearing some traditional dances that they will be performing for the tourists later this season. We were the only people in the place, so it was like having our own private dance show.

Tongan dancers

We did try to pay attention to the race and the game but ended up paying the most attention to the dancers.

Volunteer Night

There are 14 volunteers in Vava'u from three different countries—10 Peace Corps volunteers, three Japanese volunteers and one Australian volunteer. We all know each other and hang out when we can, but it's rare when we all get together. Friday night, the Aquarium Cafe invited all of us to a special "Volunteer Night."

The Aquarium Cafe has expanded and is under new ownership. The new owners invited us to help train their new staff. We received a big discount on food and drinks, and the Tongans gained some experience, which hopefully will help them do a better job during the season.

We stayed until the cafe closed. As volunteers, we have to watch our expenses pretty closely, so it was great to have a night where we could all get together at a restaurant and not have to worry as much about the bill at the end of the night.

It was a pretty amazing day! And just in case you are wondering . . . I also did a lot of work last week, including a workshop for 26 Tongan business owners.

THE FUTURE OF TONGA
Sunday, June 21, 2009

When I first arrived in Vava'u in October, 2007, I met an American tourist who had also just arrived. He was surprised to find out that there were Peace Corps volunteers serving in Tonga. As he put it, "This place is pretty first world."

At the time, I didn't think much about it, but over the past two years, I've thought a lot about his comment and also about whether Peace Corps should still be in Tonga after more than 40 years. At first glance, Tonga has many of the qualities you would expect to find in a first world country. Most of the country has electricity, running water, cell phones, television and Internet. There is no hunger or homelessness in Tonga, and the literacy rate is almost 100%—much higher than that of the United States and other developed countries. Many Tongans are bilingual, speaking Tongan and English, and on average, Tongan men have a life expectancy of 73 years and women, 69 years.

Those statistics don't seem to describe a place where you would expect to find the Peace Corps, which only works in developing countries. But as is often the case, there is a different story once you look a little closer.

The economy here is completely supported by foreign aid and by remittances from Tongans living abroad. Almost everything is imported, except for the crops that are grown to provide food for the families here. There are very few exports, and those items that are exported, like kava and Tongan handicrafts, are often sold to other Tongans living overseas.

I believe there are products which could be sold overseas and which could help Tonga reduce its reliance on handouts. However, two very big changes need to occur before that can happen.

First, Tongans would have to decide that they want financial independence. The people here are so used to simply receiving the things they ask for that there is little incentive for them to work really hard. Currently, the flow of remittances from overseas has slowed due to the economic problems in the United States and to a lesser extent, Australia and New Zealand. This means that some Tongans are not getting the support from overseas to which they have become accustomed. If that trend were to continue, would that be enough to convince Tongans to try and live more independently?

The second major change that would have to occur before Tongans can export products is a major improvement in the country's infrastructure. During the pineapple season this year, many farmers who wanted to sell their crops outside of Vava'u were unable to do so because the two boats that run weekly between the islands were not operating. For more than a month, there was no boat, limiting the ability of anyone to send anything out of here and also causing many items to disappear from store shelves. There are planes, but that is expensive, and the shipping costs can increase the price to a level where it is no longer competitive.

And there are issues with planes. In March, Air New Zealand cancelled several flights to Tonga, causing a backup of fish that was scheduled for export. Finally, the airline got its flights back late on a Saturday, but because everything in Tonga is closed on Sunday, they couldn't land at the airport until Monday. The fish was no longer fresh by then. And the prices for inter-island flights are very high. It is cheaper to fly from Tongatapu to New Zealand than it is to fly from Tongatapu to Vava'u.

It's not just the transportation infrastructure that has challenges. At different times in the past week, I have been without water, electricity, cell phone service and Internet service. I don't know the reason for any of the outages except that they happen pretty often.

I believe that until Tonga can come up with a way to fix its infrastructure, and especially the transportation infrastructure, it will be very difficult for the country to reduce its reliance on outside money.

There are certainly other challenges besides infrastructure here. Right now, there is no foreign investment in the country because of strict laws concerning land and business ownership. I am not sure that those laws are bad. They keep foreigners from taking advantage of the Tongans and are probably why the wonderful Tongan culture is so well preserved after so many years.

Unfortunately, I think that would change. If foreign investors were allowed to come to Tonga today, even in a limited capacity, I believe the good-natured Tongans would lose out. It has become such a part of the Tongan culture to accept "free money" that I fear the Tongans would take the quick cash instead of thinking about the long-term consequences of giving up their land and their businesses.

This is why I think it is important for Peace Corps to stay in Tonga. With the right volunteers, we can help educate the Tongans about business and try to teach them to think longer term. Hopefully, we can convince Tongan entrepreneurs to cultivate crops and create products that can be exported and encourage them to lobby the government to provide a reliable infrastructure to ensure their success.

However, change won't happen quickly. Peace Corps has decided to focus its efforts on educating the next generation of Tongans about business instead of working with the current business owners. Beginning this fall, Peace Corps is eliminating the business advising program where I work and replacing it with a business education program for students at the secondary and tertiary levels. There is no curriculum yet for this new program, and it will be up to the volunteers who arrive here later this year to help develop it. Let's hope that the process of developing and implementing this curriculum doesn't take too long because I do think there are some significant changes coming to Tonga soon.

Probably the most significant will be allowing Tongans to have more say in their laws. The current king, George Tupou V, has signed away some of his powers, and beginning next year, average Tongans will be better represented in Parliament.

While there are still many questions to be answered about how much influence Tongans will have in their government, there is little doubt that change is coming. And hopefully, part of those changes will be programs to focus on business and make Tonga more independent of foreign money.

LOOKING FORWARD
Friday, July 3, 2009

It has been more than two years since I received my invitation to become a Peace Corps volunteer in Tonga. That invitation had the date I would begin. Another big date was the day I announced I was leaving my company after 15 years. Having specific dates made those decisions seem final.

Now, with less than five months left to go, I have another date. That's the date when I'll be leaving Tonga and wrapping up my volunteer service in the Peace Corps. That will happen on Thursday, November 26, 2009. It now seems very final. Others in my group will start leaving November 13th.

In my case, leaving a little early will allow me to meet a friend in South Africa. I'll be flying out the morning of November 26th to Sydney and then on to Hoedspruit, South Africa and the Kruger National Park. From South Africa, I'll head home to West Palm Beach. When I get back, I will have flown all the way around the globe.

At various times during my Peace Corps experience, I've thought about extending my service or even signing up for another stint in a different country. However, as much as I've enjoyed my experience here, I've realized that the best thing for me right now is to get some "USA time." I would like to continue with Peace Corps in some capacity and will be exploring that option as the time for my close of service gets nearer.

So, while I've got a final date, I've also got a lot of things left to do. I just started work this week on a video project for the Tonga Development Bank. The bank plans to air the video on local TV and also use it to promote the bank at workshops in the future. In addition, I have several new clients with whom I'm working, and it happens to be tax time in Tonga, which means I'll be helping a bunch of people with their taxes. I never would have guessed I would be giving tax advice in Tonga. Finally, I've still got some vacation time left, and I am hoping to make one more big trip before I leave.

So the adventure isn't over, but the end is near. I'm very thankful for the experiences I've had, and while I didn't plan it this way, it seems appropriate that my last day in Tonga, Thursday, November 26th, is Thanksgiving Day.

Note

Soon, there will be just 19 of us remaining out of the 33 who started. Two more volunteers from Tongatapu are leaving on Tuesday.

THEY CALL THIS CHEATING IN THE USA!
Tuesday, July 7, 2009

Monday night, just after 10 p.m., I was lying in bed. The doors were closed and the lights were out. I had just finished watching a movie, and I was going to sleep. The phone rang. I looked at the caller ID, and I didn't recognize the number. However, I quickly thought it might be a friend who just got a new phone number, so I answered it.

"Hi Steve, I'm a teacher at the side school and I need your help." (The side school is the all-English speaking school where my neighbor James works.)

"What kind of help?" I asked.

"I have to write an essay, and I want you to help me. I'm outside your house right now."

I quickly had several thoughts before I answered. Why was this woman outside my house at 10 p.m.; why was she calling me instead of James; how did she get my number and why did a teacher need help writing an essay? I told her that I had already gone to bed and asked if we could meet in the morning. I suggested she come to the bank at 9:30 a.m., and I would try to help. She said okay and we hung up. I then heard the sound of a car engine starting, I saw headlights come on and heard a car drive away. Yep, she really was outside my house. It often happens that people, even complete strangers, show up, and if my doors are open, I'm usually glad to help—but not after I'm in bed unless it's an emergency, and this was not!

The next morning, just after walking out the door of my house at 8:30 a.m., a car pulled up with a woman inside. She told me she was the woman who had called last night. In the United States, I might have felt like I was being stalked, but in Tonga I actually didn't think much about it. The woman, who didn't tell me her name, gave me a little more detail about the essay she had to write. She said her cousin was a student at Vava'u High School, and he had an assignment to write an essay about the overpopulation of Tonga. He wanted her to write the essay, and now she wanted me to write it.

I politely told her that I couldn't do someone else's homework but that I would be glad to help him write it. I suggested he come by the bank or by my house that evening, and I would work with him to get it done.

"Oh no," she said. "I told him I would write it, and I need you to help me."

I then told her that I was not going to write the essay for her but that I would help her write it. I didn't see any point in completing a high-school assignment for two people when neither was going to learn from it. "OK, but how about if I give you the information, and you can just write down the important points, and then I'll write it from that?"

She handed me a notebook.

Clearly, she was not going to give up, so I took the notebook and told her I would make some notes for her and that she could pick it up later at the bank.

I walked to work and then opened the notebook. It was filled with questionnaires that had been filled out by other Tongans concerning overpopulation. Evidently, this was not just a simple essay; it was an exercise in analyzing data and writing about it. (By the way, one of the people who answered the survey said the solution to overpopulation was sterilization for everyone.)

So what did I do? I did as I said I would do and wrote some notes. But the notes were about how to analyze the data and compare people's opinions to the facts. She would still have to work to complete the assignment. I doubted her cousin, the student, would learn anything from the assignment. I also assumed she would take the notes I had written and give them to someone else to write the essay.

As it turned out, that was exactly what happened. I left my notes and her notebook at the bank for her to pick up. When I got home, I went over to James' house and guess what? The notebook and my notes had now been given to James.

That's just the way things tend to happen in Tonga.

A Big Bank Robbery in Tonga

On Friday, someone left the door to the vault open at the head office of the Tonga Development Bank in Nuku'alofa. That by itself isn't actually that unusual. I worked there for two months when I first became a Peace Corps volunteer, and I remember noticing the door was often open. However, on Friday, someone walked in and helped themselves to TOP$500,000, which is about US$250,000. That's pretty much everything that was inside the vault. On Monday, the staff here at the bank branch in Vava'u were all buzzing about this, and most believe it was probably someone at the bank who took the money.

From TV to Tonga

I was surprised and humbled this weekend by a story called "From TV to Tonga" on the website of WCPO-TV in Cincinnati. It was written by Larry Handley, who is a meteorologist at the station. As he mentions in the story, which I've pasted below, he and I used to work together.

From TV To Tonga
Thursday, July 2, 2009

It was a beautiful March day in 1989 when I arrived at TV20 in Gainesville, Florida (at my own expense) to interview for a weather anchor position that I heard was open at that station. Steve Hunsicker, the station's news director, greeted me warmly and proceeded to politely listen to me blather on about why someone with no credentials or real weather experience should be given a chance. For reasons I still can't explain, he hired me and the rest, as they say, is history. Despite his apparent lack of sound judgment some 20 years ago, his recent decisions are much more impressive.

About a year and a half ago, Steve resigned his position as a big-time television group executive to join the Peace Corps. He left his nice home in South Florida, his powerful and high-paying job and all the comforts of America to help businesses in the Kingdom of Tonga succeed. His blog is a favorite bookmark on my computer, and I always look forward to his newest entry. I must admit that I'm living vicariously through his adventures on the other side of the world. He tells tales of beautiful geography, people and traditions. He shares adventures that could only be experienced in that setting. He had to learn a new language in just a few months, and he lives on nearly nothing. He chose to do all of this in his upper 40s, and he seems genuinely happy and content.

His two-year commitment to the Peace Corps ends later this year, and he has no idea what he will do when it's over. However, he seems totally unconcerned and relaxed. I believe that's the way it works. The more you give of yourself—freely and honestly—the less you worry. Maybe helping to solve other people's problems and making their lives better increases your own faith that things will work out. Thanks to Steve, things worked out for me 20 years ago when I was desperate for a job like they are working out now for the people of Tonga. And there's no doubt in my mind that things will work out for Steve as he transitions back to life in America.

Thanks Larry for such kind words.

Independence Day in Tonga

On Saturday, July 4th, I celebrated the United State's independence by eating hotdogs, hamburgers and drinking beer while sitting on the ocean. While it was a lot different than the way I spent last July 4th, it probably wasn't that different than the way many Americans spent the day. But there were a couple of differences . . . I was eating hot dogs from China, beef from New Zealand and drinking beer from Germany. I wasn't in the United States, I was in Tonga. And the ocean? It was the beautiful blue South Pacific.

THE GREAT VAVA'U CLEANUP
Wednesday, July 15, 2009

When you walk around Vava'u today, the island is immaculate. It hasn't been this clean since the king's coronation last August. There is no litter in sight, all the yards are mowed, junk has been taken out of the yards, and the sidewalks in the main town of Neiafu are spotless.

My landlord and his family have been spending hours every day working in the yard, planting flowers and scrubs, weeding and even putting Tongan flags on ribbons across the front of my home.

Steve Hunsicker's house in Vava'u cleaned up for the Princess

As this photo of my house shows, both the house and the yard look great, and I had nothing to do with it.

Last week was National Environmental Awareness Week, and all across Tonga, students were encouraged to learn about the environment, pollution and renewable energy. Here in Vava'u, the Tonga Development Bank awarded a TOP$250 prize to the winners of a contest among all the high schools. Teams had to answer questions, and the team that got the most correct answers received the check.

Vava'u High School won the competition and walked away with the money.

So it might be a natural conclusion to assume that the reason the island looks so great is because of National Environment Awareness Week. Unfortunately, that is not the case.

The Tongan princess, the sister of the king, is visiting Vava'u this week, and the reason that everything is spotless has everything to do with her visit and little to do with Environment Week. She is visiting both outer villages and the main city. In the case of my neighborhood, I live just a block from the Vava'u royal palace, so my Tongan neighbors want to make sure everything is clean as she comes and goes during her stay.

It would be nice if the island could stay this clean, and I'm sure the focus on the environment in the schools last week will help, but unfortunately there are no easy solutions. In my opinion, the biggest problem is that nothing that is imported to Vava'u ever leaves here. All of the cans, bottles, cars, oil, tires, etc. that are brought here in the name of progress stay here forever. All this stuff is either burned or put in junk piles. Until there is a viable recycling program, an island-wide garbage collection and garbage bins, the problem will remain.

Peter's Photo

Here's a photo of my landlord's grandson, Peter. He is a great kid and has really warmed up to me. I think he was a little intimidated by me when I first moved here. Now, he comes over and jokes around.

Peter Tupou

When I took the first photo of the house, Peter spotted me and immediately ran over and posed for this photo. It's also interesting to see how much he has grown in the past 15 months.

A WHALE OF A DAY
Tuesday, July 21, 2009

This morning, I was calling on bank clients in the small outer island village of Matamaka. I was with Oholei, one of the loan officers at the Tonga Development Bank. We had arrived by boat, and he and I were making our way through the village while the boat's driver, Ha'ukau, stayed with the boat.

We had been in the village for less than 15 minutes when I saw Ha'ukau walking quickly toward us. This was pretty unusual as he always stays with the boat when we are visiting clients.

As he got closer, he yelled:

"*Ha'u* Steve *ha'u vave*!" That means, "Steve, come here quickly!" He motioned me to follow him to the beach and when we got there he said in English just one word: "whales."

I kept looking but couldn't see them, so we headed back toward the boat while Oholei finished up with our client. We waited at the dock, my eyes peeled for any sign of a whale. Finally, way off in the distance, I saw a little black hump appear. If I hadn't been looking, I would have missed it.

That was the last we saw of the whales until Oholei made his way back to the boat. We got in the boat and started heading to our next stop when we saw not one, not two, but three whales dead ahead.

We moved closer, then turned off the boat's motor and waited. A few minutes later, we saw a giant whale swim directly under our boat. If it had surfaced it would have capsized the boat, but clearly the whale was just as curious about us as we were about it.

Humpback whale in Vava'u

We didn't want to disturb the whales, so Ha'ukau started the engine and put the boat in reverse. Almost immediately, a large whale breeched directly in front of the boat. All you could see ahead was black . . . no water, no shoreline, just the side of whale. It was THAT big. If the boat had been going forward, we would have hit it; it was that close.

We stayed in the area for a while longer, and the whales continued to play. We think it may have been a mother, father and baby as two of the whales were very large and the third looked smaller.

I've seen whales before but never this close. There are about a dozen companies in Vava'u that offer whale-watching trips or a swimming with the whales experience, but we were the only ones around to share this experience, and we didn't pay for it.

The whales soon swam away, and we continued on to another village and more visits with clients. But it was our visit with the whales that the three of us will remember most.

SPENDING THE NIGHT AT THE POLICE STATION
Tuesday, July 28, 2009

I woke up last Tuesday morning in a Tonga police station. In fact, I ended up spending 15 hours with the police at the station, and it was NOT my decision to be there. There were no handcuffs, no Miranda rights (those don't exist here) and no free phone call to an attorney or even the Peace Corps.

It all worked out fine, but the story of how I got there and why will take a little explaining.

Last Monday, I began a visit to many of the outer island villages here in Vava'u. I was joined on the trip by two Tongans, a loan officer and a boat driver. These two make the trip every month to see clients on the outer islands, but I came along because the bank was planning a workshop on Hunga, which is one of the outer islands.

We left the old harbor of Neiafu and soon arrived at Olo'ua. This village is pretty close to the main island but is a world apart. As we made our way from the dock up to the village, there were no sounds, no people, not even the chirps of any birds.

We found our client and then headed back to the boat and on to Taunga. This was my second trip to this village, and it is a really pretty spot with a beautiful sandy beach and friendly villagers.

Our next stop was Ovaka. This island is one of the furthest from the main island, and it is also home to my fellow Peace Corps volunteer Scott. We found him helping the women of the village.

In Ovaka, we started inviting people to the workshop that we had planned for two days later. Since this was my first visit to Ovaka, I went to check out Scott's house.

By outer island standards, Scott has a pretty big house. It has two bedrooms and a large open living area. There is no electricity or running water, and the only furniture is a single twin bed. Not even any chairs. I didn't know it at the time, but a comment I made here was the first step in my eventual stay with the Tongan police.

From Ovaka, we got back in the boat and went to Hunga. There is a huge lagoon in the middle of Hunga that connects to the outer ocean in just two places. The entrance closest to Ovaka can only be used at high tide. It was low tide, so we ventured out into open ocean and around to the other side.

The first thing you notice when you arrive in Hunga is the new road. New Zealand Aid has paid for a road to be built from the water up the hill to the village.

The Hunga highway to nowhere

This might seem like a pretty good deal until you discover that there is just one tractor and one truck in all of Hunga. That's it! Two motorized vehicles.

While making our client visits and handing out more invitations to our workshop, I saw something I had never seen before—an octopus hanging on

a pole to dry. They do this to preserve it.

By the time we were finished in Hunga, it was late in the afternoon, and we had completed our work for the day. At this point, Oholei, the loan officer with whom I was traveling, suggested we make a stop at the nearby Blue Lagoon Resort.

A number of years ago, the bank helped the owner build this resort, and he seemed glad to see us, buying us both a beer and telling me to look around. It's a nice place. It's powered by windmills and solar power and looks like a perfect place to spend a relaxing vacation or even a honeymoon.

So what does all this have to do with my overnight stay with the Tongan police?

When we first left the main island, both the driver and Oholei had asked me if I was planning to spend the night in the islands. I said sure and told them I was prepared with a sleeping bag and other gear. I told them I could sleep anywhere.

Since I've been in Tonga I've slept on floors, in a kava hall, on sofas and I've camped plenty of times. I assured both of them I could stay wherever they were staying.

Now remember I mentioned the comment I made at Scott's house? I pointed out that he only had one bed. Oholei apparently took this to mean that it was not acceptable for me to stay with Scott. There is only one other Peace Corps volunteer in the islands, and that is Amy. Because she is a single woman, it would not be culturally appropriate for me to stay with her. Oholei was worried that I might not have an acceptable place to stay.

Finally, the two Tongans told me that we were going to stay in Falevai. Falevai is the only outer island village with both a medical center and a police station.

We arrived there as the sun was setting, and they went inside and quickly arranged for me to spend the night at the police station. When I asked why I was staying at the police station, they told me that it's the only place they knew of that had a bed. I stated again that I would be fine sleeping anywhere, but there was no arguing with them, and so for the first time in my life, I spent the night at a police station with the one police officer who works in the outer islands.

My room was a small room with a single bed, but it was not behind bars. I was just a few steps away from the jail, so I can say I slept AT the jail, but I did not spend the night IN jail. There is a big difference.

A Cool Camping Spot

The Friday before my night at the jail, I went camping for the first time in almost two months. I joined five of my fellow volunteers for an overnight camping trip and beach bonfire.

One of the great things about Vava'u is that you can find a beautiful beach and have it all to yourself.

The beach we found was a bit of a hike, but well worth it. It was below the village of Holonga, and it's rare to see anyone there. I camped last year at Utula'aina point, which is just above this beach, but this was the first time I had camped at this particular location.

Peace Corps Tonga Group 75

The Peace Corps office in Tonga is expecting 27 future volunteers in a few months. That's a slight increase over the 24 who started with Group 74 and down from the 33 who started with my group, Group 73. Of the 27 new trainees who are coming in October, the staff is expecting one teacher trainer volunteer, six primary school volunteers, 10 secondary and tertiary institute volunteers and one community development volunteer.

A VERY SAD DAY IN TONGA
Thursday, August 6, 2009

Early this morning, one of the ferries that operates between the Tongan islands sank with 79 people on board, almost all of them Tongans. The boat left the main city of Nuku'alofa yesterday in route to Vava'u.

Fifty-three people have been rescued and the remaining 26 are believed to have drowned. It appears that no women or children survived, just men. (Update: Ninety-five people are presumed dead out of 141 who were on board the ship.)

The boat, the *MV Princess Ashika*, was put in service just a few months ago to temporarily replace another boat that was determined to be unsafe. The *Ashika*, which was actually older than the boat it replaced, was to remain in service until late next year when a new boat, paid for by the Japanese government, is to begin connecting the islands.

It may seem odd that only the men survived, but as is normal in Tongan culture, it is very likely that the men were in a different part of the boat or outside. Men and women do not normally socialize or even sit together in public. The women and children normally sit inside the boat, and the men stay outside and drink kava and smoke.

All over Vava'u today, the accident was all everyone was talking about. At the market, one of the women selling vegetables was in tears after just learning that her son may have been one of the victims. There were similar stories all over the area, as it was likely that the majority of the people on board were either from Vava'u or were related to someone who lives here.

One of the missing men was a JICA volunteer. JICA is the Japanese version of Peace Corps.

The area where the boat went down is not far from Nomuka, which is part of the Ha'apai Island Group, but is actually closer to the main island of Tongatapu.

The survivors had been picked up by the other ferry that serves Tonga and taken to the main island in Ha'apai.

There is no word on what caused the boat to sink, but one rumor claims that the boat was having troubles even before it left Nuku'alofa and that the crew was told not to make the trip.

Steve Hunsicker

GRIEF TURNS TO ANGER IN TONGA
Sunday, August 9, 2009

For the most part, Tongans are a happy people who love to laugh and take most things in stride. "*Sai pe*" may be the most uttered phrase in the kingdom and it simply means "It's okay." But things are not sai pe in Tonga today. The grief that first hit the country when the *MV Princess Ashika* ferry sank last week is now turning to anger.

All over Vava'u, the destination point for the *Ashika*, people are asking how this could have happened and why the government put such an old boat into service. The *Ashika* was older than the boat it replaced. Another story being reported here says the government was urged NOT to put the boat into service because it did not pass safety checks.

There is also a lot of anger directed toward the king. In Tonga, it is illegal to criticize the king in public or to print anything negative about him. A few years ago, the owner of one of the independent newspapers was jailed for making negative comments about the government.

But that's not stopping Tongans now. The anger today is because just after the ferry sank, the king left the country for a vacation in Scotland. It seems abhorrent to the Tongans that their king would abandon them like this in a time of crisis.

When the survivors of the ferry disaster arrived back on the main island of Tongatapu, they were not consoled by the king, but instead met by his sister, the princess. The king has not issued any statements about the disaster and has done nothing to show support for the victims and their families.

Complicating things even more, the prime minister of Tonga was out of the country at a meeting in Australia when the boat sank. However, instead of returning to Tonga immediately, he stayed at the forum, saying he had important agreements to work out that would benefit Tonga in the future.

Even in peaceful Vava'u, some Tongans are talking about protests and an Australian news organization reported that an angry crowd gathered in Nuku'alofa outside the offices of the shipping company that operated the ferry. That should make people nervous, as Nuku'alofa is just now being rebuilt following riots in 2006 by people unhappy with the king and his government.

As is typical in Tonga, a lot of the information is passed through word of mouth, via the coconut wireless. That means you hear many different stories about what is actually happening. The official word from the Tongan police is that there are 93 people still missing, most of them women and infants. All but six of the missing are Tongans.

In villages around Vava'u, the impact is particularly hard. In one village of just over 100 people, six people are presumed dead . . . meaning the ferry disaster has wiped out 6% of the entire village's population. There are similar stories everywhere in Vava'u. Just about everyone either knows or is related to someone who was on that boat.

So far, just two bodies have been recovered. The boat sits in water that ranges from 36 to 110 meters deep, much of it too deep for divers.

There is also concern about how a small place like Vava'u is going to handle so many funerals. There is talk of having one large funeral for everyone instead of many smaller services. And Tongans want to know who is going to pay for the services. Funerals are very expensive, and Tongan families are expected to feed everyone who shows up and to give gifts to those who attend. This could be a major financial hit in an already struggling economy.

While it is extremely unlikely that there are any survivors, some families are hoping that perhaps their relatives never got on the ferry.

In addition to being the primary way that Tongans travel between the islands, the ferry is also the way that most food and freight get to the outer islands. On board the ferry when it sank was an ambulance and medical supplies donated by a USA organization to provide emergency transportation for the hospital here in Vava'u.

Some speculate the ferry disaster will serve as a wake-up call for Tonga and could help the pro-democracy movement gain momentum, especially if it is determined the king's government allowed this ship to sail knowing it was unsafe. If that's the case, it certainly was not sai pe.

HELP ON THE WAY FOR TONGA FERRY VICTIMS
Monday, August 10, 2009

There is often a strained relationship between Tongan business owners and the Chinese business owners who operate here. The Tongans like the cheap prices and the regular hours of the Chinese stores, but there is resentment because they have put many Tongan shops out of business.

By law, only Tongans can operate grocery stores in the kingdom. But a few years ago, the former king sold Tongan passports, which effectively allowed many Chinese to become Tongan residents and business owners. Even though the practice of selling passports was quickly stopped, the Chinese continue to take market share away from the Tongans.

Today, the owners of all the Chinese stores in Tonga announced that they were going to donate TOP$50,000 to help pay for the funerals of the 93 people who are still missing and presumed dead after the sinking of the *Ashika* ferry last week. In addition, a local money transfer company is kicking in an additional TOP$10,000 and a local Tongan Kava group has raised TOP$300 to assist. (TOP$2 is about US$1.)

Here in Vava'u, a fund has been created by many of the local tourism-related business owners. So far, thanks to contributions from tourists who are here and from those businesses, that fund has about TOP$800 in it.

There is also talk that the Tongan government may help with some of the funeral expenses, and the boat was insured by Lloyds of London, which could provide additional funds.

A funeral is very expensive in Tonga. A family will easily spend TOP$3,000 to TOP$5,000 to bury a loved one and sometimes even more. It is expected that the government will declare the missing "officially dead" later today or tomorrow. The funerals will start all over Tonga immediately afterwards, with a photo of the deceased substituting for their final remains.

The Washington Post has a comprehensive story about the Tonga ferry disaster today. And all around Vava'u, many people, myself included, continue to wear black in memory of those lost.

THE "FACTS" ABOUT THE TONGA FERRY SINKING
Saturday, August 15, 2009

By definition, a fact is something that is proven to be true. Ideally, it would be nice to think that the information Tongans receive about the sinking of the *Ashika* ferry last week would all be factual. But in a place like Tonga, where the media is controlled by the government, getting the "facts" can be difficult.

While there are some independent media voices, you still need a newspaper-publishing license from the government. If you upset the wrong person, your license to publish will be terminated. For the most part, the government can decide what it will release to the public and what it will keep secret. Neither the public nor the media have any formal right to gain access to official documents and reports in Tonga.

The coconut wireless—word of mouth—is still very much alive in Tonga, but that system has its faults because you often hear so many conflicting stories that it is hard to know which are true and which are speculation.

But times are changing. Tonga may be a remote island country, but it is no longer an island lacking information. Media from other parts of the world are covering the ferry sinking, and unlike the Tongan-based news organizations who may be fearful of criticizing the government and the king, these foreign news organizations can ask the tough questions, and what they write is available in Tonga via the Internet.

In last week's post, I talked about the anger that some Tongans have directed toward the Tongan king, who left on a four-month holiday the day after the *Ashika* ferry went down. After that post, I exchanged e-mails with another volunteer who lives in Tongatapu, who said he hadn't heard any criticism of the king, instead saying people were mad at the prime minister. And one of the independent Tongan newspapers, Matangi Online, has not made a big deal out of the king's departure. The editor of that paper was quoted in the *New Zealand Herald* last week.

Matangi Tonga Editor Pesi Fonua yesterday said that Tongans living at home appeared untroubled by King George's rapid departure for Edinburgh.

"There's no uproar by the people who lost loved ones. There doesn't seem to be any feeling about that."

In Scotland, where the king is beginning his four-month vacation, a news organization had a very different story.

Playboy king's Scottish holiday sparks anger

Heilala Delasau, a Tongan human rights activist, said: "The king is partly to blame and should be held liable. He should have stayed to help. He is a leader and should be helping his people at this time."

Sitiveni Lilo, a retired Tongan journalist living in Wellington, New Zealand, said: "Tonga is not a full democracy and people are afraid to speak out. People are concentrating on their loss, but there is also deep anger that the king left instead of staying to command the rescue operation and attend memorial services."

Protesters say they are exasperated by the wealthy playboy king, who earned the nickname "Oddball" because of his habit of riding around his Pacific island nation in a London taxi.

With his penchant for elaborate uniforms and remote controlled boats and toys, (King) Tupou has a reputation as an eccentric out of touch with reality.

Closer to Tonga, the *New Zealand Herald* had the following in their Sunday edition this morning.

Tongan king's critics hit out

Mateni Tapueluelu, editor of the independent *Taimi o Tonga* newspaper, said yesterday he was infuriated by the reports from Scotland and expected the Tongan public to feel the same way.

"It's just going to make people angry, they're going to see the monarchy as useless and an expensive irrelevance. At best he's a waste of money," said Tapueluelu.

"When the going gets tough, he gets going: Leaving his people to swim or sink." Tapueluelu said there was growing dissatisfaction with the Tongan, royal-dominated government as well over its handling of the Ashika tragedy.

"I'm beginning to hear talk that we should have an interim government," he said, adding that he hoped a "peaceful transition of power is ensured."

The Latest "Facts"

Now to the "facts," or what I think are the latest "facts."

Officially, there are still 93 people missing and presumed dead. The ship was located last week in 330 feet of water, making it too deep for divers to recover the bodies of those who perished. One report said it would cost 25 million New Zealand dollars (about US$17 million) to do a full recovery of the ship—money that Tonga does not have. Right now, Tongans have accepted that their loved ones are not going to be coming back, but they are still waiting to learn whether they will get the bodies back before they do any funerals. The Tongan transportation minister has resigned from his job, and

Tongans are doing their best to support each other in this time of tragedy. And yes, the king is on vacation in Europe.

FOOD GLORIOUS FOOD
Monday, August 24, 2009

One of the first things you learn as a Peace Corps volunteer is that no matter how hard you try, your eating habits are going to be very different. Some volunteers who have been vegetarians for years soon find themselves eating meat. Those who may have been picky eaters in the United States now find themselves eating things they could never have imagined, while others try to come up with creative ways to add some variety to their diets.

There are really two problems with food in Vava'u. The first is that Tongans pretty much eat the same foods every day without a lot of variety. There are a number of root crops that are grown here, and those are part of the Tongan daily diet combined with some kind of very fatty meat.

The second problem is that Tonga is an island, and if it doesn't grow here, it has to be imported. If there are no tomatoes at the market, you are not going to get a tomato even at the best restaurants. "If it ain't here, it ain't here."

For the first year or so of my Peace Corps service, I either shared meals with other volunteers who knew how to cook or I ate stuff that I was comfortable cooking. In the past year, I've gotten a little more ambitious; trying to actually learn to cook with what is available.

The good news is that in Peace Corps you have lots of free time so you have the time to cook.

I thought I would tell you about two things that I made recently. I would never have attempted either of these meals in the United States. It was too easy to go Publix or Polo Tropical and pick up chicken. Want a pizza? I would have ordered from one of the many places that deliver to your door and if I was desperate, I might have even popped a frozen pizza into my oven.

So when I show you this picture, you have to understand this is a big accomplishment for me.

Steve Hunsicker's home-cooked meal

This is pepper chicken . . . meaning it is cooked with pepper and a few other spices. The key to the chicken in Tonga is to remove all the fat and skin before you cook it. Often, you end up cutting away almost half of what is in the package.

The biscuits were made completely from scratch. (I was really proud of myself when I discovered I could make biscuits.) The stuff that looks like mashed potatoes is actually mashed ufi, which is a Tonga root crop. I boiled the ufi, which was given to me, mashed it up and added milk, hot peppers and salt.

Vava'u Shopping Tip

A shopping habit you quickly learn in Vava'u is that when you see something you want in a store, you buy it . . . because you may never seen it again. We once has fresh broccoli. It lasted about a week, and I haven't seen it again. That was more than a year ago. Another time, a stalk of celery showed up— yes, there was just one—when I went into the store. I didn't buy it as it was expensive and didn't look very good. It's not just fresh food that's random, we occasionally will run out of staples like rice, flour and boxed milk. (There is no fresh milk in the stores.)

This creates even bigger challenges when you are in the mood for something because it might not be there.

I now wonder if I'll still take the time to cook when I return to the United States or if you'll be bumping into me at the deli counter of Publix.

Changes in Peace Corps Tonga

The Peace Corps Tonga country director is leaving. The country director is the top position in each country, and in the case of Tonga, he is also the top-ranking American here since there is no embassy.

Jeff Cornish is moving to a new country director post in The Gambia, West Africa. In his e-mail announcement to the volunteers he said:

> *It has been my honor to serve with you here in the kingdom. Together we have done much to improve post operations, programming and volunteer support. I am proud of the role each of you has played in supporting each other, as well as those you serve in your respective communities. I am also proud of the fact that you have remained committed to your service and to the fulfillment of both Peace Corps and local community goals for development.*

No word on a replacement. He begins his new job on October 25th. Best of luck Jeff!

The Wreck of the *Clan McWilliams*

More than 80 years ago, a steam-powered tanker came into the harbor at Neiafu, Vava'u. The 300-foot boat was on fire and sank before the captain could run it aground. The wreck now sits in about 100 feet of water at the bottom of the harbor. Last week, I had a chance to dive on the wreck. Because of its depth, I was limited to just 20 minutes on it, but it was amazing to see how intact this boat is after all these years.

You can still see the portholes and where the doors used to be. The ladders are still there as is the railing along the side of the ship. We only explored the first half of the ship, as the remainder is in even deeper water.

10 QUESTIONS (AND ANSWERS) ABOUT PEACE CORPS
Wednesday, September 2, 2009

I was recently asked by the Peace Corps press office to answer 10 questions about my Peace Corps service. This is the information they will use to put together a news release to different news organizations about my service.

A couple of the questions prompted me to talk about some things that I've not mentioned before, while a couple of other answers may sound familiar. Here are the 10 questions and answers:

1) What one particular experience/moment highlights your Peace Corps service? I've helped more than 300 Tongans learn new business skills in both workshops and one-on-one consultations. In some cases, I taught community members how to start a business. One memorable success story was when I worked with a Tongan business owner who had run up a TOP$20,000 (about US$10,000) overdraft at a local bank and was on the verge of having to close his business. He kept no records and was giving away too much stuff from his store to friends and family and also for his own consumption. I went in, examined his records and made suggestions on ways to turn his business around. He immediately did everything I suggested, including tracking what he was giving away. Once he realized how much he was giving away, he was able to reduce that amount. He started paying down his overdraft and keeping records for the first time.

He even started writing down all of the cigarettes that he was taking and smoking. He told me that once he saw on paper how many cigarettes he was smoking each day, it forced him to cut back on his smoking.

He has now paid his overdraft down, his business is doing much better and he has even started a new business—running a taxicab service. His mother is sick, and he has been able to afford to hire an employee to run the store so he can be with his mother. That employee continues to keep good business records for him.

When I think about success stories, this is the one that jumps out at me. All he needed was a little push, and he did the rest on his own.

2) How have your values shifted, if at all? I think that by putting yourself into a culture that is so completely different you can't help but get a better understanding of the world. As a person who spent most of his life in the news media and living in a multi-cultural place like South Florida, I always thought I had a pretty good worldview, but coming to Tonga, I realize that I didn't really have a clue. It's not so much that I understand the world better, but I think I understand people better. By living in a foreign culture you really do learn that people are much more alike than they are different.

I'm not sure that any of my "core" values have changed, but hopefully I understand the world a little better now because of my Peace Corps experiences.

3) **What have you accomplished for the Tongan people?** See the answer to the first question above. Hopefully, some of the business people with whom I have worked now have the skills to do better and perhaps be more successful.

4) **Have you made local friends? Share a 'friendship' moment.** I went fishing one Saturday with two Tongan friends. Both have a lot more experience fishing than I have, and I was keen to get out and enjoy the day. As it turns out, I caught the only fish of the day, a small grouper that I landed shortly after we threw our lines in the water.

However, the trip was a great Tongan experience. My two friends, like most Tongans, don't have rods and reels. They have fishing line, some fish hooks and some weights. My weight was a small piece of rebar with the hook tied about 12 inches above it. We used pieces of smaller fish as bait.

I felt a tug on my line, but didn't really think I had a fish. However, when I pulled it up, there was a fish. Six hours later it was still the only fish we had caught, but we did do a great job of feeding the fish underneath us because they kept eating the bait.

The fish weren't the only ones eating. When we first got out on the water, my friends pulled out a big container of probably 20 sandwiches for the three of us. Then, once we got to the spot where we dropped anchor, out came more food—a big can of fatty meat and a huge bowl of root crops. Tongans love to eat and even when fishing, we had more food than the three of us could eat.

As we headed back to shore, we ran out of gas. We were near the shore, but still a good distance from where the car was parked. We ended up spending more than an hour swimming the boat back.

5) **What local customs drive you crazy?** Probably funerals. The Tongan word is *putu*. When someone dies, the family is expected to throw a big feast and feed everyone who shows up. While it is also customary for people to bring a gift to a funeral, the family responds by giving gifts to everyone who comes. The family of a loved one never comes out ahead. At the bank where I work, we have people come in immediately after a loved one has died seeking to take out a loan to pay for the funeral. In some cases, a family will go into debt for years just to pay for the funeral.

This all seems crazy to me. It is certainly important to pay your respects to your loved ones, but not to this extent.

I was out visiting bank clients one day when we happened to drive by a funeral. One of the bank's employees asked me if I was hungry. I knew he meant that he wanted to stop and eat at the funeral. I asked him if he knew the person who died or the family. He said no, but it was okay, because at a funeral, you feed everyone who shows up. I told him I wasn't hungry and suggested we go back to the bank. I didn't feel right about sitting down and taking free food from someone who had just had a relative die.

It seems to me the money spent on a funeral would be much better spent on school fees for a family member than on a lavish feast and gifts. Because there is often free food, when someone dies, people will take an entire day off of from work to attend the putu. Certainly that is fine for family members, but is it necessary for an entire village? This means you might go to the grocery store and find it closed because the staff is all attending a funeral that day.

6) **How does technology fit into your experience?** On my second day as a volunteer in Vava'u, I introduced myself to the manager of ANZ bank here. As we were talking, she asked me if I knew how to program a cash register. I had never done that before, but I figured I would be able to do it, so I told her that I could. Within a week, I was programming a cash register for that business and training the staff how to use it. Next, I did the same for a bar. A month later, another business called and wanted me to help with their cash register and train their staff, and then a month later, a restaurant that was under new ownership called asking for the same assistance. In all four cases, these were businesses that had a cash register, but didn't know how to use it. Not only are the businesses now using the cash register, but it is helping them improve their recordkeeping.

The same thing has happened with computers. Once I was able to help one person with her or his computer, then another would call. Next, I helped a computer lab, and then I built websites for two different clients. Once the word got around that I could help, I started getting lots of calls. When possible, I tried to show people how they could do some of the tasks themselves, but often the people I helped barely knew how to use a computer, so it was hard to teach them how to repair one.

In the case of the websites I built, I tried to design them so that the Tongan staff could easily update them without the help of a web person. All of the sites are for tourism-related businesses. Hopefully, the sites will help these businesses attract more customers from overseas.

The funny part of technology has been helping Tongans with their digital cameras. Many now have either cell phones that take photos or digital cameras, but they have no idea how to use them. It's amazing to see their faces when they take a picture for the first time and then get to see it right away.

7) **Why should more Americans apply for PC service?** I think all Americans should have a chance to live in a foreign culture—whether it is through Peace Corps or some other program. If more Americans had the chance to be exposed to different cultures, I think we would be a much more

accepting society. When you remove yourself from all the things we consider normal, you realize what an "American-centric" view we have of the world.

Joining Peace Corps is also a chance to do something rewarding. I don't think many volunteers get to "save the world" or do huge major projects, but I think most, if not all, make at least a small difference in the lives of the people in their host country.

I will say the Peace Corps is NOT for everyone. If someone is thinking about joining, they should research it thoroughly and make sure it really is right for them. It's pretty easy to find the contact information for many volunteers online. Find some volunteers who seem to be similar to you and start up an e-mail exchange with them. Ask questions and get a lot of different opinions. I think most volunteers will be happy to tell you about their experiences. Some have had bad experiences while others, like me, have had great experiences.

8) **Describe your village site in detail: What is attractive/difficult about it?** I actually live in the town of Neiafu, and it's not really what you would imagine as a typical village. I live on the property of my landlord, Kepu Tupou, and his family. In addition to Kepu's house, there is the house where I live and right next to it, is another house where James Barbour, an education volunteer, lives. James and I live 10 feet from each other, but we each have our own house. Our situation is unique in Peace Corps Tonga because no other volunteer lives that close to another anywhere in the country. Some volunteers have to take a boat to see another volunteer.

I like my living situation a lot. Kepu and his family are great, and they feed me Tongan food almost every Sunday. That's a big part of the culture here, not only sharing food, but having a big meal on Sunday after church. It's also nice to have another American so close, and I'm thankful to have a person like James right next door. I'm also very close to work. It's a 10-minute walk down the hill to my job at the Tonga Development Bank. The walk home isn't quite as nice, as I have to climb back up the hill and it is steep. However, the road offers a great view of the harbor, so the view helps make up for the steep climb.

9) **When were you most frightened?** Only once was I really frightened. The story is a bit long, and it happened just one month after I became a volunteer. One Thursday, my friend and fellow volunteer Craig and I had lunch together at the Catholic Basilica in Nuku'alofa. They have a small restaurant in the basement of the church, and I had eaten there a few times previously. I usually order the special, and on this day it was fried tuna. I would have preferred to have it lightly seared, but was just happy to get tuna, as it is one of my favorite meals. Craig did not order the fish and ate something else, which I don't remember. When I got back to work, I wasn't feeling great and told my supervisor at the bank that I was going home. I told Craig that lunch hadn't sat well with me. He was surprised that I was feeling

bad so quickly after we ate, even mentioning that normally food poisoning takes a while to become symptomatic after you eat.

I went home and stayed in bed the rest of the day and called in sick on Friday. I did not eat anything at all either Thursday night or all day Friday. I never vomited but just felt bad. I was not really nauseous; I think queasy would be the best way to describe it.

I woke up early Saturday morning, reached for my water bottle and discovered I did not have the strength to pick it up. My first thought was that I was weak from not eating, but I quickly realized this was much more serious. I couldn't lift anything with my left hand, and I couldn't even raise my arm and hand over my head. For all practical purposes, I had lost use of my left arm and hand.

This terrified me as you can imagine. Clearly this was not the result of something I ate. It was a much more serious problem. I called the Peace Corps medical office and the assistant Peace Corps medical director came over. She checked my blood pressure and pulse, which were both normal. She asked if I was in pain, to which I replied no. I had numbness in the fingers on both hands and also had numbness on my tongue, but I wasn't uncomfortable. The director told me that she would get me to a doctor first thing on Monday, but there wasn't much she could do for me on a Saturday unless things got worse.

On Monday, when we got to the doctor's office, I was unable to write or sign my name. (I am left-handed.) Jacinta Tonga, the nurse who is the Peace Corps medical officer, had to fill out the forms for me. Once I got into the exam room, the doctor diagnosed that I had just one-fifth of my normal strength in my arm. In other words, I had lost 80% use of my hand and arm. The doctor said I might have had a stroke but thought it could also be something muscular. She even checked me for diabetes. I really didn't believe I had suffered a stroke.

The doctor was an Australian doctor, probably in her late 50s. After examining me, she suggested acupuncture to see if that would help my arm. While Jacinta, the Peace Corps medical officer who accompanied me to the doctor was skeptical and wasn't sure I should have it, I agreed to give it a try. I figured it certainly wouldn't do any harm.

At the clinic, there was only one exam room, so the doctor moved me into the clinic pharmacy, which opens onto the waiting room and has a big open window between the rooms. She stuck six needles in me—one in my head and the rest in my hand, arm and shoulder. I asked for a glass of water and was left alone in the pharmacy. After about five minutes, I started to feel faint. I screamed for help, and a stampede of people came rushing in, including other patients who were waiting to see the doctor. They grabbed me before I fell and put me on the floor. I spent the next 20 minutes lying on the floor of the pharmacy with needles sticking out of me. I can only imagine what would have happened if I had fallen on top of one and jammed it into my body. Afterward, the doctor told me that about one out of every 50 people get faint when they get acupuncture. It's hard for me to imagine that those little needles could cause me to feel that way.

Peace Corps was now making plans to send me to Brisbane, Australia for a full exam and an MRI. Jacinta told me: "Steve, I know you really love Peace Corps, but if you have to be sent home, it's because you need to take care of your arm. That is what is really important." Of course she was right, but just hearing someone say out loud that I could be sent home and medically discharged from the Peace Corps was pretty scary. I went home and spent the rest of that day and night wondering what I would do back in the United States, especially with no use of my left arm and hand. I couldn't even type or use the computer easily. However, the practical side soon kicked in, and I decided I would go back to the United States and find the very best doctor and hospital for treatment of problems like mine. It didn't matter to me where it was in the United States, just that I would go to the best place possible. Peace Corps would be paying for my treatment, and I figured I could easily absorb the costs of living somewhere until I got better. And there was always the chance that the hospital was near my home in Florida or near my family in Virginia.

On Tuesday, my arm was better. Not normal, but I had more use of it and could almost bend my elbow into a right angle. I called Jacinta, who told me she still did not have an appointment for me in Australia, but that she was happy to hear I was doing better. She told me I was to stay home for the rest of the week and didn't even want me to go out of my house.

Two days later, my arm and hand were doing much better, and Jacinta called and said, "You were poisoned." That was the official verdict from the Peace Corps medical office in Washington, DC after reviewing my case. I was skeptical at first. I couldn't believe that everything that had happened was the result of eating fish. But after reading the Peace Corps medical handbook and looking online, I came to believe that it was a proper diagnosis. I was probably suffering from ciguatera fish poisoning, paralytic shellfish poisoning or scombroid fish poisoning. And it probably was not anyone's fault that I became sick. All three of the poisons mentioned above are impossible to detect, and the fish comes out of the water that way.

Because I was getting better every day, I no longer had to take a trip to Brisbane, Australia, and I had no need for any further medical attention. I went back to work the following week and two weeks after I had first eaten the poisoned fish, I decided my arm was 100%. However, it does still scare me to think how much poison I had ingested to have that kind of impact on me. It also changed my perspective and made me appreciate the fact that I was still in Peace Corps.

10) How will you move your service forward upon your return to the United States? As I mentioned earlier, I think I have a better view of the world, or at least people, because of my Peace Corps experience. Ideally, I would like to continue with Peace Corps in some capacity. I'm pretty passionate about helping small businesses and would love to find an opportunity where I could do that within the Peace Corps organization.

WILL YOU BUY THIS FOR ME?
Wednesday, September 9, 2009

It's no secret that Tonga survives on the generosity of others. The country's main source of income is from overseas remittances and foreign aid. But times are tough and people aren't as generous. For the first six months of this year, the amount of money sent by Tongans overseas to their relatives in Tonga dropped by 14%, and tourism is down 6%.

Foreign aid is also drying up. One of my fellow Peace Corps volunteers was just turned down by New Zealand Aid for a project because New Zealand has put all of its aid to Tonga on hold for the rest of the year. Other countries are doing the same.

This is a big adjustment for Tongans, many of whom are very used to asking, "Will you buy this for me?" You can go almost anywhere in Tonga, and you'll see signs like the one on a rainwater collection tank saying who provided the money for the project.

For years, the money has flowed freely, and all kinds of projects have been funded. For example, early last year I heard about a school that had a shortage of textbooks and no computers, but instead of asking for money to get books, school supplies or computers to help the kids, they instead got the European Union to buy them a very expensive riding lawn mower. And the school doesn't have a very big yard.

The island of Hunga just finished building a very expensive road from the waterfront up to their village. There is just one vehicle on the entire island, a truck that was also paid for with grant money. The road was built so that the truck could go down this road to pick up supplies from boats. The road is all poured concrete with a sidewalk on each side, but if you look closely, you'll notice some obvious problems. There is no drainage, so all the water pours down the road into the harbor below. You can see where the mud has already started to collect. It's also not straight and it is much more difficult to walk up the hill to the village than if they had built a set of stairs. I was initially told the project was funded by New Zealand, then was told it was paid for by India. You have to wonder if the money wouldn't have been better spent installing electricity or running water on the island, of which it has neither.

And then there are the grants that go for great projects, but they end up being a waste of time.

The village of Falevai has a beautiful medical center. It's the only place outside of the main island where people in Vava'u can go for medical issues. The center was paid for with grant money. There is just one problem. There is no money to pay doctors and nurses to work there. So the building, which is actually nicer than the Vava'u hospital, sits empty. Villagers now use the fence around it as a clothesline to dry their laundry.

On the surface, all three of these projects probably sounded good on paper: a lawn mower to help a poor school, a road to improve the infrastructure of a village and a modern medical center to help people who live on small outer islands. It just didn't work out that way.

And in fairness to the countries that provided the grant money, they did so out of a desire to help the people of Tonga. It can be hard to say "no" when a friendly Tongan with a big smile on his or her face comes up and says, "Will you buy this for me?"

A TONGAN TRADITION I DON'T LIKE
Wednesday, September 16, 2009

I like most Tongan traditions. One of the really cool things about Tonga is how well its culture and traditions have been preserved. But, as I briefly stated in a previous post, there is one tradition I don't like, and that's the way Tongans say their final goodbyes. It's not that I don't appreciate the importance of a putu (funeral), either in Tonga or in the United States. I know how important it is for the friends and family to say goodbye to those they love, but I also think it isn't necessary for a family to spend their life savings to pay their final respects.

In Tonga, there is nothing modest or inexpensive about a putu. A Tongan family feels enormous cultural pressure to throw a huge expensive funeral every time someone dies.

A Tongan funeral is not just a funeral ceremony. The family is expected to throw a big feast and feed everyone who shows up. While it is also customary for people to bring a gift to a funeral, the family responds by giving gifts to everyone who comes. The family of a loved one never comes out ahead. A typical putu can cost more than most Tongans make in a year.

At the bank where I work, we have people come in immediately after a loved one has died seeking to take out a loan to pay for the funeral. In some cases, a family will go into debt for years just to pay for the funeral. Many turn to their relatives overseas to cough up the money, so they can have a "great" funeral for their loved one.

Some families even hire bands to play at the funeral and to march with the body from the house to the cemetery.

There are many other ways that the family responds when someone dies. How close you are to the deceased will determine how long you wear black and huge funeral mats.

It's also traditional for a woman's hair to be cut in memory of her loved one. A higher-ranking woman in the house will tell a lower-ranking woman to cut her hair. The hair is usually woven into a belt that can be worn to hold up one of the large funeral mats.

Now in all fairness, putting on a putu is a work of art. There are no funeral homes here, so all of the work—from preparing and dressing the body to digging the grave—is done by friends and family. The preparations are lavish, with many people helping to cook the food and set up tables so everyone has a place to eat. During the day, the men sit and drink kava while the women sing. The kava drinking and singing will often last for days—from the time the person dies until they are finally put into a grave decorated with quilts, flowers and plants.

When you attend a funeral it all goes like clockwork, and it's truly amazing to see the end result of so much work.

One more interesting note about death in Tonga: If you ask a Tongan why someone died, they will usually say they were sick or they were old. There are no autopsies and the cause of death is rarely known.

TOGETHER FOR THE LAST TIME!
Tuesday, September 22, 2009

Almost two years ago, on October 2, 2007, I first met the people who would become known as Peace Corps Tonga Group 73. These 33 strangers would soon become friends, sharing the experience of serving as Peace Corps volunteers in Tonga.

We spent a grueling three months together during training before becoming volunteers and heading out to our job assignments. We reunited twice for Peace Corps conferences and along the way, many of our friends left Tonga, each having his or her own reason for leaving early.

Last week, for the last time, the members of my group got together on the main island for our close of service conference. Unlike past conferences that focused on our service, this one was really all about the volunteers and was designed to prepare us for our life after Peace Corps. For the 19 of us who have remained in Tonga, it was also our last time together. While we all arrived in Tonga on the same date, most of us will be leaving on different dates. I'm officially leaving Tonga on November 23rd, exactly two months from today. Many of our group will leave before then. For those of us who don't live on the main island, that means we will not see the volunteers who leave before us again.

The remaining members of Tonga Group 73

We spent our last few days together as a group reminiscing about our service, talking about those who had left early and discussing our plans for the future. There was also talk about a reunion once we all get back to the United States.

On our last night, Peace Corps provided us with a delicious feast and Tongan entertainment. It was a fun night. At the end of the evening, we did a group dance, with everyone coming up on the stage for one last dance together. And then one last group hug.

It's certainly not the end of my Peace Corps experience, but a major milestone in my Peace Corps service. I'm now back home in Vava'u and realize how many things I still want to do in my remaining two months.

ANOTHER AUSTRALIAN ADVENTURE.
Tuesday, September 29, 2009

For the second September in a row, I ventured south from Tonga to Australia. Last year it was Brisbane. This year, I explored the southern coast of the only country that is also a continent, visiting Melbourne, Adelaide and Kangaroo Island.

Kangaroo Island

Without a doubt, the highlight of my trip was a two-day tour to the very appropriately named Kangaroo Island. Kangaroo Island is located east of Adelaide and is actually quite large. At 4,400 square kilometers, it is five times larger than the total land mass of every island in Tonga combined.

And yes, there are kangaroos everywhere.

It was so amazing to see animals in the wild that I had either never seen before or had only seen in a zoo. This koala bear (see next page) was high in a tree and almost looked like a stuffed animal, but he was very real, munching away on a eucalyptus tree.

This is an Australian seal. It is one of two types of seals on the island. The other is the New Zealand fur sea, which we also saw. The fur seals actually swim from New Zealand to Australia and can live in the water for months at a time. I spent two days on the island as part of a tour with a company called Surf and Sun. I was very impressed with this company and would highly recommend them to anyone planning a trip to Kangaroo Island.

I was joined on the trip by a couple from Germany, five women from Europe and a woman from Korea. They were all in their 20s except for the German guy who was 30. At dinner the first night, I found myself surrounded by six single women. One of them said, "So Steve, I guess you are not used to having dinner with so many girls." I responded by saying, "Well actually I am used to that. Where I live I'm surrounded by women all the time." And another said, "But I'm sure they are much older." To which I replied, "Actually not, I spend a lot of my time with single women in their 20s." I then went on to explain that I was one of just three male Peace Corps volunteers on my island and that the rest were all women. (They thought that was interesting, but when I told my female friends in Vava'u that story, they all laughed.)

I suspect that when I first got on the tour bus, this group wasn't sure what to make of me—this older guy who was on their trip. But that quickly changed, and I know the exact moment that it happened.

As part of the tour, we went to a place called Little Sahara. It's a huge sand dune that is not on the water, but inland. We came there to sand board, something I had never done before. I was the second one down the hill, and it was fascinating to see how the attitudes of my group changed once they saw me get on that board. One other comment about the stay on Kangaroo Island: We ate really well. The Surf and Sun tour provided all the food, and we took turns cooking and cleaning.

Wine Tasting

I've never been to a vineyard before. When I went to New Zealand in April, I had planned to go, but never made it. This time, I was determined not to let that happen and signed up for a tour of the Barossa Valley, outside Adelaide.

We visited five wineries, and I sampled 30 different wines all in one day. South Australia, where the region I visited is located, is the top producer of Australian wines.

We didn't get to taste it, but I did get to smell a 100-year-old port wine. A taste of that would have cost me something like AUD$50 (about US$40). And that wasn't for a glass, that was just for a taste.

In addition to the wines, I ate kangaroo for lunch, along with other assorted meats and salad. I thought the kangaroo was delicious. It had obviously been marinated and was quite tender, with a consistency closer to beef. (I had expected it to taste more like deer.)

One stop that was pretty interesting was at what is called the Whispering Wall. It's actually not a wall, but a dam for a reservoir. However, the acoustics are amazing. I stood on one side of the dam and in a very low whisper was able to carry on a conversation with someone on the other side, who was also whispering. It was pretty cool to see that sound could travel that far.

I enjoyed the wine tasting and the visit to the Whispering Wall, but I can't recommend the tour company that I used. The firm, called Groovy Grape, was an hour late picking us up. At two of our stops, we were told that because we were so late, they had to cut short our time there. And then the kicker was that we ended up getting back 20 minutes early.

Melbourne

I spent five days and four nights in Melbourne. It's a really cool and culturally diverse city. But what is really fascinating about the place is the location of some of its coolest spots.

If you've ever worked in any business that depends on customers coming to your location, then you know how important it is to have the right location. If customers can't find you, you won't survive very long.

Apparently someone forgot to tell the folks in Melbourne that because there are tons of bars and restaurants that are located in places where most Americans wouldn't venture—mainly down dead-end alleys. These alleys are all over Melbourne, and the city is known for having successful businesses in spots that are not so easy to find.

Cumulatively, I've now spent almost a month in Australia, and I'm not done yet. Once I complete my Peace Corps service, I'm heading to Cairns, to go diving on the Great Barrier Reef and then down to Sydney before heading back to the United States.

Steve Hunsicker

THE TSUNAMI IN TONGA
Thursday, October 1, 2009

The islands of Niuatoputapu and Niuafo'oa in Tonga have been devastated by a tsunami that hit the region Wednesday morning just before 8 a.m. local time following an earthquake.

This is the same tsunami that did so much damage in Samoa and American Samoa. (Samoa is on the other side of the dateline so it hit there on Tuesday.)

Unlike Samoa, these Tongan islands, which are commonly known as the "Niuas," are pretty remote. A boat takes supplies to the islands just once a month, and there is no regular plane service.

The Tongan Development Bank has an office on each of the islands. Its office in Niuatoputapu was one of many buildings destroyed.

Earthquakes are not uncommon in Tonga. There are active volcanoes throughout the South Pacific including here in the island kingdom. However, they are rare enough that you still notice when they happen. That was the case Wednesday morning, just before 7 a.m. I was awake, but still in bed when the shaking started. It lasted a long time, and I knew immediately it was the strongest earthquake I had felt since moving to Tonga two years ago. I also didn't think the quake was strong enough to do any damage here.

At no point was anyone in Neiafu really worried. Vava'u is very hilly and the harbor is one of the most protected harbors in the South Pacific. Yacht owners will often leave their boats here during cyclone season because it is so well protected, and after the warning was issued, many of the boats that were out on the water returned to dock.

My friend Scott, who is a Peace Corps volunteer on Ovaka, one of the outer islands of Vava'u, is the only person I know in the Vava'u region who actually saw any impact from the tsunami. I spoke with him on the phone, and he said the water went over the wharf on his island, something he had never seen before, and then went down to sea level. He said the tsunami lasted for about 30 minutes. He described it to me as "more interesting than scary."

This is the second major disaster to hit Tonga in the past 60 days. The ferry *Ashika* sank in August killing more than 70 people.

FIRST HAND ACCOUNT OF THE TONGAN TSUNAMI
Friday, October 2, 2009

The only person I know in the part of Tonga hit by the tsunami is Mafi, the manager of the Tonga Development Bank office in Niuatoputapu. She and the rest of the bank staff up there are all fine.

Below is her account of what happened when the tsunami struck Tonga. Part of this was originally written in Tongan, and I've translated it to the best of my ability.

Here is her story:

> Someone called out that fateful morning, "The ocean is coming ashore."
> So the first thing I thought of was to get to the bank, which is two minutes from my house in order to check on our things. I got my elderly mother-in-law and daughter into the van, and we drove towards the bank.
> Halfway down, I saw the big wave coming towards us. It was moving across the bank, and I saw it being destroyed. All I could do was go into reverse gear, flooring the gas.
> I picked up all the people running on the road and headed towards the high ground. The wave was about 10 meters (30 feet) behind us. I just kept praying and asked God to live, and I thought I just have to keep the van in control.
> I left the people in a safe high place and came down again to see if I could help some people on the lower ground, but the wave had gone back and all I could see was ruin.
> We kept the people on the mountain all night in case another wave came back. People were so frightened . . . and we tried to calm them.
> We picked up all the food and staff from the store, and that's what the people ate that day and night. Hika (a woman) was able to survive because she managed to swim with the wave without hitting anything.
> The bank's building is all gone, including the strong room with everything in it. There is no equipment remaining from the bank. Everything is destroyed.

The bank has an emergency plan, and they have already sent supplies and people up to Niuatoputapu to assist with the recovery.

We have had several more earthquakes since this one, but none have been major. I thought I felt one yesterday, but it wasn't very strong, and I thought perhaps I was imagining it. But when I checked the USGS earthquake website, it turns out it really was another one. They also list some other earthquakes in Tonga that I didn't feel.

It will take a long time for Niuatoputapu to recover, but for the rest of the country it is pretty much business as usual. The earthquake had no impact at all here in Vava'u (or in other parts of Tonga), and everything is open and running.

A SCARY WELCOME TO TONGA
Saturday, October 10, 2009

The future Peace Corps volunteers who will replace the members of my group in Tonga are now here. Tonga Group 75 arrived Thursday morning on the main island of Tongatapu to begin three months of training.

Within hours of landing at the airport, a tsunami warning was issued and all volunteers and the trainees were told by Peace Corps to stay away from coastal areas and to remain at their sites. In the case of the trainees, they were all secured in a guesthouse until the warning passed. What a welcome to Tonga.

As you might imagine, the warning on Thursday was taken a lot more seriously after a tsunami devastated Niuatoputapu 10 days ago. In Vava'u, the schools immediately closed, most businesses closed, and the streets were eerily empty. The response from Peace Corps was also much swifter this time than when the tsunami warning was issued 10 days ago. Then, I never received a phone call from anyone at Peace Corps. This time, I had multiple phone calls from both Peace Corps staff and fellow volunteers.

Of course, last time, I also felt the earthquake—something we didn't feel in Vava'u this time.

Job Training

My friend Emily, who is a volunteer in Tongatapu, has been visiting us here in Vava'u this week. Emily works for the Ministry of Training, Employment, Youth and Sports. (Yes, one ministry does all four things.) Emily is here to teach Tongan youth how to apply for jobs and how to interview. On Wednesday, she conducted a workshop for those interested in getting a job.

Volunteer Emily MacGruder conducts a workshop

Emily also went around to many of the businesses here interviewing them to find out what opportunities they have for Tongan youth.

Fun Friday in Vava'u

Friday, my friend Scott and I went diving around a small island called Lotuma, which is located near the entrance to the main harbor in Vava'u. Lotuma is the same island where we had a very fun July 4th celebration two years ago.

Steve Hunsicker dives near the island of Lotuma

This dive, while not spectacular, was still pretty interesting because there are many giant clams along the reef. I started playing a game to see how close I could get to the clams before they would close. I was never able to get near enough to touch one before it shut its shell.

After the dive, I joined my fellow volunteers for our monthly meeting, and then we went out to a new restaurant that just opened here. This place, called Laredo's, has just started advertising an all-you-can-eat-ribs dinner for TOP$30. That's more than we get in an entire day for food but is only about US$15. However, we couldn't pass up the chance to splurge. When we got there, we found that after just two days of offering the special, they had increased the price to TOP$35. We still decided to "pig out," and we did . . . joking that after the Peace Corps volunteers left, the restaurant would have to increase the price to TOP$40. Three times the waitress came to take away my plate, and each time I stopped her and told her I wanted more ribs. They were really good and were grilled right in front of us on an open fire.

After that we headed out to a couple of nightspots before calling it a night.

It was a fun Friday and a nice break to have some time with my fellow Americans here in Vava'u. I have just 40 days left.

SWIMMING WITH WHALES—ABSOLUTELY AMAZING!
Friday, October 16, 2009

How do you describe the experience of being just feet away from one of the largest mammals on the planet?

How do you describe the experience of watching a baby whale calf play under the watchful eye of its mother?

And how do you describe the feeling of being pushed by gentle turbulence as a giant humpback softly swings its tale creating a mini wave?

Words can't describe it. Swimming with whales is one of those rare events in life that must be experienced firsthand to fully understand and appreciate it.

After a day swimming with whales, something that very few people ever get a chance to do, I feel truly humbled by these gentle giants and at a loss to find the appropriate adjectives to describe the experience.

The Humpback Whale Experience

I spent the day with Dolphin Pacific Diving. The day started a bit slow, and I started to wonder if we would actually encounter any whales. It's late in the season, and many of the whales that have been here all winter have left.

Humpback whale giving Steve Hunsicker the "eye"

I have been close to whales before, but this was the first time that I had planned to dive with them.

We had stopped for an early lunch break, when one of the guys on the boat asked, "Is that a whale?" I didn't see it at first but it was. We quickly made our way toward the whale, and as we approached, we saw a baby calf jump completely out of the water, spinning as it landed back in the water. It was a terrific start to a great experience.

When we got in the water, we swam out. The water was dark, and then I noticed what I thought was a reef on the ocean bottom. But as we got closer, I realized I was looking down at a giant humpback whale directly below me. This was NOT the baby we had seen jump out of the water, it was the mother, taking a rest. And she wasn't on the ocean floor, she was floating.

The first stop was short, as the whales swam away, but on the next stop, the whales were in a playful mood—especially the baby who seemed to almost be chasing us. At one point, I felt like the calf was putting on a show just for the five of us who were in the water.

"Mama" had her eye on us and on her baby. I looked her straight in the eye and wondered what I must look like to her.

On the last stop of the day, we probably spent 45 minutes in the water just watching the whales play. I had been taking a lot of photos, but finally just shut off the camera and floated there, watching these two go about their lives. It was peaceful, tranquil, and they seemed to exert a calmness in us like nothing I've experienced before.

Whale Videos

I shot two videos while in the water with the whales. The first video was taken with my Canon A710 still camera in video mode. That camera doesn't have the resolution of my other camera, but it is much easier to use underwater.

http://vimeo.com/shunsicker/whales

The second video was shot on my Sony SR-11 video camera. The camera quality is much better, but it is almost impossible to see anything through the viewfinder underwater, so I just point the camera in the general direction and hope it comes out.

http://vimeo.com/shunsicker/whales2

One note about the videos: It may look like I've slowed the videos down, but the videos are in real time and not slow motion.

A TONGAN DRAG SHOW
Thursday, October 22, 2009

The Kingdom of Tonga is often described as a conservative and Christian country, rich in tradition and culture. That's very true. But some people who consider themselves conservative, Christian and traditional in the United States might be very surprised at one of the traditions in this island nation.

As I have mentioned in previous posts, in old Tongan culture, when a family did not have any young girls to do "women's work," they raised a young boy, called a fakaleiti, to do that work. While this tradition probably still happens, the fakaleiti of today are more often than not gay men who dress like women and often perform jobs that are traditionally done by women.

I should make it clear that not all fakaleiti are gay. And not all gay Tongans are fakaleiti.

Some fakaleiti are married to women and have children of their own.

If you go to a restaurant or store in Tonga, it is not uncommon to be helped by a man who is wearing women's attire. You will also see these men walking around town just like anyone else except for the way they dress. It is an accepted part of the culture here.

Every Wednesday night during the winter tourist season, some of the fakaleiti ham it up for the tourists at a local Vava'u bar called Tonga Bob's. The fakaleiti show is a must-see for many visitors to Vava'u, and while the show is not a traditional Tongan event, it still brings out plenty of locals to watch.

The way the men dress during the show is NOT the same way they dress in town. This show is for the audience, and the guys go out of their way to entertain.

The tourist season is winding down, and this week marked the final fakaleiti show of the year. It was my second time to attend. I went to the first show of the season last year and the last show this year. It was a fun night and because many of the tourists are gone, a lot of Tongans squeezed into the bar to watch.

Tongans love to laugh and yes, they laugh at the fakaleiti. But that's the point—to have a good time and not take it too seriously.

Also in the audience for the final show of the year were some members of the French Navy who have a small boat docked here this week.

One other note: Every year there is a fakaleiti festival on the main island of Tonga called the "Miss Galaxy Festival." It's a huge mainstream event that features fakaleiti from all over Tonga and attracts major international sponsors like Air New Zealand and WestPac Bank.

TONGA DEVELOPMENT BANK VIDEO
Wednesday, October 28, 2009

For the past several months, I've been working on a video for the Tonga Development Bank. This video will air on television throughout the kingdom and will also be shown at future bank workshops. It is designed to promote the bank's business advisory service, which is the area where I work. On Wednesday of this week, it was shown publicly for the first time at a bank workshop in Neiafu.

The project turned out to be a lot harder than I expected. I produced the entire 10-minute video in Tongan. In order to make the video work, I wrote down the questions in English, and those were translated to Tongan. Once the interviews were finished, I had someone translate the transcript of the interviews into English, and from that I wrote the script. The bank approved the final script in English, and then it was translated for me back into Tongan.

Even though I worked in TV news for 23 years, video editing was never one of the jobs I performed. Since I've been in Tonga, I've taught myself the basics of editing on a computer. But this project was even more complicated because I had to make sure the video matched the Tongan script. Thankfully, I had a Tongan-English dictionary to help.

MY FRIENDS IN TONGA
Wednesday, November 4, 2009

I believe we are all influenced by the people with whom we associate. If you hang around negative people, it tends to make you more negative. If you find yourself around someone who is cynical, eventually, you may start to question everything.

I'm very fortunate that for the past two years, I've been surrounded by a lot of friendly and positive folks. And I hope that their influence on me continues long after I leave Tonga.

Just like in the United States, I have several groups of friends here, ranging from my work friends to my personal friends to my fellow volunteers.

Steve Hunsicker with his Tongan co-workers

These are my colleagues at the Tonga Development Bank in Vava'u. I've seen each of these people almost every working day since I moved here.

They are a great group of folks, and they love to laugh at me almost as much as I like to laugh with them. (Okay, sometimes I laugh at them too!)

The man in the middle on the first row is my great friend Fuka, who is the manager of the branch. He has been such a great help to me during my service that I can't imagine being a volunteer in Tonga without him around. We are the same age, have a lot in common, and we shared a memorable fishing trip last year.

My fellow volunteers have also been an important part of my life, especially those who arrived with me. Our training group, Tonga Group 73, initially started with 33 volunteers. There are now just 18 of us left, and next week, the remaining group members will start to leave for good. (November 12th is the first day we are allowed to leave, and we have until December 12th to depart unless we request an extension.)

However, the volunteers to whom I've been the closest are the ones with whom I've shared an island. Group 71 and Group 72 were both here in Vava'u when I arrived. They are now gone, replaced for the past year by the members of Group 74.

The final camping trip for Vava'u group 73 volunteers

Two weekends ago, we had a final camping trip with the eight Vava'u volunteers (and some other friends). It was a last chance for us to hang out together for an extended period of time. We spent two nights camping on an uninhabited island.

There were originally eight people from my group in Vava'u. James, Shannon and I are the only three who remain. (Shannon is in the white top, and that's James in at the far right next to me.)

The members of Group 75, who are all now in training, will arrive after we have all departed. Six of them have been assigned to Vava'u, but none will be replacing James, Shannon or myself.

Some Random Notes

• I obtained my Advanced Open Water SCUBA certification last week. This follows my basic Open Water certification in March. My final dive was a night dive, and it was such a difference experience than diving during the day. We also encountered a three-foot shark who seemed a lot less interested in us than we were in him.

• My last day at work is November 19th. I fly to the main island on November 20th, and then I leave Tonga for good on November 23rd.

• I've been sick for the past six days and have rarely left the house. It's frustrating because there are so many things I want to do before I leave Vava'u and losing six days when you only have three weeks left sucks. However, I've been pretty healthy during my service, so I guess it was my time.

WRAPPING THINGS UP
Wednesday, November 11, 2009

With just over a week remaining for me in Vava'u, there isn't much left for me to do at work. Today was my final business development workshop, the 20th workshop we've done since I've been a Peace Corps volunteer in Tonga.

The workshops are designed to help Tongans better understand how to run a business and how to keep records. I estimate that more than 500 Tongans have participated in these 20 workshops. Some of them, like a woman I featured in the video I produced for the bank, have made big improvements because of the skills they learned at the workshops. Hopefully these businesspeople will continue to improve in the coming years. Wouldn't it be great to come back to Tonga one day and see that one of the past participants has done great things?

The Week Ahead

My final day at the Vava'u bank is next Thursday. I fly to the main island of Tongatapu on Friday to say goodbye to the folks at our head office and to do my exit interviews with Peace Corps.

I leave Tonga for good on Monday the 23rd, when I'll fly to New Zealand for about 30 hours before heading to Australia for a couple of weeks. I'm meeting my friend Shannon there, and we have a lot planned for Australia—including a five-day dive trip on the Great Barrier Reef. On Thanksgiving Day, we've arranged to have a traditional American dinner with turkey and all the trimmings. While in Australia, we will also be going to a place called Cape Tribulation before wrapping up the trip with five days in Sydney. It's my third trip to Australia. I went to Brisbane in September 2008 and to Melbourne and Adelaide/Kangaroo Island in September of this year.

I fly back into West Palm Beach late on December 8th.

STEVE'S ADVENTURE ENDS TODAY
Sunday, November 22, 2009

It has been more than three years since I first applied to join the Peace Corps, and what an adventure it has been. I filled out my application on September 26, 2006; I arrived in Tonga on October 4, 2007; and today, November 23, 2009, I am leaving Tonga, no longer a Peace Corps volunteer.

Officially, I'm now called an RPCV, or a returned Peace Corps volunteer, but since I haven't actually returned yet, it seems a bit strange to use that acronym just yet.

A Video Journal

As of today, I've written 160 entries about my Peace Corps experience, with the vast majority written during my two years of service and my 10 weeks of training. But written words and still photos have only allowed me to share a portion of my journey. Therefore, I decided for my last entry from Tonga, I would produce a video journal about some of the things I've found most interesting and some of the things I've done. The video is little long . . . almost 16 minutes, but I just couldn't cut anything else out. I have more than 20 hours of footage, so it was quite an accomplishment to get this down to 16 minutes. I hope you enjoy it.
http://vimeo.com/shunsicker/stevesadventure

I shot almost all of the footage in the video except for the interviews. Those were shot by my friend Chad, and I sincerely appreciate his help.

My Future Plans

When I left my job more than two years ago, I knew that once my Peace Corps service was over, I would be coming back to the United States with no job. That day has now arrived, and I can happily say that I am now searching for my next opportunity. I don't know what that will be, and I don't have anything lined up. The good news is that I'm very open to just about anything. My hope is to find something that I will enjoy as much as I have enjoyed my time in Tonga.

Saying Goodbye

Much of what I've been doing for the past two weeks has involved saying goodbye to all the people I have met in the past two years. My last three Sundays were spent at different Tongan homes eating umu, which is the traditional Sunday feast. I have been humbled by the many thanks and gifts that I have received . . . too many to even begin to mention here. And I was honored to have not one, not two, but three going-away events—two in Vava'u and one at the head office of the Tonga Development Bank.

The folks at the Vava'u branch of the bank went "all out" to say goodbye last Thursday, my last day working there. We had a lavish morning tea ceremony and some really wonderful gifts. After everyone said their goodbyes, we invited customers to come and join us, and they helped us eat all the food the staff had prepared.

At our head office on the main island of Tongatapu, the bank put on another tea for me Friday with the managers and staff saying goodbye. The managing director presented me with a whale carving made of sandalwood.

And on Thursday night, I spent my last few hours in Vava'u hanging out with my fellow volunteers and other friends at the Aquarium Cafe.

A Final Thought

Many years ago, I heard President Ronald Reagan give a speech and in it, he said, "We're not here to congratulate ourselves on what we have done but to challenge ourselves to finish what has not yet been done." As I think about my service in Peace Corps, I hope that this has just been the beginning. I hope to challenge myself and others to accomplish more in the future.

'Ofa lahi atu! (With much love to you!)

Steve

THE ADVENTURE CONTINUES
Saturday December 8, 2012

It has been three years since I left Tonga, and I doubt there has been a single day when I haven't thought about my 27 months in Peace Corps and all of the wonderful people I met. When I left Tonga, I wrote a blog entry entitled "Steve's Adventure Ends Today." I could not have been more wrong. Returning to the United States, I now realize that the adventure never ends. Peace Corps is a part of me.

When people ask me what I liked best about Peace Corps, it is a very tough question. But I usually answer that I'm most proud of the relationships I made with my Tongan friends, my fellow volunteers and the volunteers from other aid organizations.

For my birthday last year, I traveled to Japan with a friend from Miami. Even though it had been two years since I last saw any of the four Japanese volunteers I served with, all of them traveled from all over Japan to help me celebrate. It was the first time the four of them had all been together, and it was a great reunion.

Steve Hunsicker with four former JICA volunteers

The year before, I traveled to the Dominican Republic where I got to visit with Alice, one of the volunteers with whom I served. She was working there as an English teacher, continuing the work she had done in Tonga. And right here in the USA, I've gotten together with many of my former volunteer friends. To date, five of them have visited me at my house, and I've seen another 10 since my return.

It is harder to keep in touch with my Tongan friends, but many of them are now on Facebook, and I still occasionally email or chat with them. I even occasionally get a question from some of my former clients, and I'm of course happy to still help.

I've also collaborated on a travel guide about Tonga with three of my former volunteers. That book was published by Other Places Publishing, a company founded by returned Peace Corps volunteers.

But the real surprise since returning to the United States has been meeting so many other returned Peace Corps volunteers. And I've learned that no matter where they served and when they served, we have a lot of similar stories and shared experiences. It's also refreshing to see how many of these returned volunteers are still active in helping others.

I now work for Peace Corps as the South Florida-based recruiter. I spend most of my time talking with people who are thinking about applying to Peace Corps. It gives me a chance to help continue the more than 50-year legacy of Peace Corps, but it also allows me to talk about my own experiences in Tonga.

My work has also inspired me to compile all of my own experiences into this book. Many of the entries in the book are taken from the blog I kept during my service, but I've also included some private journal entries that were never published on my website.

In putting together the book, it was fascinating for me to read many of the early entries about my frustration with the application process. As a recruiter, I now have a little more insight into that process, and I know that some of the assumptions I made when I was an applicant were not always correct. However, I hope that it makes me a better recruiter because I do remember what it is like to hear nothing for such a long period of time.

I also like to tell people that I have "a one-country perspective." As I have learned since returning, there are many similarities in all the Peace Corps experiences worldwide, but they are also all different. These are my stories and my experiences.

I wouldn't change anything!

If you enjoyed reading this book, please consider adding a review at Amazon.com.

For more information about Peace Corps:
http://www.peacecorps.gov

To donate to a volunteer project:
http://www.peacecorps.gov/index.cfm?shell=donate

ABOUT THE AUTHOR

Steve Hunsicker is the South Florida recruiter for Peace Corps. Before being hired by Peace Corps, Steve was a business development volunteer in the Kingdom of Tonga.

As a volunteer, Steve helped more than 500 small-business owners start or expand businesses in one-on-one settings and workshops. He created websites for four Tongan businesses; he tutored students on business topics at the University of the South Pacific; and he produced several videos, including one for Peace Corps to introduce Tonga to incoming volunteers.

Steve is the co-author of a travel book about Tonga, published in 2011 by Other Places Publishing.

Before volunteering with the Peace Corps, Steve spent 23 years in television news, including 15 years with Freedom Communications, the company that owns WPEC CBS 12, in West Palm Beach. At WPEC, Steve was the executive news director, responsible for eight hours of local news every day on WPEC and WFLX Fox 29. Prior to joining WPEC, he was the news director at Freedom's WTVC's NewsChannel 9, the top-rated station in Chattanooga, Tennessee. Steve began his TV career in Tallahassee, Florida and has also run TV news departments in Gainesville, Florida, Harrisburg, Pennsylvania and Honolulu, Hawaii.

Steve enjoys volunteering with the United Way, SCUBA diving and talking with other people interested in Peace Corps service. He is a graduate of West Virginia University and lives in West Palm Beach.

Steve Hunsicker (far right) with two of his Tongan friends. He is dressed in typical Tongan business attire.

EXCERPT FROM "OTHER PLACES: TONGA"

Invariably, whenever anyone tells a Tongan that they are going to Vava'u, have been to Vava'u, or want to go to Vava'u, the Tongan will respond by saying, "fakaofaofa," meaning "beautiful." Vava'u's hilly terrain marks a sharp contrast to the mostly-flat Tongatapu and Ha'apai island groups. Furthermore, the island's hills, along with its close proximity to neighboring islands, provide Vava'u with a rare commodity: extremely calm, well-protected waters year-round.

Vava'u boasts some of the most protected waters in the world; this makes it a favorite place for yachts from all the world over. Add in the magnificent clear blue ocean and amazingly secluded beaches, and it is easy to understand why the population of Vava'u swells during the winter season.

The name, "Vava'u," can be pronounced three different ways, but there is really only one correct way to say it. It's "va-VA-ooh." The most common mispronunciation is "Va-Vowel" or, occasionally, "va-va-OOH." Though Tongans almost never correct anyone who says the name incorrectly, they certainly appreciate all efforts to say it properly.

HISTORY

When Captain Cook first journeyed to the islands of Tonga, he did not visit Vava'u.

At the time, the Tongans told him there was no safe place to harbor there, thus steering him away from one of the most protected harbors in the South Pacific. The people of Vava'u are very proud of their differences from Tongatapu; this tradition stretches back many, many years. When William Mariner wrote his history of the Tongan Islands, he tells how the King of Tonga came to Vava'u to "conquer the island group." To his great surprise, the king was greeted peacefully by the people of Vava'u, who offered him a deal. According to the proposed agreement, the people of Vava'u would recognize him as king, as long as he promised never to come back to the island.

The King rejected the deal, and a very bloody battle ensued, which ended when the King eventually conquered the island.

Even today, although the people of Vava'u will often tolerate the things which are decided on the main island of Tongatapu, the people of Vava'u prefer to do things their own way. That is, the people of Vava'u are not only far removed geographically, but also politically, from Tongatapu. For example, in 2006 when Tongatapu was exploding with protests over education, the people of Vava'u were holding a parade to celebrate their schools and teachers.

More so than any of the other islands, Vava'u has felt a large impact from tourism, which has affected the history and development of the island. Visitors come to visit to see the island's beauty, and many then choose to stay and live on Vava'u, because they enjoy the Vava'u lifestyle so much. By law, palangis, or non-Tongans, are limited in what they can do in Tonga. For instance, the law allows non-Tongans to run businesses only in fields in which Tongans do not possess the requisite practical expertise to run that kind of business. This generally means that palangi operate most of the tourist businesses on the island. There are, however, also a few expatriates who work in fields like architecture and computer technology. However, foreigners often find that running a business in Tonga can be risky. Most palangi business owners will note that they must "tread lightly," so that they won't upset the wrong person and get their business license revoked.

MTYHS

As in most Polynesian cultures, and for that matter, the rest of Tonga, myths abound throughout Vava'u.

One legend tells that the island of Lotuma used to be the top part of Mt. Talau. Looking at Mt. Talau, one of the highest places in all of Vava'u, the island's flat top, not to mention its location proximate to Lotuma, certainly make the story plausible.

According to the legend, evil spirits from Samoa came to Vava'u to steal the top of Mt. Talau. However, they only made it a short distance when they saw a bright light, which they thought was the rising sun. Fearful, the spirits fled, dropping the mountain top into the ocean, forming the present-day island of Lotuma. The bright light, however, was not the rising sun; it was in fact a Tongan woman exposing her buttocks, "mooning" the evil spirits, reflecting the light toward them and frightening them away.

Read more about Vava'u and the rest of the Kingdom in "Tonga", published in 2011 by Other Places Publishing. The book is available at Amazon and other booksellers.

Printed in Great Britain
by Amazon.co.uk, Ltd.,
Marston Gate.